Plant Combinations for an
Abundant Garden

CRE☗TIVE
HOMEOWNER®

Plant Combinations for an Abundant Garden is a collection of new and previously published material. Portions of this book have been reproduced from *Home Gardener's No-Dig Raised Bed Gardens (978-1-58011-748-7, 2016)*, *Home Gardener's Small Gardens (978-1-58011-746-3, 2016)*, and *Home Gardener's Garden Design & Planning (978-1-58011-729-6, 2016)*.

Plant Combinations for an Abundant Garden
Vice President–Content: Christopher Reggio
Editor: Laura Taylor
Designer: David Fisk
Indexer: Jay Kreider

ISBN 978-1-58011-827-9

The Cataloging-in-Publication Data is on file with the Library of Congress.

We are always looking for talented authors. To submit an idea, please send a brief inquiry to acquisitions@foxchapelpublishing.com.

Printed in Singapore

Current Printing (last digit)
10 9 8 7 6 5 4 3 2 1

Creative Homeowner®, *www.creativehomeowner.com*, is an imprint of New Design Originals Corporation and distributed exclusively in North America by Fox Chapel Publishing Company, Inc., 800-457-9112, 903 Square Street, Mount Joy, PA 17552, and in the United Kingdom by Grantham Book Service, Trent Road, Grantham, Lincolnshire, NG31 7XQ.

Shutterstock: Alexander Raths (106–107); Alexey Stiop (63 top left); AlinaMD (4–5 background); Alison Hancock (11); AnEduard (59 bottom); argus (back cover bottom); Artazum (40 top); Chen Liang-Dao (63 bottom); Del Boy (138–139); Dora Zett (front cover); Elena Elisseeva (141 bottom, 229 bottom); EQRoy (120 top); Grisha Bruev (62 bottom); JPL Designs (44 bottom); karamysh (12); Karin Jaehne (112 left); loflo69 (back cover top); Maria Sbytova (38–39); Matthew J Thomas (225); monticello (182–183); Naphat_Jorjee (53 bottom); nikolaborovic (42 top); NORTH DEVON PHOTOGRAPHY (64 top); OlgaPonomarenko (226–227); Ozgur Coskun (37 bottom); PhotoSGH (31 right); ppa (30); Romolo Tavani (back cover middle, 6–7); rootstock (58 bottom); Scott E. Feuer (24); Sofiaworld (2–3); somyot pattana (63 top right); stockfour (37 top); Stock Rocket (5 inset, 142); Thomas Barrat (13 bottom); Toa55 (4 inset, 21); V J Matthew (69 right); White78 (78–79)

Plant Combinations for an
Abundant Garden

Design and Grow a Fabulous Flower and Vegetable Garden

David Squire
Alan & Gill Bridgewater

CRE**A**TIVE
HOMEOWNER®

Contents

No-Dig Gardening

Deciding What to Plant

Tips for Growing Vegetables and Fruit

Care and Troubleshooting

Getting Started

No-Dig Raised Bed Troubleshooting

QUESTION	ANSWER
Does it matter how we align the crops with the sun?	Much depends on the location of your plot, the shape of the land, and how the plot is shaded. For example, we live in the UK on a sloping site that is shaded by large trees on the western boundary. So the plot gets full benefit of the sun right from sunrise through to late afternoon, and from then on in the plot is in the shade. This being so, we try to arrange things so that lines of tall plants such as runner beans run from east to west – so that at least the lines get to have sun on both sides. The orientation of small, low plants like zucchinis is not so important, as long as they are not overshadowed by taller plants. The whole object of the exercise is to try to ensure that all the plants get their fair share of the sun.
Last year my parsnips took so long to come through that the bed spent weeks looking empty and bare. Could I have planted some sort of temporary crop to fill the space?	Yes, the best advice with a slow-growing crop like parsnips is to intercrop (see page 20) with something that you know is going to swiftly grow up and be finished before the parsnips really get going, such as radishes and salad leaves.
My large 36 in (90 cm) square wooden compost bins are completely full and there is too much compost to use this year. Can I plant them up with zucchinis?	Good idea. Simply top off your compost bins with a good 6 in (15 cm) of well-rotted farmyard manure and plant them there. You should get a lovely crop!
My leeks became lanky and did not do very well over winter. What should I do next time?	The best option is to plant them in holes as described on page 54, and then gradually add additional bed frames and layers of mulch, so that by the time the leeks are fully grown they are more or less buried. This technique supports the plants as they grow, increases the quality of the growing medium, and protects the plants so that they can better survive a difficult cold winter.
Is there any swift and easy way of stopping slugs and snails from attacking my raised beds?	Like most gardeners, we have tried everything from slug pellets, broken egg shells, beer in jam jars, to stretched cotton wiped with garlic, and so on. What seems to work best is copper wire (although why it works is a mystery). Strip the copper wire out leftover power cable (maybe begged from friends and neighbors) and then staple the lengths so that the tops of the beds are completely ringed. The slugs and snails slide up to the copper, give it a look over and then slide off.
Is it really worth all the effort of keeping poultry just to ensure a steady supply of manure?	There is no denying that keeping poultry is a bit of a chore, but there are manymore pros than cons. You will have as many fresh eggs as you can eat, you will be able to give eggs to friends and family, the poultry nicely takes care of gluts of fruit, salad, cabbages and so on, and you will have as much organic manure as you can handle. Keeping poultry nicely completes the growing, eating, waste and recycling loop. Just think – you could be eating freshly picked zucchinis from the garden and fresh eggs all swiftly fried in olive oil and served up with lumps of new brown bread!

INDEX

WHY GARDEN?

The moment you take people out into the garden, they immediately become more relaxed and expansive. Their smiles get bigger, they talk more loudly, their hand movements are broader, and they generally stride around looking happier. Whoever said that the great outdoors is our natural habitat certainly knew what they were talking about. Gardens are uniquely wonderful.

What could be better after a hot, sticky day at work, or a long drive home, than to relax in the garden? Gardens are all things to all people – a place for reading, a place for growing tasty vegetables, a place for playing out private fantasies such as building a log cabin, digging holes, building ponds or breeding chickens, a place for whatever takes your fancy. Patios, ponds, sheds, gazebos, barbecues, vegetable plots and lawns … there are so many exciting options.

Your garden might not be much bigger than a small room, but this does not mean that you cannot turn it into the best room in the house – a room with a ceiling that stretches right up to the sky. This book will gently guide you through all the stages, from planning and making drawings through to selecting tools, digging, building walls, planting, stocking and much more besides. No more dreaming … now is the time for turning fantasies into realities.

Measurements

Both metric and U.S. measurements are given in this book – for example, 6 ft (1.8 m).

Seasons

Because of global and even regional variations in climate and temperatures, throughout this book planting advice is given in terms of the four main seasons, with each subdivided into "early," "mid-" and "late" – for example, early spring, mid-spring and late spring. These 12 divisions of the year can be applied to the approximate calendar months in your local area, if you find this helps.

ENJOYING YOUR GARDEN

Although you might start out with preconceived notions – the garden has to be formal, or you want to grow vegetables, for example – the finished garden will of necessity be a coming-together of what you dream of having and what you actually have on the ground – the location, the size of the plot, the character of your home, and so on. The best way of getting started is to list your needs, think hard about the possibilities, and take things from there.

How do I get the best out of my garden?

YOUR NEEDS

List your needs in order of priority. Your needs might be unspoken, but you probably know absolutely for sure what you don't want. If this is the case, then list what you don't want, and then, by a process of elimination, gradually work through to what you would like to have.

THE POSSIBILITIES

Look at the size and location of your plot, and the size of your bank balance, and consider the possibilities accordingly. You might want a huge lake, but if you only have a modest-sized garden, with a modest-sized bank balance to match, it is probably better to modify your "needs" and opt for a good-sized pond.

IMPROVING AND EVOLVING

Gardens generally improve and evolve simply with the passing of time. Plants get bigger, new plants can be grown, lawns can be changed into flower beds, and so on.

Even the smallest patch can be turned into a gentle, soothing haven.

GARDENING STYLES

Although there are only two basic styles of garden, informal and formal, there are many variations on these styles. For example, you could have an informal cottage-orchard type garden, or an informal wild garden. Much the same goes for a formal garden. You could have a classic garden with all the features relating to a symmetrical ground plan, or you could have a Japanese garden that is formal in its layout.

INFORMAL

A natural patio complete with apple trees and meadow grass.

Wildlife areas introduce a new dimension to gardening, and are perfect for a small, quiet, out-of-the-way position.

FORMAL

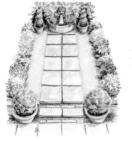

A small formal garden which has been designed so that the plants can easily be changed to follow the seasons.

A single stone ball can be an eye-catching feature.

THEMED

Areas of gravel create the perfect base for a Japanese garden.

ASSESSING YOUR GARDEN

Where do I start?

Asuccessful garden is nearly always a marriage of what you actually have and what you would like to have. The first step is to spend time in the garden. Look at the space, the levels, the walls and so on, and then decide what you want from your garden. Do you like gardening, or do you simply want to enjoy being outdoors? Consider your finances and your physical capabilities. Generally think through the possibilities and then slowly begin to make plans.

SIZE

Garden size is relative. If you are not very keen on gardening and just want a space to relax and read a book, half an acre (0.2 of a hectare) is a huge area, but if you want to grow all your own vegetables then the same area is perhaps a bit poky. Big, small, long or wide, treat the space like a room in your house and make the most of all the existing features.

SHAPE

Making the most of an unusually shaped space – thin, wide, triangular, L-shaped, or whatever – can result in a uniquely exciting garden. A difficult corner plot can be a problem, but then again such a shape offers you the chance to create a really unusual garden, one that stands out from its neighbors.

EXTREMELY SLOPING SITES

Extremely sloping sites can be great fun. You have three options. In ascending order of sweat and expense, you can make something of it as is, you can build raised decking to create level patio areas, and, most difficult of all, you can create one or more terraces. If you want terraces but need to keep costs down, and don't mind hard work, the best option is to dig out and move the existing soil.

ORIENTATION

Stand in the garden at various times of the day, and look at the house and the trees and the position of the sun. As you cannot move the house within the site, you have no choice other than to design the garden so that it makes the most of what is on offer in the way of sun, shade and privacy. Decide, for example, if you want the patio in full sun, or the vegetable plot in full sun and yet out of sight of the house.

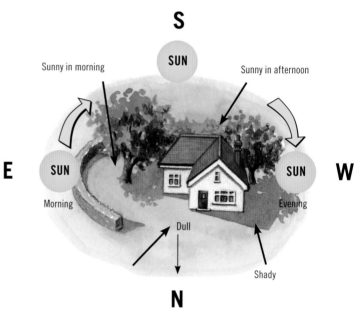

Design the garden so that it makes the most of the sun.

Balcony gardens

The best way of coping with a cramped balcony garden is to use a variety of containers; these may be fixed to the balustrade, used as window boxes, hanging from the walls, arranged in tiers or in groups on the floor, placed in groups just inside the door to the house, and so on. Use container plants to blur the boundaries between the inside and outside space.

Roof gardens

Much depends upon the size of your roof garden, but as a generalization it is always a good decision to spend on a quality floor such as tiles or decking, really good furniture, and as many pots and containers as you can get into the space.

EXPOSED SITES

Ordinary garden plants hate wind. The key to creating a garden on an exposed site is to build as many windbreaks as possible – walls, fences, sheds and the like – and then to grow tough plants on the lee or sheltered side of the breaks. Once the plants are established, the enclosed space will be that much warmer and draft-free – a good environment for a whole range of medium to fully hardy plants.

SOIL TYPES

To a great extent, you have no choice but to work with your soil – its particular type and conditions. The soil type will influence what you can grow. Don't worry too much about its pH (whether it is acid or alkaline); just take note of whether it is sandy, wet, dry, clay or rocky, and then look around at your locality and choose plants that will thrive in that type of soil.

LARGE PERMANENT FEATURES

In most instances, you have to work around large permanent features such as a huge tree, the back of a neighbor's shed, a tall wall that overlooks the garden or a streetlight. If you don't like the back of the neighbor's shed, then why not block it out with a shed of your own, a trellis covered with a vigorous climbing plant, or a tall, attractive fence? Try to use the back of the shed to your advantage.

YOU AND YOUR GARDEN

The wonderful thing about gardens is that they give you the chance to create your own private haven. Of course, you do have to consider the needs of friends and neighbors, but first and foremost you must start by identifying your own needs – all the things that you do and don't want.

Ideas suited to the types of garden

Your garden might well be, in some way or other, uniquely tricky, but the good news is that there will be all sorts of exciting ideas and options that you can use to best advantage.

Small shady garden with moist soil Try a woodland theme with a small sitting area or "glade" positioned to catch available patches of sunshine. Go for woodland plants that positively enjoy damp shady conditions, like ferns, ivies, some grasses and bamboos, hostas, *Polygonatum*, primulas and hydrangeas.

Small shady garden with dry soil A good idea is a woodland glade theme with shrubs and trees like fuchsias, *Parthenocissus* (Virginia creeper) and *Acers* (Japanese Maples) around the borders. Have a large patch of lawn for the "glade." Extend the woodland glade theme by spreading a mulch of woodchip around the shrubs and trees.

Small sunny garden with dry soil Position a gazebo or arbor so that it catches most of the sunshine, and then have a small pool with appropriate planting. You could have *Eichhornia* (Water Hyacinth), *Aponogeton distachyos* (Water Hawthorn) and a whole range of lilies.

Sloping garden with stony soil Take advantage of the stony conditions by making the garden into one large alpine rock garden. Bring in large feature rocks and stone troughs, and grow alpine plants like Thyme, *Sedum* (Stonecrop), *Iberis* (Candytuft) and *Phlox subulata* (Moss Phlox).

Large garden with wet clay soil Turn the whole garden into one big water garden with a large natural pond at the center and areas of bog garden to catch the runoff from the pond. Have all the usual plants in the pond, with the marginals

around the pond blurring into bog plants like irises, primulas, ferns and *Hemerocallis* (Daylilies).

Garden with back-to-back houses Position a pergola at the bottom of the garden, with trellises to each side, and then plant climbers to grow over it. You could concentrate on *Clematis* – search out the various spring, summer, autumn and winter varieties – so that you have foliage, buds and flowers all year.

Garden sloping down from the house Create a flat terrace area close to the house with steps running from the terrace down to the lawn and flowerbeds. You could have a cottage-garden feature in the lower garden with wildflowers like *Viola odorata* (Sweet Violet), *Lythrum salicaria* (Purple Loosestrife) and *Lychnis flos-cuculi* (Ragged Robin).

Garden sloping up from the house Dig out the ground close to the house and build a patio. You could have steps leading up the slope with ponds and waterfalls at various levels. The idea is that you can sit on the patio and view the water and plants as they cascade down the slope.

Small garden ringed by high walls Fix wires and trellises on all the walls and then plant a whole range of climbing plants. You could have *Parthenocissus* (Virginia Creeper) and *Pileostegia viburnoides* on the shady walls, and plants like *Wisteria* and *Lonicera* (Honeysuckle) where there is sun.

Small walled courtyard garden Build a pergola that more or less fills the space. Cover the top of the pergola with clear plastic sheet so that the courtyard is roofed over. Put a small wall feature on one wall, and plant grapevines on the underside of the pergola so you can sit out in all weather.

Wish list

Every good idea starts with a wish list. The very act of sitting and dreaming about what is possible is a good part of the pleasure of gardening. I wish I could have …

Barbecue: a brick-built barbecue is a good option. All you need is a patio area, the barbecue itself and seating all around.

Beds and borders: beds and borders are like an ever-changing film screen – places that you can stuff full of color.

Bird bath and bird feeder: bird baths and feeders are a must. What better way to enjoy the garden in winter than to put food out and to watch the birds feeding and bathing?

Chickens: going to the chicken house and listening to that very special sound that hens make when they are about to lay … it's a thought!

Fruit trees: apples and plums are good, but when they are fresh from the tree they are very special – a gift from nature.

Gazebo: lots of people dream about having a gazebo. Just think about it – a place for the kids, or a place for sleeping when the weather is hot and sticky.

Greenhouse: if you want to be able to get out into the garden from very early spring until early winter, you are going to need a greenhouse.

Herb garden: a sunny patio is good, but a patio planted with herbs such as thyme, sage, marjoram and so on is better.

Kids' garden: children need a place to play. A jungle gym is fine, but a place to dig and make a camp, and make a mess, is so much better.

Lawn: an area of lawn is essential. The mowing may be a bit of a chore, but the scent given off by the freshly cut grass, and the pleasure of sitting on the lawn, are experiences that should not be missed.

Log cabin: if ever there was a dream feature, this is it. It can be just about anything you care to make it – a workshop, a weekend cabin, a place for the kids, or a potting shed.

Patio: what could be more pleasurable on a warm sunny day than to sit on a patio with friends and family? A good patio is a choice item.

Pergola: a well-placed pergola is another great option – good for providing shade over the patio, for growing grapes and for blotting out eyesores.

Pond: water has irresistible magical qualities that give us pleasure – the sight and sound of moving water is fascinating.

Raised beds: raised beds not only make for easy gardening – with less strain on the back – but they are also good for keeping small toddlers and pets away from the plants.

Summerhouse: a summerhouse is a delightful setting for having afternoon tea, reading a good book or just indulging in some quiet contemplation.

Vegetable plot: this is the age of the vegetable plot. If you enjoy fresh food and/or want to go organic, then a vegetable garden is for you.

Wildlife: birds, bugs, frogs, toads, newts and small mammals … a wildlife garden is one of life's great pleasures.

GATHERING INSPIRATION

Where do I start?

In much the same way as poets and artists draw inspiration from their interests and passions – romantic love, the glories of nature, the wonders of technology, travel – so the garden designer needs to draw inspiration from his or her experiences and passions. Whatever your interests may be – trees, roses, water, travel, eating in the garden, watching your children at play – your best starting point is to draw inspiration from the things that give you pleasure.

LOOKING AND COLLECTING

Note the large, permanent objects and items that you have to live with, such as the house, boundary walls and large trees, and then look around you at the things you have collected. For example, you might have a collection of nautical bits like anchors, glass floats and chains, old street lamps, old farm items, special plants or perhaps even your holiday photographs to inspire you.

A collection of bamboos could well be inspirational.

Favorite plants can also provide great inspiration.

Try found objects such as Victorian street lamps.

Postcards of beautiful gardens will give you something to aim for.

Books, magazines and television programs

Once you have come up with the bare bones of a scheme, follow through your research by looking through books and magazines, and by watching television. It is a good idea to make a collection of the ideas that you would like to include in your design – colors, plants, materials, structures, furniture, in fact anything and everything that strikes your fancy.

Keep a scrapbook. Save photographs from magazines and catalogs that show things like grand houses, flowers or sculpture.

Garden centers and nurseries

Garden centers and nurseries are great places for searching out ideas. Arm yourself with a digital camera, paper and pencil, and take note of everything that looks interesting. Gather a body of data to flesh out and back up your ideas – names of plants, colors, growing habits and so on. If you have in mind to go for a theme, say a Japanese garden, search out plants, materials and products that you know to be variously useful, traditional or characteristic.

Wander around the garden center or nursery keeping an eye open for anything that might spark an idea, such as unusual containers.

As you walk slowly around the various displays, take photographs of plants, products and features that you think might fit well into your scheme.

Visiting gardens

If you have a friend who has created a beautiful garden, when you next visit ask them to tell you about how they got started and how the design has evolved.

It is also a good idea to visit world-renowned gardens that are open to the public. In the US, for example, there are the Brooklyn Botanic Garden, Missouri Botanical Garden, Atlanta Botanical Garden, Denver Botanic Gardens and Leach Botanical Garden, to name a few.

A fine example of a traditional English pergola, with solid square-section brick columns topped off with oak beams.

A well-planted border can be a joy to the eye – so stunning that you might want to copy it in every detail.

Sometimes a particular arrangement of plants and structures, such as this piece of statuary placed beneath a rose arch, is inspiration enough.

Plants you like

List your favorite plants, with common names and botanical names, and brief details about their growing habits. Try to get magazine images as a reference. Ask friends, family and neighbors to tell you as much as they can about them.

Unsuitable plants

Look at your list in the light of your designs, and cross out ones that are obviously unsuitable. You might like the color and the scent, but if it is going to grow too big for your space, or it is too prickly for say a child's play area, then it is no good. Size and habit are particularly important if you are designing a small, enclosed garden.

Other sources of inspiration

Famous paintings Paintings are inspirational. For example, how about a garden design based on one of Monet's lily-pond paintings?

Memories Rolling around in your grandfather's apple orchard, flirting under a particular type of tree … these types of memories can be particularly inspirational.

Fantasies If, for example, you have fantasies about living in a hut on a tropical island, you could build the fantasy into your designs.

Country walks A bend in a river with a quaint wooden bridge and willows … country walks are another rich source of ideas.

Cultural influences If you have experienced the pleasures of sitting in a Mediterranean garden, or under a loggia in India, why not create one of your own?

PUTTING THE ELEMENTS TOGETHER

Something for everyone in the family

It is important to include the whole family in the design process – adults, children and even pets. Make sure everyone is happy with the end design.

Deciding what to drop If you have worries, such as the kids falling into the pond or plant allergies, then simply leave these elements out of the design.

Eclectic or sweet harmony? Most gardens veer towards harmony but, if you know what you like and you want a glorious unrelated mishmash of styles and forms, the choice is yours.

Scaling down Sometimes you do have to compromise. If an element is dangerously large, or there just is not enough room for all those oak trees, you have no choice but to scale down.

Cost and time When it comes down to it, most designs hinge on money and time. You could spread the creation time over several years, get friends to help with the work and beg and borrow plants, but you might also need to cut basic material costs – stone, wood, cement and the like.

DESIGN TECHNIQUES

How can I use my inspiration?

This is the exciting bit. You have visited grand houses and show gardens, taken many photographs, developed a passion for just about everything, and generally looked, collected and clipped until your mind is racing with ideas. When it comes to good design, it helps if you follow the rule that says "form follows function." This means that your final design should be a balanced blend of both your functional needs and your ideas and passions.

A long, formal pond or canal links the patio with the rest of the garden. The natural earth-colored bricks and symmetrical layout give this design a traditional or classic feel. The planting is less formal.

A decking patio with seaside overtones – the matching raised beds are topped with turquoise crushed stone to draw the eye. This is an entirely modern design that focuses on color, texture and function.

GOOD DESIGN, POOR DESIGN, TASTE AND STYLE

In the context of design, a good starting point is to say that things and structures have to work – gates must open, seating needs to be comfortable, steps must be safe, and so on. If you are worried about what constitutes good taste or good style, then the best advice is to relate to tried and trusted classical forms. If you go for untried, cutting-edge forms and imagery, then you may risk, certainly in the short term, your design being described as being in poor taste or poor style – sometimes possibly for no other reason than that it has not passed the test of time.

Harmony and contrast

Taken literally, the term "harmony" describes forms, colors and textures that are similar one to another, to the extent that they look happy together. Red brick, stone and wood might be described as being in harmony. The term "contrast" describes forms, textures and colors that are dissimilar or opposite. The strange thing is that contrasts – say dark against light, or rough against smooth – can be a joy to the eye. For example, polished marble can look all the more exciting when it is set against a contrasting material like rough-hewn oak.

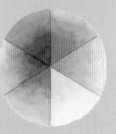

You can use a color wheel like this to help you make informal decisions.

DRAWING INSPIRATION FROM AN EXISTING DESIGN

There is a fine line between drawing inspiration from an existing design and copying a design. If you visit a garden and are so excited by it that you go away and create a garden that pays homage to it, you are drawing inspiration from it. If, however, you replicate it stone by stone and flower by flower, you are merely copying it.

FRESH, ORIGINAL IDEAS

Using fresh, original ideas is always good. Try to be original with the small things – the little details – and big original ideas should follow. There is no credit in being original just for the sake of it, however. Of course, it is always good to aim for originality, but do not worry too much if you fail.

GARDENS EVOLVE

The wonderful thing about gardens is the way they evolve. You start by putting in structures – paths, walls, and hard areas – and gradually as plants grow in size and number, and as your behavior changes, so you will find that you will, almost by necessity, modify the shape of the structures to fit.

Work with what you have: do your best to keep and use what you have – mature trees, dips and hollows in the ground, natural features like rocks and pools.

Soil stability: be wary about making big changes with wet or waterlogged soil, or soil on a sloping site. Take advice if you have doubts.

The house must look comfortable: aim for a landscape that holds and nestles the house, so that the house looks "happy" in its setting.

Get the best viewpoint: shape the garden so that it looks its best when seen from the house. If you get it right, the house will also look its best from various vantage points around the garden.

Draw inspiration from nature: the easiest way forward is to draw inspiration from a slice of nature – a forest glade, a valley, the side of a hill.

Materials in harmony: all new materials look their best when they are drawn from the locality – local bricks, local stone, local wood.

Scale in harmony: aim for structures that complement the house in size, rather than structures that overwhelm the house.

If you liken planting to painting colors on a canvas, you can take the analogy one step further by saying that you must hold back with the planting until the canvas – the structure of the garden – has been well prepared.

Climatic conditions: the plants must be suitable for your climate – it is no good going for delicate plants if your site is windy and subject to frosts.

Soil conditions: the plants must suit the soil – you must not choose chalk-loving plants if your soil is predominantly clay.

Sun and shade conditions: look at the way the sun moves around the garden, note the areas that are sunny and shady, and position the plants accordingly.

Scale: take note of the potential size of plants – the width and height when fully grown. Be especially wary of some of the fast-growing conifers.

Year-round color: aim for a broad selection of plants, so that you have year-round foliage, bud, stem and flower color.

Container-grown plants: these can be purchased and planted all year round.

MAKING NOTES AND SKETCHES

It is a good idea to go out into your garden, with a stack of colored pens and a pad of graph paper, and to make sketches. Take measurements of the garden, decide on the scale – say one grid square equals 2 ft (60 cm) – and then draw the garden in plan and perspective view, with close-up details showing special areas of interest (see right). Draw what you already have, and then draw in any desired changes. Try to visualize how the changes will affect how you use the space. Place markers around the garden so that you can more easily visualize changes.

A perspective view of the garden is more difficult to draw than a plan view, but is nevertheless the best way to visualize your design.

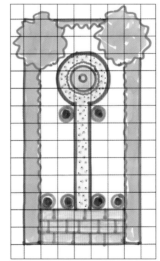

A plan view of the garden (viewed from above) can be drawn to scale over graph paper. Coloring in areas can be helpful.

Important features can be drawn separately and in more detail.

Use a rope, hose or chain together with some stakes to help you plot out an irregular shape.

CHOICE OF INFRASTRUCTURE

Are special designs possible?

When planning the infrastructure of a small garden, there is usually more money available for the construction of each square yard or meter than for a large garden, where economies generally have to be made. Additionally, because the area is small, immediate and more distinctive visual impact is needed. Garden centers and builder's yards, as well as catalogs from magazines and newspapers, will give you an idea of the materials available.

FENCING CHECKS

You may have inherited an attractive small garden and initially decided not to make radical changes, but if you have children and dogs it is worth checking fences.

- Fencing posts broken at ground level can be repaired by cutting off the base and fitting a spike-ended, metal, post-base. Alternatively, bolt a concrete or wooden post to sound wood and re-concrete into the ground.
- A wide variety of materials and styles are available for fencing. For a more formal setting, use cast iron. For a casual, Western look, choose split rail fencing. If the fence is more than just decorative, as in keeping in pets, opt for appropriately sized fencing.

Walls smothered in flowering climbers, such as Roses, Clematis and Honeysuckle, create color as well as informality.

Problems with clay

Increasingly, high temperatures combined with limited summer rain causes clay to shrink radically. Where foundations of buildings are deep, this creates few problems but, when paving slabs on a patio or path have only a thin concrete base, eventually they deform and buckle. First-aid treatment is to lift and re-cement individual slabs. For a longer-term solution, you will need to lift all the slabs and provide a thicker base for the complete patio or path.

Structural elements to consider

- **Decking:** raised or at ground level.
- **Edgings:** wide range, including concrete and wood.
- **Paths:** surfaces and durability.
- **Patios, courtyards and terraces:** wide choice.
- **Pergolas, trellises and arches:** for small gardens.
- **Porches and entrances:** decorative features.
- **Sheds and greenhouses:** practical features.
- **Steps:** practical yet attractive.
- **Walls and fences:** garden perimeters.

DISPOSING OF RUBBISH

There are several solutions for disposal:

- **Rent a rollaway bin** – check that the company is insured, that they know about your city's codes about placement of the rollaway, and that the size they deliver is appropriate for your needs.
- **Builder's bags** – these are increasingly used to deliver building materials, as well as collecting rubbish. They are about a yard/meter square and deep. Check with your local builder's merchant.
- **Local authority** – may provide a trash-collection service.

THINK ABOUT THE PLANTS

Don't separate the selection of plants from getting the infrastructure right.

- If you like relaxed plants such as bamboos, ferns and ornamental grasses, you will want an informal garden to complement them.
- For clinical and regimented displays of summer-flowering bedding plants, you will need a formal garden.

MAKING THE MOST OF BALCONIES

These are more sheltered than a roof garden, and with a base that is firm and secure. However, a sun-facing position will rapidly dry compost.

- If the balcony does not have a roof, fit a collapsible sunshade.
- Where a balcony has a roof, but strong, late-evening sunlight still causes dazzle, you can fit a sun shade to the balcony's upper edge.
- Always make sure that water cannot drip on people or balconies below. Wherever possible, stand pots in large, plastic saucers.

Infrastructure for roof gardens

Persistent and buffeting wind combined with strong sunlight make roof gardens difficult but exciting places for gardening. Additionally, consider the following constructional questions.

- Permission may be required from the building's owner, as well as from local authorities. Also, check the thoughts of neighbors – it may not impress them.
- The weight of the flooring needs to be light but strong – check with a structural engineer if in doubt.
- The weight of pots and other containers – when full of soil and after being watered – may be excessive.
- Don't damage felt roofs.
- Make sure excess water is adequately drained.
- A sturdy screen is usually needed to filter strong wind. Make sure it cannot be blown away and cause damage to people and property.

INFRASTRUCTURE EXAMPLES

A SMALL GARDEN

Within informal gardens, a surprisingly wide range of features can be included in a casual yet purposeful manner. The pergola acts as a focal point.

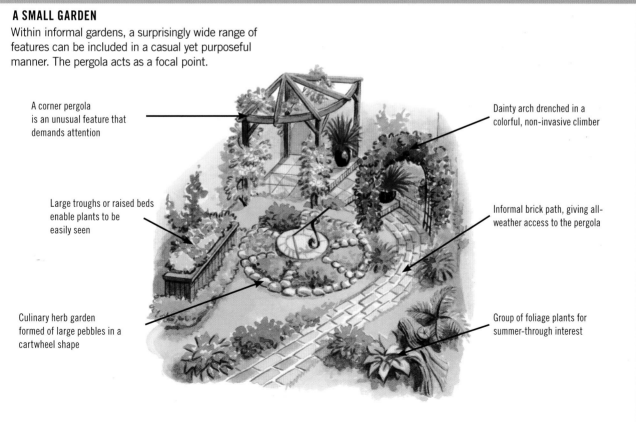

A corner pergola is an unusual feature that demands attention

Dainty arch drenched in a colorful, non-invasive climber

Large troughs or raised beds enable plants to be easily seen

Informal brick path, giving all-weather access to the pergola

Culinary herb garden formed of large pebbles in a cartwheel shape

Group of foliage plants for summer-through interest

A SMALL FRONT GARDEN

Most small front gardens have a formal character, with plants in rows and neat roadside edgings. Porches help to create focal points for paths.

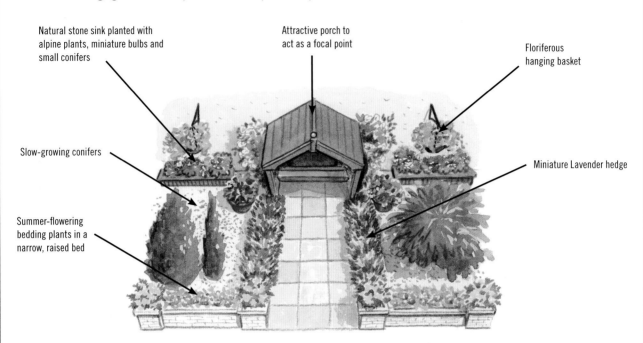

Natural stone sink planted with alpine plants, miniature bulbs and small conifers

Attractive porch to act as a focal point

Floriferous hanging basket

Slow-growing conifers

Miniature Lavender hedge

Summer-flowering bedding plants in a narrow, raised bed

A SMALL COURTYARD

Courtyards are summer-leisure areas as well as places where plants can be grown. By their nature, courtyards are private areas, with complete seclusion.

Gap in courtyard floor for a small, woody climber or shrub to be grown

Corner wall baskets and other wire-framed plant supports

Collection of wall pots and baskets, packed with summer flowers

Bricks in herringbone pattern, contrasting with paving and pebbles

Pebbled area, contrasting with square paving slabs

Miniature water feature, with water gushing into a brick-made, waterproof base

GETTING IT DOWN ON PAPER

If you want the project to run smoothly, you need to plan everything out and make drawings. The procedure is as follows: first, make a rough sketch on a scrap of paper, showing the existing garden with measurements. Next, transfer these details onto graph paper to make a "site plan" (drawn to scale). Then, set a sheet of graph paper over the site plan and make a "master plan" of the new garden, tracing the boundaries and existing items as required.

MAKING THE SITE PLAN

About graph paper You will need a pad of graph layout paper – meaning thin paper that has been printed with a grid – the biggest size of pad that you can obtain. Look at the size of your garden; say it is 100 ft (30 m) long and 80 ft (25 m) wide, and decide on the scale of your graph paper. Count the squares on the long side of the paper and divide them by the length of the garden. Work to the nearest whole square. So, for example, if the paper is 100 squares long, then you could say that one square on the paper equals 1 ft (30 cm) in the garden.

Measuring your garden Use a long tape measure to measure your garden. Start by measuring the length. Plot this measurement on the long side of the paper. Repeat the procedure with the width of the garden and plot it on the short side of the paper.

Right angles – 90° angles Check for right angles by measuring the diagonals. For example, if your garden is in any way square or rectilinear, then the crossed diagonal measurements should more or less be equal.

Awkward shapes You can plot an awkward shape by drawing a straight line from two fixed points – say between two trees. Step off at regular intervals along the straight line and measure how far the curves of the awkward shape are out from the stepped-off point.

Paths and drives

If the site plan is a record of items and structures that you have no choice but to leave unchanged, you have the option here of whether or not to mark in the position of the paths and drives. You could say that, since the position of the front door and the front gate are fixed, it follows that the paths will also stay the same. This does not necessarily follow, however. That said, it is usually a good idea to draw them in.

Slopes in cross-section

The easiest way of recording a slope is to draw a cross-section view. Draw the length of the slope on a piece of graph paper and label the line "top." You need a spirit (carpenter's) level taped to a 7 ft (2 m) long board. Working from the top of the slope, hold one end of the board on the ground so that the level is true, and measure the vertical distance from the overhanging end of the board down to the ground. Mark this in on the drawing. Continue down the slope until you have a record.

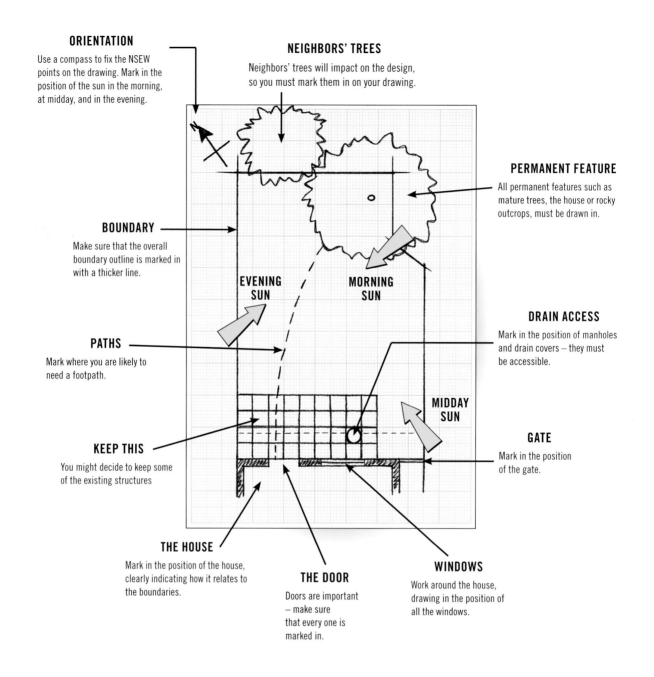

ORIENTATION
Use a compass to fix the NSEW points on the drawing. Mark in the position of the sun in the morning, at midday, and in the evening.

NEIGHBORS' TREES
Neighbors' trees will impact on the design, so you must mark them in on your drawing.

PERMANENT FEATURE
All permanent features such as mature trees, the house or rocky outcrops, must be drawn in.

BOUNDARY
Make sure that the overall boundary outline is marked in with a thicker line.

EVENING SUN

MORNING SUN

DRAIN ACCESS
Mark in the position of manholes and drain covers – they must be accessible.

PATHS
Mark where you are likely to need a footpath.

MIDDAY SUN

KEEP THIS
You might decide to keep some of the existing structures

GATE
Mark in the position of the gate.

THE HOUSE
Mark in the position of the house, clearly indicating how it relates to the boundaries.

THE DOOR
Doors are important – make sure that every one is marked in.

WINDOWS
Work around the house, drawing in the position of all the windows.

ITEMS THAT YOU NEED TO MARK ON THE SITE PLAN

- NSEW
- Midday sun
- Outline of boundary
- Items that you want to keep or modify
- House
- Mature trees
- Neighbors' trees
- Underground pipes and cables
- Doors on house
- Windows on house
- Drain access points
- Main gate

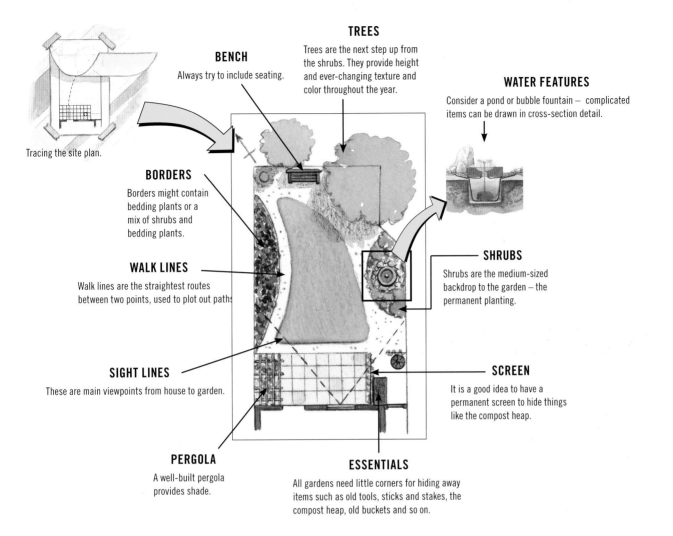

TREES

Trees are the next step up from the shrubs. They provide height and ever-changing texture and color throughout the year.

BENCH

Always try to include seating.

WATER FEATURES

Consider a pond or bubble fountain — complicated items can be drawn in cross-section detail.

Tracing the site plan.

BORDERS

Borders might contain bedding plants or a mix of shrubs and bedding plants.

WALK LINES

Walk lines are the straightest routes between two points, used to plot out paths

SHRUBS

Shrubs are the medium-sized backdrop to the garden – the permanent planting.

SIGHT LINES

These are main viewpoints from house to garden.

SCREEN

It is a good idea to have a permanent screen to hide things like the compost heap.

PERGOLA

A well-built pergola provides shade.

ESSENTIALS

All gardens need little corners for hiding away items such as old tools, sticks and stakes, the compost heap, old buckets and so on.

MAKING THE MASTER PLAN

Tracing the site plan Put a sheet of graph paper over the site plan and use the underlying plan to work out what you want in your new garden. You might well have to go through this procedure a dozen or so times before you have a drawing that suits all your needs.

Penciling in your design Once you have achieved a good preliminary plan, set it under another sheet of graph paper and trace it off with a pencil. This new drawing is your "master plan." You should now have two finished drawings – the site plan that records the bare bones of the garden, and the master plan that sets out the design of the new garden. You can photocopy the master plan so you have lots of copies.

Separate details Some items are so complex in themselves that they will need working drawings. So, for example, with a water feature, you will need a plan view, a front view and a cross-section showing how it is constructed.

Coloring in Some people make colored drawings to show how the garden might look at various times of the year. To make a colored drawing, set a sheet of plain paper over the master plan – hold it against a window and make a tracing. Tint this drawing with colored pencils or watercolors.

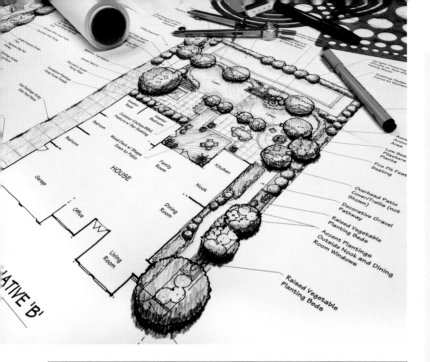

The best plants for the job

With thousands of plants to choose from, the challenge is to get the right plants to suit your location. See the Deciding What to Plant section of this book on pages 138–181 for some of the best choices in each category.

Trees: Small trees offer good year-round color and texture – foliage, blossom, fruit and bark.

Hedges: Hedges make good boundaries, attract wildlife and add year-round color and interest.

Herbaceous perennials: These are the plants that last a few years before being lifted and divided.

Shrubs: Shrubs are ideal for small gardens.

Wall shrubs: Wall shrubs are a good option for small courtyard gardens.

Climbing plants: Climbers are essential when walls and fences ring your garden.

Annuals, biennials and bedding plants: Summer bedding is formed mainly of these plants.

Bamboos and grasses: Bamboos and grasses are good when you want plants in small raised borders and containers.

Water plants: You will need plants for the margins, for the areas of bog, and for the water area.

Other plants: These include rock, alpine and desert plants, container plants, herbs, fruit and vegetables.

Calculating materials

Save time and money by calculating quantities and ordering in bulk.

Area

Rectangle – Multiply the length by the breadth to give you the area. A plot 100 x 50 ft = 5,000 square ft (30 x 15 m = 450 square m).

Circle – Area of a circle is pi x radius squared, with pi being 3.14. For example, with a 10 ft (3 m) diameter circle the sum is 3.14 x 1.5 squared, meaning 3.14 x 25 = c.80 sq ft (3.14 x 2.25 = c.7 sq m).

Irregular – Draw a square grid over the shape. Find the area of a single square. Gauge how many whole squares you have and multiply them by the area of a single square.

Volume

The volume is the area of the base multiplied by the height. For example, a tank measuring 3 x 3 x 3 ft has a volume of 27 cubic ft (90 x 90 x 90 cm = 729,000 cubic cm).

Turf is sold as regular shapes – usually about 12 in (30 cm) wide by 18 in (45 cm) long

Soil is sold in cubic meters, by the jumbo bag or truckload

Gravel is sold in cubic meters, by the jumbo bag or truckload

Bricks are sold individually or by the thousand

Stone is sold by the piece or in cubic meters

Concrete is sold ready-mixed in cubic meters or by the jumbo bag

PLANNING THE WORK

The key to good garden design is planning. If you want the project to run smoothly, you must work in a carefully thought-out, step-by-step sequence. It is no good simply rushing in and hoping for the best; you must work out the order of tasks to the very last detail. The best method is to start by establishing the boundaries, and then to work in and up, sorting out the tasks in order — ground levels, infrastructures, features, lawns and finally planting.

STEP-BY-STEP ORDER OF WORK

**STEP 1
BOUNDARIES**

Have one last talk with neighbors about precise positions and heights, and then measure out and build the walls and fences.

**STEP 2
GROUND LEVELS**

Dig holes for ponds, and generally move the earth around to suit your needs. Be careful not to bury the valuable topsoil. Put in drainage trenches, water pipes and power cables.

**STEP 3
PRIMARY
INFRASTRUCTURES**

Build the primary infrastructures — retaining walls, main paths, drive and foundations.

**STEP 4
FEATURES AND DETAILING**

Build the main features — ponds, pools, sheds and patios — and follow up with details such as steps, small paths, gates and edgings for lawns and borders.

**STEP 5
LAWNS**

Make sure that the lawn areas are well drained. Level, rake and roll the ground, and then either sow seed or lay turf.

**STEP 6
PLANTING**

Prepare the borders and the other planting areas, and plant your chosen shrubs, climbers, trees and bedding plants.

EMPLOYING LANDSCAPERS VERSUS DIY

Of course you can call in landscape contractors, but it will be expensive, and worse still you will miss out on all the fun. By far the best all-round option is to do the work yourself. If you follow the DIY route, you can control the costs, make modifications as you go along, get lots of healthy exercise, save on gym fees, take as much time as you want, ask your friends and family to join in the fun – the kids will love digging holes – and, possibly best of all, the workers can have countless barbecue parties.

STEP 1: **Boundaries**

Being mindful that most neighbor disputes are about things like tall hedges and fence posts, carefully identify your boundaries. Tidy up the hedges and/or build secondary fences in front of them. If you are rebuilding a fence or wall, be sure to talk to your neighbors along the way. Replace only short lengths at a time, so that neither you nor your neighbors lose sight of reference markers.

STEP 2: **Ground levels**

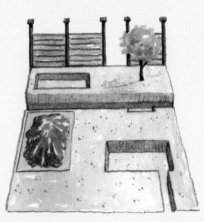

You have three choices with a sloping site: you can leave it as a feature, you can build low retaining walls and make a series of terraces, or you can build one or more retaining large walls and level the whole site. Be aware that changing levels will have an impact on your neighbors' drainage. You must not build the earth up against house walls or fences. Dig out ponds and bury pipes and cables.

STEP 3: **Primary infrastructures**

Build up the various primary retaining walls to hold back the earth, and then follow on with walls for raised beds. Make sure that primary retaining walls are broad-based with drainage points and good foundations. Retaining walls higher than about 3 ft (90 cm) will need to be reinforced with iron bars set into the foundations. Build paths and drives, and foundations (for things like sheds, steps, edges of flower borders and lawns, and brick gate posts).

STEP 4: **Features and detailing**

Put in the main features, such as pond liners for sunken ponds. Build walls around raised ponds, lay patios, tidy up paths and erect sheds; then follow up with small details like steps, small paths and edges around ponds and trees. Build brick gateposts, hang gates, erect pergolas and trellises, and put down lawn and border edgings. If you have got to do anything else that involves digging holes or making a mess, now is the time to do it.

COMMON PROBLEMS AND HOW TO AVOID OR SOLVE THEM

Fence disputes Talk things through with the neighbors at every stage. Leave old posts in place as markers. Leave their fences alone.

Neighbors' trees You cannot do anything about neighbors' trees, other than to trim them from your side. Remember to ask the neighbors if they want the trimmings.

Big rocks Keep rocks as a feature, or get a specialist to remove them.

Clay soil Live with clay soil. Look at neighboring gardens and see what grows best. For vegetable gardens, make raised borders and buy compost and horse manure – so that you are working above the level of the clay.

Contaminated ground Build over gravel and/or use it as filler. If it is something nasty like asbestos or oil, seek specialist advice.

Waterlogged ground Build a pond, lay drainage pipes and create a water garden complete with bog plants.

Unwanted structures Carefully salvage bricks and use them for walls.

STEP 5: Lawns

Having seen to it that the lawn areas are well drained – with perforated pipes or trenches filled with gravel – bring back the topsoil and carefully level the ground. Spend time getting it right. Finally roll the ground, and put down seed or lay turf. Keep off the lawn until the ground has settled.

STEP 6: Planting

Now comes the exciting bit – the planting. Take your time and do your research. You can make considerable cost cuts by phoning around and comparing prices.

- Have a good long look at the finished garden and plan out the planting positions. Prepare the planting areas with just the right soil. Make a plant list.

- Call nurseries and garden centers, and generally make enquiries about availability. Make contact with specialist nurseries for items like roses, fruit trees, climbing shrubs, pond plants and fuchsias.

- See if you can cut costs by buying in bulk or by getting all the plants at the same time. Compare prices.

- If you are buying large, mature, container-grown trees, make sure that there is adequate height and width access.

- If you have doubts about the total planting pattern, start by planting the main trees and shrubs.

PROBLEMS AND OPPORTUNITIES

Can all sites be made attractive?

With all sites there are problems and opportunities, and sometimes areas that initially appear totally inhospitable eventually produce the most interesting and distinctive gardens — unique and full of character. Creating height through arches, trellises and pergolas draws attention away from exceptionally narrow or short gardens, while a levelled area on a steep slope becomes idyllic when turned into a leisure feature, especially if illuminated at night.

Use climbers to cloak eyesores and barren walls. Hanging baskets and window boxes can be used in a similar way.

Annuals are sown in spring each year to create an inexpensive yet vibrantly colored feast of flowers.

Raised decking is ideal for creating a distinctive feature, perhaps alongside a stream or a colorful garden pond.

TOO SMALL?

Logically, there is a size when it is near impossible to create an area in which plants can be grown. Yet many successful gardens are created in areas at the entrances to basement apartments, where both space and light are limited. In small areas ideals are limited, but a few decorative pots, a hanging basket and window box can be just as cherished as an extensive and well-manicured lawn is to a croquet devotee.

SEEING THE OPPORTUNITIES

The ability to recognize hidden opportunities in potential gardens is, in part, gained by looking at other gardens, both locally and nationally. Some large display gardens even have areas where a range of small gardens are featured; even if one of them in its entirety does not suit you, an amalgam of several elements may be practical in your garden. Have a sketch-pad or camera handy and take a few notes that later give clues to opportunities.

LEGACY PROBLEMS

Often there are existing structures in a garden left from the previous owners (or even before them). It could be poles set in concrete to hang out the wash, or the foundation of an old shed. Regardless, former owners often let these existing obstacles restrict their garden design. When first taking possession of a new garden, the time is now to remove these old structures so you can start from a clean slate.

TERRACING SLOPES

Brick retaining walls have a formal nature and are suited to relatively open areas, whereas old railroad ties are better for relaxed and informal settings with beds of grasses and deciduous azaleas. Peat-blocks are another solution to soil retention, but not on steep slopes. In open areas, slopes can be grass, with level areas interspersed with 45° slopes. Powered edge trimmers are ideal for cutting grass on slopes.

STEEP SLOPES

Slopes provide added interest in a garden, although moving from one level to another can sometimes be difficult – especially as age progresses. Flights of 6–8 steps – with a resting landing between them – make slopes easier to negotiate.

Creating a flattened leisure area on a steep slope helps to split it up. Where possible, position this feature level with head height when viewed from a patio around the house.

SHORT AND WIDE

Accentuate the shortness by erecting a head-high screen of leafy or flowering climbers across the garden, so that the boundary cannot be seen. Ensure that the screen is not too high, because a glimpse of openness beyond the garden removes any feeling of claustrophobia. A well-kept lawn creates an impression of space, while a bench positioned close to the screen forms a focal point.

LONG AND NARROW

Create the impression of a shorter garden by dividing it into several units, each with a unique feel. In a small garden, a free-standing trellis, perhaps combined with a leaf-drenched arch, takes up less space than a dense hedge. Create mystery by varying the position of a linking path, making it impossible to see the back of the garden from the house.

A garden's aspect is not usually the first consideration when moving to a new house. Whether it is fully exposed to sunlight or shaded by trees or neighboring buildings can be a lottery that brings both problems and opportunities. There are plants that delight in full sun, while others prefer to grow in shade. The light or shade preferences of many plants are detailed in the plant directory (see pages 34–59).

The degree and nature of light and shade in a garden varies from one part of a day to another.

- **Full sun:** many plants thrive in full sun, especially if regularly watered. Those native to hot countries and with hot-climate adaptations such as silvery, hairy or aromatic leaves are first choices, but even these need help when getting established. Regular watering and yearly mulching are two moisture-saving tasks.

- **Light shade:** most plants thrive in a combination of dappled light and full sun. Unless there is a large, overhead canopy of leaves from a tree (which also deprives other plants of moisture and nutrients) the brightest time is during the middle part of a day.

- **Heavy shade:** most decorative garden plants do not grow well or exhibit attractive qualities when in deep shade. Unless the shade comes from a building, thin out an overhead canopy created by trees.

SOIL PROBLEMS

Soils vary in their nature; most are neutral and neither acid nor alkaline. Others are well drained, some waterlogged. Occasionally they are hot and dry. Plants that prefer specific soils are indicated in the plant directory (see pages 34–59).

- **Acid soils:** these are soils with a pH below about 6.5. Acidity can be corrected by dusting the surface with hydrated lime or ground limestone in winter, after digging. However, some plants – such as Rhododendrons and Azaleas – demand acid soils.

- **Alkaline (chalky) soils:** these have a pH above 7.0. Chalky soils can be corrected by used acidic fertilizers such as sulphate of ammonia, plus applications of peat. Many plants grow well in chalky soils.

- **Neutral soils:** these are soils with a pH of 7.0, although most plants grow well in a pH between 6.5 and 7.0.

Exposed and windswept sites

Newly planted as well as established plants are often damaged by cold, searing winds. Hedges filter the wind and can be used to make gardens more congenial for tender plants. Walls create barriers and encourage swirling eddies on the lee side, as well as buffeting on the windward face.

Coastal gardens

Salt-laden wind is present along coastal strips as well as a few miles or kilometers inland. Some plants tolerate these conditions, while others have their leaves damaged. Coastal plants for forming attractive hedges in warm areas include *Fuchsia magellanica* (Hardy Fuchsia) and *Tamarix ramosissima* (Tamarisk; also known as *Tamarix pentandra*).

TOOLS AND MATERIALS

Although you can borrow tools and use found, salvaged and gifted materials, such as old bricks and left-over sand, you will inevitably have to buy some new tools and things like cement and wood. Tools and materials come from DIY outlets, builder's merchants and local suppliers. You can find savings in time and energy if you buy the best tools for the task, and in money if you purchase the materials in bulk from local suppliers.

What will I need to buy?

TOOLS

MEASURING AND MARKING

You need a basic kit for measuring, marking, checking levels and setting out the site. Spray paint or chalk can be used for marking out straight and curved lines (not illustrated).

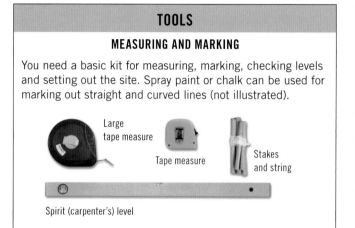

Large tape measure

Tape measure

Stakes and string

Spirit (carpenter's) level

PREPARING THE SITE

These tools will enable you to dig, move and level earth. You can rent a power tamper for preparing large patio foundations (not illustrated).

Spade

Fork

Shovel

Sledgehammer

Rake

Gloves

Bucket

Wheelbarrow

BRICK AND STONE

This toolkit will allow you to break, chop and cut both stone and brick. You may want to rent an angle grinder or a cement mixer for big projects.

Club hammer

(Stone) mason's hammer

Brick chisel

Masonry drill bit

Bricklayer's (mason's) trowel

Safety

Always follow the manufacturer's instructions. Always protect your eyes, ears and hands when using power tools. Wear a dust mask when using cement powder. Wet cement is corrosive. Always keep children out of harm's way.

TOOLS

WOOD

If your designs include fences, gates, pergolas, sheds or decking you are likely to need the tools shown here.

GARDENING

Apart from items like a spade, a fork and a pair of gloves, you may also need a mower and a small number of dedicated tools like those shown below.

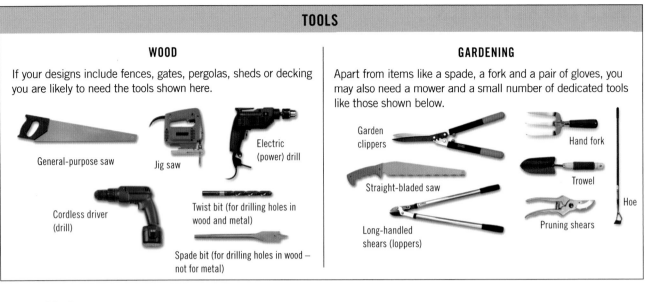

General-purpose saw

Jig saw

Electric (power) drill

Cordless driver (drill)

Twist bit (for drilling holes in wood and metal)

Spade bit (for drilling holes in wood – not for metal)

Garden clippers

Straight-bladed saw

Long-handled shears (loppers)

Hand fork

Trowel

Pruning shears

Hoe

MORE TOOLS

Often the best way of getting tools is to buy them when the need arises. For example, you have a spade and fork, but you soon find that you need a shorter, lighter spade, or a fork with a more comfortable handle, so you get another one. If you are less keen on the construction aspects, larger and/or more specific tools like a power tamper or cement mixer are best borrowed or rented. You could also borrow a few tools, and then buy your own when you know what it is about the borrowed tools that you like.

MATERIALS

BRICK AND STONE

Brick and stone can be purchased direct from the producer, from builder's merchants and from architectural salvage companies.

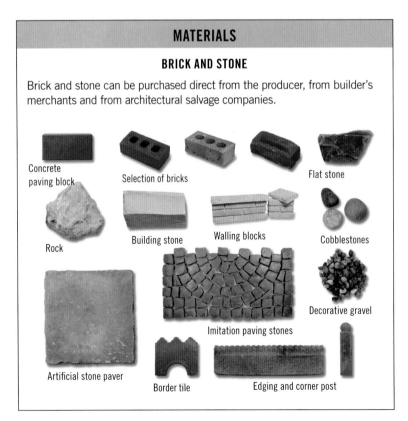

Concrete paving block

Selection of bricks

Flat stone

Rock

Building stone

Walling blocks

Cobblestones

Artificial stone paver

Imitation paving stones

Decorative gravel

Border tile

Edging and corner post

Buying earth and turf

Earth is best purchased by the cubic meter or yard in a giant bag or by the truckload. The more you get, the cheaper it will be. Be careful that you do not buy poorer-quality stuff than you already have.

Turf, or sod, is sold in rolled-up strips about 1 ft (30 cm) wide and 2–3 ft (60–90 cm) long. The cheapest way is to buy it direct from the grower. They are usually quite happy for you to pick up a small number of strips.

MATERIALS

WOOD

Wood in all its forms can be obtained variously from lumber yards, builder's merchants, garden centers and specialty suppliers.

Useful wood sections

Trellis

Bark chippings

Log roll

Railroad tie

CONCRETE AND MORTAR

While there are as many "best" recipes as there are builders, the following work well. The numbers signify the ratio of ingredients (by volume) to each other, measured in the same manner (such as by the shovelful).

Concrete	Mortar
3 aggregate + 2 sand + 1 cement	3 sand + 1 cement

MORE MATERIALS

As garden design is becoming more and more popular, so many materials and products, such as decking, garden shelters, butyl pond liners and concrete sculpture, are being sold by dedicated specialty suppliers. The recent popularity of decking has meant that decking companies and companies only selling decking materials are springing up everywhere. You can make contact via local directories or by the internet; that said, however, one of the pleasures of garden design is travelling around searching out good suppliers.

Ponds and water features

All the items and materials needed for creating ponds and water features can be obtained from garden centers, water-garden centers and specialty suppliers. For large ponds choose a flexible liner. Geotextile is a soft textile material that is laid underneath flexible pond liners and helps prevent the liner from being damaged by sharp stones. A pump is often used in small water features.

Geotextile and flexible pond linings

Rigid liner (formal shape)

Rigid liner (informal shape)

Plastic pump

Rigid cascade liner

MARKING OUT THE SITE

Will it work in practice?

At long last, you can don your work clothes and start marking your designs out on the ground. Once the stakes have been banged in and the various curves and lines have been marked out with string, you will have a clearer picture of how it is all going to look. Along the way, you will need to make decisions about such things as levels, where to put the earth, when to start digging holes, how much land to give to lawns, and so on.

USING YOUR MASTER DRAWING

Having drawn up a site plan to show existing features, and then used this to create a master design that shows how you ideally want the garden to be (see pages 10–11), take several photocopies of both plans, and put the originals safely to one side. To transfer the master design to the garden, read off the scale (say one grid square on the plan equals 1 ft or 30 cm on the ground) and work out the actual measurements that will be needed in the garden. Mark out the shapes using stakes and string, sand trickled from a bottle, or a can of spray chalk.

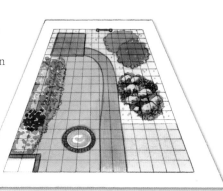

A master plan

SHED OR GAZEBO

Make sure, when you set out the size and shape on the ground, that there is room all around for maintenance. Visit the site at various times throughout the day to get a feel of how it is going to be.

All your measurements should relate to one or more fixed points, such as the house, the front gate and mature trees. Start by marking out what you consider is the most important feature — say the path that runs the full length of the garden — and then fill in with the other features. Live with the bare bones of the marked-out design for a day or so to see if it works.

ROCK GARDEN

It is always a good idea to site the rock garden on high ground — it looks more natural and it saves on stone. Make sure that there is easy access for stone delivery.

PATIO

Mark the shape of the patio, and carefully consider how you will level it. Try it out at various times of the day to see how it fares for sun, shade and shelter.

FLOWER BORDERS

Transfer irregularly shaped "boundary" flower borders from the design to the garden by measuring out at regular intervals from the boundary fences and then joining up the resulting points.

POND

Identify the center of the pond with a stake, and then mark the edges out from this point. Go for the biggest possible pond, because it will look smaller when it is finished.

PATH

Paths are important. Make sure that they are wide enough for things like the wheelbarrow, mower and kids' ride-on toys. Walk the route and live with it for a day or so. Be prepared to change it to suit the needs of the whole household.

Slopes and holes

Assessing the degree of slope: Bang in two stakes, at the highest and lowest points, so that they are flush with the ground. Bridge the stakes with a length of wood and check with a spirit (carpenter's) level.

Levelling a slope: If you do not mind hard work, you can either bring in materials to level the low ground or dig into the slope and move the soil from the highest to the lowest point.

Easy options with slopes: Incorporate the slopes into your design using steps, terraces and waterfalls; alternatively, build a raised deck that stands above the slope.

Dealing with holes and mounds: Turn holes and mounds into exciting design features such as ponds, bogs and rock gardens, or use the earth from the mounds to fill the holes.

Marking out squares and rectangles

Use stakes and string to fix the position of one side. Bang in subsequent stakes to fix a second side in relation to the first, and so on. Use a tape measure to check that opposite sides are equal in length, and parallel. To achieve perfect squareness, measure the diagonals and make small adjustments to the sides until the diagonal measurements are identical.

Marking out circles

Make two marks on the ground – one to fix the center of the circle, and one to fix the most critically placed point on the circumference. Pound a stake in at the center. Cut a length of string and tie a loop at one end and slip it over the stake. Tie a loop at the other end so that it centers on the critical circumference point. Slide a bottle full of sand, lentils or rice into the loop, and use this to scribe the circle out on the ground.

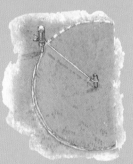

Marking out ellipses

Pound in two stakes to mark out the total length of the ellipse, and one to fix the center. Pound in two stakes to mark the total width of the ellipse. Tie a length of string to make a loop that tightly encloses the two end stakes, and one or other of the width stakes. Slide a bottle full of sand, lentils or rice into the loop at one or other of the width points, remove the two width stakes, and scribe the ellipse out on the ground.

Marking out curves

Take a pile of stones and mark the curve out on the ground. Stand back, look at it from different viewpoints, and make adjustments. Live with the curve for a while. When you are happy with the curve, mark it in with sand or chalk and remove the stones.

Remember that long, broad-sweeping curves are generally easier on the eye than small, tight ones.

REMOVING TURF

Use a tape measure, stakes and string to mark the area out on the ground. Use a spade to slice the whole area into a spade-width grid. One square at a time, hold the spade at a low angle and slice under to remove the turf.

MOVING EARTH

As the precious topsoil always needs to finish up on top, start by using a wheelbarrow and spade to put the topsoil safely to one side. Use the subsoil to fill in holes or boggy areas, or to build up banks. Spread the topsoil over the subsoil.

DIGGERS

A rented digger will certainly get the job done fast, but will it fit through your gates? Will it damage the drive, lawns, trees and/or shrubs?

FORMWORKS

A formwork is a box-like frame – made from 1 in (2.5 cm) thick planks – that is used on soft ground to hold back the sides of a foundation hole. The formwork can be left in place.

FOUNDATIONS AND DEPTHS

A foundation is a construction below ground that distributes and supports the weight of the structure. The basic rule is the greater the load (the weight and size), the larger the foundation needs to be.

PATIOS

A basic foundation for a patio that is being built on firm, well-drained ground.

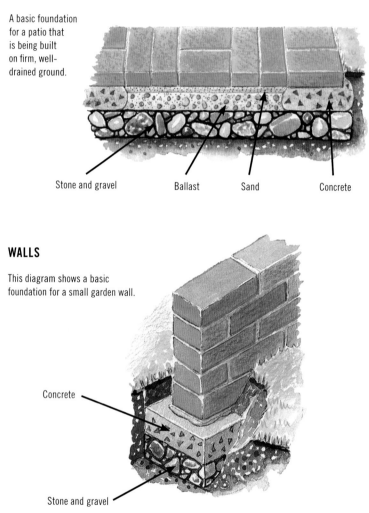

Stone and gravel   Ballast   Sand   Concrete

WALLS

This diagram shows a basic foundation for a small garden wall.

Concrete

Stone and gravel

Garden
Construction

WALLS, FENCES, HEDGES AND GATES

What are the options?

Building walls, erecting fences, planting hedges and hanging gates are all little-by-little procedures that involve you doing your best at every stage. Of course, you might have trouble to start with, but if you follow the directions and remember to take your time, then not only will you end up with a good finished product but you will also have lots of fun along the way. The best advice is to take it slowly – undertake a small project over several days.

BRICK WALLS

There is something very enjoyable about building a simple brick wall – the process of trowelling slices of smooth soft mortar, and placing one brick upon another, is amazingly therapeutic. If you want to enhance your garden with an attractive, traditional, easy-to-use, long-lasting material, then you cannot do better than go for bricks. The procedure involves putting down compacted gravel, laying a slab of concrete over the gravel, and then bedding a pattern of bricks in mortar on top of the concrete. A basic two-brick thick wall is a good choice for most garden walls, but single brick thickness can also work well.

A low garden wall incorporating a tile and soldier course feature.

You will soon get the feel of how to apply the soft mortar with a trowel.

Arrange the bricks so that the vertical joints do not coincide with those in the row below

Stone and gravel   Concrete

A low, single-thickness brick wall with a concrete and gravel foundation.

STONE WALLS

A mixed-stone wall with feature stones for pots.

A stone wall topped with brick can be attractive.

A double-thickness stone wall with a planting cavity.

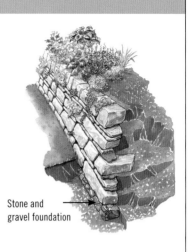

Stone and gravel foundation

Dry-stone walls are a good option for gardens – they are easy to build, strong and long-lasting, they can be built without cement or mortar, and of course they are wonderfully attractive. The traditional technique, developed over many thousands of years, involves stacking stone upon stone – with earth and small stones as an infill – so that the resulting wall is broad-based with the sides leaning in. The procedure is to dig out a trench for the foundation, put compacted gravel in the trench, and then start stacking the stones. Stone walls can also be built using mortar, in the same way as for brick walls (see above).

A traditional dry-stone wall can also be used as a retaining wall for a raised bed or border, with plants in the gaps.

FENCES

Close-boarded fencing

Horizontal lap panel

Interwoven panel

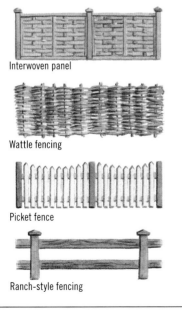

Wattle fencing

Picket fence

Ranch-style fencing

Wooden fences are a good option. Not only is there a huge selection to choose from, but better still they can be up and running in the space of a weekend. You can have traditional white-painted pickets, trellis, close boards, horizontal lap panels, interwoven panels, woven wattles, ranch-style fences, and so on. You have the choice of self-building or employing a specialty company. If you choose the latter, you need to watch out for poor-quality companies. The best advice is to ask friends and neighbors if they can make recommendations.

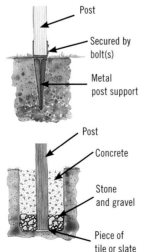

Post

Secured by bolt(s)

Metal post support

Post

Concrete

Stone and gravel

Piece of tile or slate

SETTING POSTS

A new wooden post is best set by digging a hole deep enough to meet your local codes and tamping dirt around it a little at a time until the hole is filled. You could also pour concrete to fill the hole. Metal post supports driven into the ground are often not very sturdy.

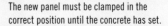

The new panel must be clamped in the correct position until the concrete has set.

HEDGES

Hedges are a great choice for boundaries and decorative features – as long as you have space and time. For example, a boundary hedge might take 4–5 years to grow to a good height, it might need to be about 4–5 ft (1.2–1.5 m) wide at the base, and once grown it will need to be variously clipped and trimmed to keep it in good condition. All that said, a good dense hedge will create privacy, provide shelter, reduce nuisance noise and generally hold back dogs, cattle, and unwanted neighbors.

A crisp, formal hedge consisting of two different foliage colors.

Hedges can be shaped to fit in the surrounding landscape, blending with nearby structures or standing out for eye-catching interest.

GATES AND GATEWAYS

Arched gateways in hedges, ironwork with roses growing over it, iron gates, picket gates, close-boarded gates – there are hundreds of options to choose from. You need to define precisely what you want from a gate. For example, do you want something small, friendly, pretty and decorative, or something large, intimidating, strong and secure?

Anti-theft gates

With wrought-iron gates, either have tops welded on the hinge pegs, or turn the top peg over so that the gate is captured and cannot easily be lifted off the hinge pegs. Use bolts instead of screws for fixing hinges to wood.

A picket gate can look nicely informal.

Close-boarded gates are good for hedges.

Wrought-iron gates are ideal for front gardens.

PATIOS

There are hundreds of ways of making patios and many materials to choose from. You could use brick, concrete slab, reconstituted stone, crushed stone, gravel or tree bark. You could have bricks in straight lines, in zigzags, as chevrons or in soldier courses. There are countless options for each material. Look at the materials and forms in your locality – your house, and neighboring houses, walls and paths – and then do your best to follow on.

Does it have to be paving slabs?

A patio made from a mixture of materials – concrete slabs, found stone and old bricks – looks good in the right setting.

This rather formal stone patio is uplifted by the planting wall.

A small patio made with found brick blends in perfectly here.

An existing patio extended with gravel, cobblestones and stepping stones.

This patio has been created using a mixture of old bricks, stone and tiles.

An unusual patio made from worn slate inside a hexagonal border.

If you want something a bit different, the strong shape of this circle looks great set within lawn and plants.

For a decorative patio, you could try mixing plain paving stones and cobblestones in a pretty pattern.

SHAPE, STYLE AND PLACEMENT

Gone are the days when the best you could hope for in patio comfort was eight gray concrete slabs and two old armchairs; now you can have a patio in just about any shape, color and style that strikes your fancy. A patio is now considered to be more an extension of the house than just a level area in the garden. Just as you want to make the best of the various rooms in your house, now you can shape and decorate the patio to suit your desires and needs.

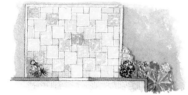   

A basic rectangular patio is a good low-cost option for a small garden.

Geometric combinations – circles and rectangles are wonderfully dynamic – can be used to create separate patio "rooms," with some areas being set at different levels to increase the visual interest.

HOW TO BUILD A BRICK PATIO

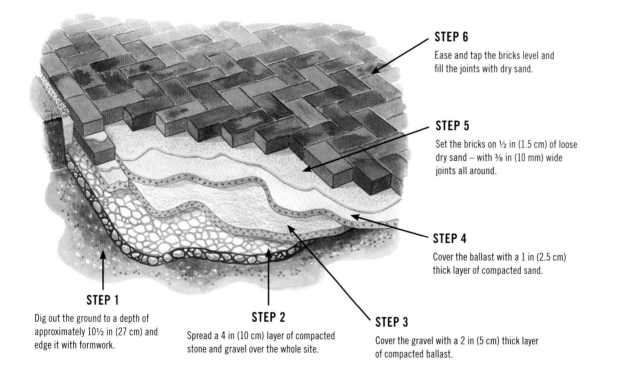

STEP 6
Ease and tap the bricks level and fill the joints with dry sand.

STEP 5
Set the bricks on ½ in (1.5 cm) of loose dry sand – with ⅜ in (10 mm) wide joints all around.

STEP 4
Cover the ballast with a 1 in (2.5 cm) thick layer of compacted sand.

STEP 1
Dig out the ground to a depth of approximately 10½ in (27 cm) and edge it with formwork.

STEP 2
Spread a 4 in (10 cm) layer of compacted stone and gravel over the whole site.

STEP 3
Cover the gravel with a 2 in (5 cm) thick layer of compacted ballast.

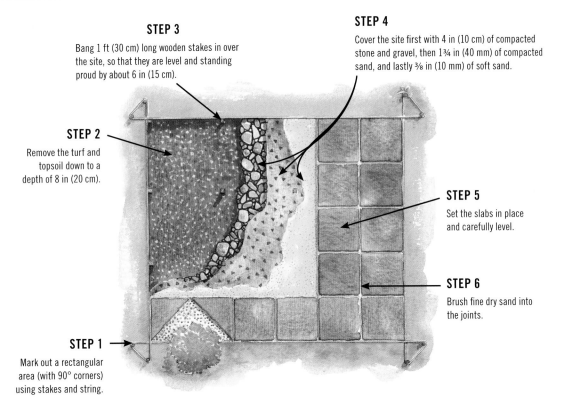

STEP 3

Bang 1 ft (30 cm) long wooden stakes in over the site, so that they are level and standing proud by about 6 in (15 cm).

STEP 4

Cover the site first with 4 in (10 cm) of compacted stone and gravel, then 1¾ in (40 mm) of compacted sand, and lastly ⅜ in (10 mm) of soft sand.

STEP 2

Remove the turf and topsoil down to a depth of 8 in (20 cm).

STEP 5

Set the slabs in place and carefully level.

STEP 6

Brush fine dry sand into the joints.

STEP 1

Mark out a rectangular area (with 90° corners) using stakes and string.

Patio additions

Pergolas A pergola not only gives a patio architectural form, and provides a framework for climbing plants, it also provides shade.

Water features The sounds of a spouting wall mask or bubbling fountain are very relaxing.

Barbecue Consider building a permanent brick barbecue.

Built-in furniture Bench seats or stone-slab coffee tables save on moving and storing garden furniture.

Quick patio

In the sense that a patio is no more than a well-drained firm area – somewhere to sit and play – a good, swift, low-cost option is to choose a well-placed, slightly sloping area, level it with a thin layer of gravel, cover it with landscape fabric, and then top it off with crushed bark.

DRAINAGE SLOPES

In the context of good drainage, a patio needs either to be exactly level, open-jointed and set on sand, or very slightly sloped. A good angle of slope is a fall of about ⅛ in (3 mm) in every 3½ ft (1 m).

NON-SLIP SURFACES

Old brick, stable pavers – like bricks but with a crisscross pattern – and stamped concrete make relatively good non-slip surfaces, as long as they are dry and kept free from algae.

DECKING

The exciting thing about decking is its immediacy. You might have to mix a small amount of concrete for the footings, but, that apart, you can simply float the deck over the existing garden – over old concrete, damp areas, rocks, slopes – and have it finished in the space of a long weekend. If you want an area for sitting, but do not have time to create a patio, decking is the perfect solution.

Things to consider

Decking is fun to build and just as much fun to use, but only if you spend time designing and planning all the details of the project. Answers to the following questions will show you the way.

- How are you going to use the deck? Do you want it for sunbathing or sitting in the shade?

- Do you want to use the deck for barbecues, or for the kids to play on?

- Do you want the deck to be physically linked in some way to the house or set in isolation?

- Do you want the deck to be raised up on legs or set more or less at ground level?

- If you plan to have a raised deck on unstable ground, will you need the advice of, say, a structural engineer?

- Does the deck need to wrap around the corner of the house like a Japanese engawa, or can it run straight out like a pier?

- Do you want a low-cost option, or are you going for the most expensive wood?

- Will your designs in any way affect your neighbors? For example, will a raised deck impinge on their privacy?

- Are there any overhead power lines that are going to be a problem?

- Some areas need planning permission for this kind of work. Will you need planning permission?

- The structure of a deck is dictated by local codes and they vary somewhat depending on where you live. Find out about yours before buying materials.

A small area of decking positioned in a sunny spot right outside the back door provides a relaxing place to unwind with a refreshing drink.

DECKING DESIGNS

This stepped decking has an integral bench and railing, together with handy underseat storage space.

Low-level decking is ideal for a pondside patio, and here the established tree will provide welcome shade in summer.

Raised porch decking with a fancy handrail and trellis – the steps also provide a pleasant way to enter the garden.

This large raised deck with steps and handrail is made more private by the addition of the trellis screens.

Dig holes and set posts to follow your local codes. Take extra care to make sure the posts are plumb. Bolt joists that run around the perimeter to the posts, ensuring the joists are perfectly level. Add the interior joists using joist hangers. Cover the joists with decking and then add decorative railings.

Plan view showing how the underframe supports the decking boards that are laid over the top.

A raised deck like this is good for a wild garden where the ground is uneven.

SPLIT LEVELS

A split-level deck is a good option when you have a slightly sloping site, or when the upper step needs to be raised up above an existing structure – such as an old foundation or underground drain.

MORE OPPORTUNITIES

A deck is just a platform made from wood, so there are lots of interesting options. You could have a decking walkway snaking across the garden, a deck made from railroad ties, decking steps, a bridge made from decking, a decking-type area around a tree, a series of terrace-like decks running up a slope, a raised deck at the water's edge, and so on.

SLOPES

Overlapping decking is a good solution for a sloping garden. All you do is build a series of decks that raise up and overlap each other like huge steps.

Codes and deck construction

Although some people consider following codes a hassle, you should remember that codes are developed to make sure your deck is up to the task of holding the weight of people and other items. A casual gathering of six friends could easily add a thousand pounds to the deck, and you want it to be sturdy. Also, if one follows the codes, it is much more likely that your deck will last much longer. Depending on the size of your deck, codes dictate the depth you must sink your support posts, the kinds of hardware you should use to hold it together and even the size of posts, beams, joists and decking. Codes dictate things like the size of gaps that are allowable in the railing to ensure a toddler doesn't topple off the deck. Contact your local building inspector to find out where you can learn about your local codes.

PLANK PATTERNS

Laying the boards in different patterns will add visual interest to the deck.

Angled 45° to the joists

Angle-cut zigzag

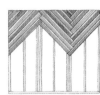
Square-cut herringbone

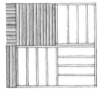
Checkerboard parquet

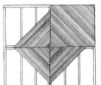
At right angles to joists

Diamond frame

BALUSTRADE OPTIONS

The design of the balustrade can also transform the appearance of a deck.

Horizontal plain

Vertical traditional

Traditional diamond trellis

Modern square trellis

Modern "Chinese" trellis

1930s sunburst

DECKING STEPS

Simple three-tread steps are good for a low deck and easy to fix.

Open-plane steps with a fancy fretted balustrade are more complicated but can look stunning.

TERRACES AND VERANDAS

> ## *What are terraces and verandas?*

Many bungalows and houses have a flat, all-weather surface at their rear which forms an outdoor leisure area. Correctly, a terrace is an open area, usually now paved but earlier grassed, that connects a house with a garden. It usually has a balustrade or low wall, especially if raised above the general level of garden. Verandas are radically different in nature, and the name has an Indian origin, meaning an open-sided gallery around a house.

Brick pillars on either side of a path's entrance onto a terrace add distinction and highlight the path's position.

FORMAL TERRACES

Inevitably, these are covered with paving slabs or companion materials such as bricks in attractive designs. Brick or reconstituted stone balusters and ornate copings create an aged appearance. They have a clinical appearance that goes well with many houses, both modern and early 1900s.

INFORMAL TERRACES

These have a relaxed feel, covered in either natural stone paving or reconstituted paving slabs with an old and weathered appearance. Occasionally, grass is used, but only where an all-weather surface is not important and the area is extremely large, so this is not really suitable for a small garden. Informal terraces look good alongside a lawn, where together they create an open-natured feature.

VERANDAS

The term *veranda* describes a gallery at ground level, on one side or completely surrounding a bungalow or house. They are a real delight, enabling a garden to be taken right up to a house. Most verandas have a sloping roof. The balustrade is usually of wood to harmonize with the rest of the veranda. Few houses are now built with a veranda and perhaps the feature nearest in design is decking.

Raised pond

If a terraced area is large, consider the construction of a raised pond; it is less easy to fall into than a ground-level pond – and the fish and plants are more easily seen.

Pergolas and trellises

These are ideal for integrating onto a terrace that in summer becomes drenched with sun for most of the day. For summer leisure, the shade these features provide will be essential.

VERANDAS

Non-rampant, flowering climbers to cloak supporting timbers

Hanging baskets suspended from strong cross-timbers

Wooden tubs or large, ornate containers planted with summer-flowering plants

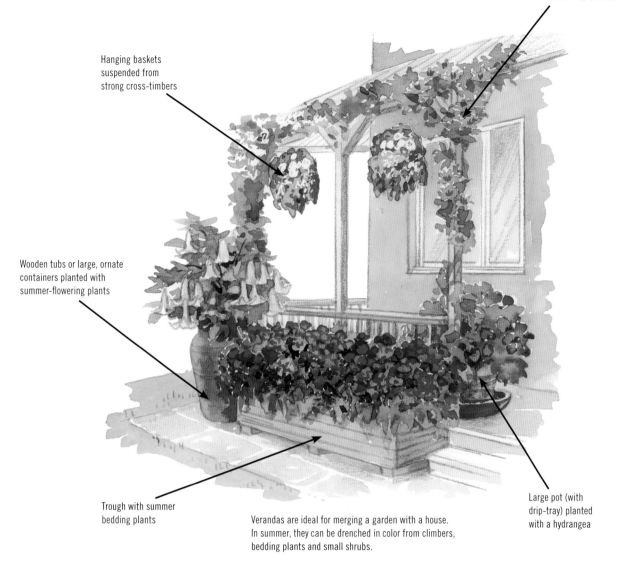

Trough with summer bedding plants

Verandas are ideal for merging a garden with a house. In summer, they can be drenched in color from climbers, bedding plants and small shrubs.

Large pot (with drip-tray) planted with a hydrangea

Planting ideas

Hanging baskets packed with summer-flowering plants are ideal for adorning the edges of verandas, while flowering climbers planted in a narrow border drench the sides in color.

Troughs and small shrubs in large pots are other interesting possibilities.

PORCHES AND ENTRANCES

> ## *Will a porch complement my house?*

A bare area around a front door creates the impression of neglect and blandness, but when a porch-like structure is added and covered in flowering or leafy climbers it brightens both the house and garden. Choose a porch that harmonizes with the house, whether formal or informal. Home-made or modified shop-bought porches are easily erected, but do need to be well secured to prevent wind dislodging them when covered with climbers.

Open-fronted porches allow light to enter the house, while protecting from rain.

Pots packed with summer-flowering plants are ideal for decorating porches.

Enclosed porches become lobbies, where many indoor plants can be grown.

DESIGN, STYLE AND MATERIALS

The design of a porch must complement the house's nature, and, while a clinically brick type may suit a modern house, a wooden one is better for older properties. Painting bricks white usually helps to impart an aged look. In narrow front gardens, a porch and fence can be treated as the same feature and constructed in similar materials.

ADDING THE FRILLS

After creating the structure of a porch, it will need to be dressed in plants to soften the hard edges and add color.

- **Flowering climbers**: choose types that harmonize with the style – those with dainty flowers for modern porches, Lonicera (Honeysuckle) for older properties.
- **Leafy climbers:** avoid creating a dark entrance
- packed with old, dusty climbers. For a summer-only display, plant the herbaceous Humulus lupulus 'Aureus' (Yellow-leaved Hop).
- **Hanging baskets:** if space allows, suspend a pair of baskets where they cannot be knocked.
- **Tubs and pots:** group a few to one side of an entrance, at a variety of different heights.

Porch with seats

HOW TO MAKE A RUSTIC PORCH

Some porches are easily made and fixed into position. Construct an informal porch from four chestnut rustic poles, each about 8 ft (2.4 m) long, and two poles (for the top), each 5 ft (1.5 m) long. Add strengthening cross-poles lower down and at the sides. Pieces of expanded trellis are needed for the sides and top. The supporting poles are concreted into the ground to a depth of 18 in (45 cm).

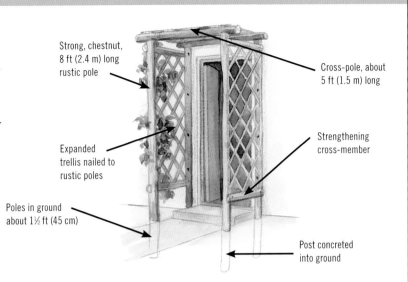

Strong, chestnut, 8 ft (2.4 m) long rustic pole

Cross-pole, about 5 ft (1.5 m) long

Expanded trellis nailed to rustic poles

Strengthening cross-member

Poles in ground about 1½ ft (45 cm)

Post concreted into ground

PATHS AND STEPS

Will these involve much work?

Much depends upon type and size, but the average traditional red-brick path will probably take 3–5 days to design and create – a day for planning and marking out, and the rest of the time for removing the topsoil and building. A wooden walkway or a path made from gravel or tree bark can usually be put down in the space of a long weekend, but a flight of brick and stone steps might take a week or more, depending on the structure of the subsoil.

This path, complete with steps, raised walls and other features has been deliberately designed to make a grand statement.

DESIGNING AND PLANNING PATHS

What do you want from your path? Do you want it to be the shortest route between two points – such as the swiftest route from the kitchen to the compost heap – or do you want it to be a slow, meandering route that takes in all the best bits of the garden? Do you want the path to be plain and functional – just a concrete strip – or do you want it to be decorative, with lots of color and different materials?

PATH OPTIONS

Following the edge of a flower border

Providing a walk around the garden

Old pieces of stone suit a country garden

A traditional herringbone brick path

Cobblestone paths are easy to lay

Leading to a particular feature

Curved paths are good for informal areas

Crazy (cleft stone) paving is suitable for a relaxed garden

Gravel and lavender are a good mix

A simple crushed stone path is just right for this scented garden, and the edges are softened by the spread of the plants.

PATH CONSTRUCTION

Gravel A gravel path is a joy – it looks good and is relatively easy to install. Remove the turf and topsoil to a depth of 8 in (20 cm), and then put down a 4 in (10 cm) thick layer of compacted stone and gravel followed by a 4 in (10 cm) layer of pea gravel.

Pea gravel

Formwork

Stone and gravel

Path construction – brick A red-brick path is a good traditional option. Remove the turf and topsoil down to a depth of 8 in (20 cm), and then put down 3½ in (8 cm) of compacted gravel, ⅞ in (20 mm) of compacted coarse sand and ¼ in (5 mm) of soft sand, followed by the bricks.

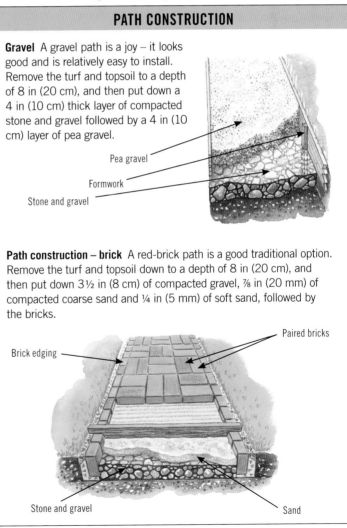

Paired bricks

Brick edging

Stone and gravel

Sand

STEPS IN THE GARDEN

These attractive formal steps have been created with stone slabs forming the treads and bricks forming the risers.

Informal steps made from reclaimed railroad ties are excellent for a country garden using natural materials.

These brick and stone steps are adjoined by buttress hand supports, complete with lights for illuminating the steps after dark.

DESIGNING AND PLANNING STEPS

A functional feature

If you have a sloping garden, you have the choice of scrambling about and just hoping that you do not slip, or you can build steps. Apart from being a good, practical solution, steps also function as a decorative feature that leads the eye from one level to another.

Calculations

Good, comfortable steps need to have risers at about 6–7 in (15–18 cm) high, with treads that measure 12–16 in (30–40 cm) from front to back.

Construction and materials

While there are lots of options – brick, stone, ties, wood, and many more beside – some materials are easier to use than others. For example, a mix of brick and stone is a good choice – the bricks are just right for the risers, and the stone can be sized to suit the depth of the treads.

Overhang of about
1½ in (36 mm)

Brick riser

Stone tread

Stone and gravel

Concrete foundation

A flight of steps leading from a path up to a patio. To a great extent, the whole flight is supported on the concrete foundation that runs under the bottom step.

STEP OPTIONS

Log and gravel steps are a good option for a country garden, as they are quick to create.

These corner steps in a path have been made from square paving slabs and bricks.

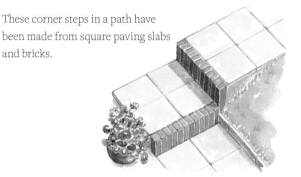

PATH AND STEP PROBLEM-SOLVING

Soft, sloping ground This flight of brick steps, with concrete over stone and gravel under every tread, is a good option for soft, damp ground. The extra-thick layer of stone and gravel and the pipe under the bottom step help to spread the load and drain off the water.

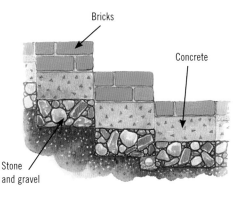

Bricks

Concrete

Stone and gravel

Boggy ground A simple pole walkway is a good option for boggy ground. The poles are supported on posts or piles – the damper the ground, the longer the piles required. If you are worried about slipping, you could also include a handrail, as here.

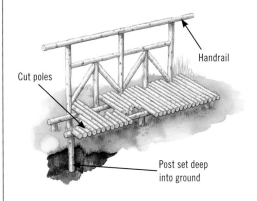

Handrail

Cut poles

Post set deep into ground

Existing concrete steps The best way of sorting out an ugly flight of concrete steps is to cover them with brick. All you do is leave the concrete in place and lay bricks over the treads. The remaining bits of concrete – the risers – can be stained or painted.

PATH CONSTRUCTION

For straight paths, use materials such as paving slabs and concrete pavers which will not need cutting and trimming. These are also best used on flat surfaces. Conversely, for a meandering path on sloping ground, choose crazy paving. Natural stone is also a possibility, but is more expensive. Because plants are often planted in the spaces between pieces of natural stone, do not use a spade to clear snow and ice away, nor put salt on the path.

LAYING PAVING SLABS

Pre-cast paving slabs are ideal for creating a firm, all-weather surface. They can be used on their own or combined with other materials, such as bricks, to create decorative patterns.

1. Prepare the area of the path by removing topsoil and adding a 4 in (10 cm) thick layer of compacted filler.

2. Spread and level a 2–3 in (5–7.5 cm) thick layer of coarse sand over the compacted filler.

3. Mark on the sand the area of the first slab and place five blobs of mortar on it – one in each corner and one in the center.

4. Carefully place a paving slab in position and check that it has a gentle slope so that surface water drains away.

5. Position the next slab and check its slope. If the slabs have straight edges, place ½ in (12 mm) thick spaces between them.

6. When the mortar is hard, remove the spaces and fill the joints with a stiff, dry, weak mortar mix (see below).

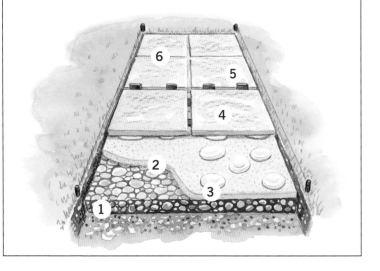

When filling joints

When filling gaps between paving slabs, take care that the mixture does not go on top of them, as it leaves marks. Instead, line the edges with masking tape; then use a stiff, dry, weak mortar mixture to fill the gaps. Tamp this level, to just below the surfaces of the slabs.

Cutting paving slabs

It is often necessary to cut paving slabs. Professionals use powered cutters (angle-grinders), but home gardeners can use a bolster (type of cold chisel) and a club hammer. Wear goggles and strong gloves and score a line on the slab (all edges and sides). Then, using the bolster and club hammer, work around the slab, several times. When complete, place the slab on a board, so that the scored line is positioned above its edge. Use the wooden handle of a club hammer to knock the slab sharply so it breaks along the line.

Cutting concrete brick pavers

Unless a squared pattern (see right) is used to lay pavers, cutting is essential. This can be done by using a bolster chisel and club hammer in the same way as for paving slabs (see above, right); when laying a large patio it is better to rent a wet saw. Don't forget to wear goggles and strong gloves.

LAYING CONCRETE PAVERS

Also known as "flexible" pavers, they gain this name because they are laid on a bed of coarse sand and can, if necessary, later be lifted and relaid. They are about the size of house bricks and ideal for straight paths. Crazy paving is better for curved paths.

1. Mark out the area of the path, remove topsoil and install 6 in (15 cm) deep side constraints. These are vital to hold the sand and bricks in place.

2. Spread and firm a 3 in (7.5 cm) thick layer of filler over the base.

3. Spread a 2 in (5 cm) thick layer of coarse sand over the filler. Select a 6 in (15 cm) deep piece of wood; cut notches at the ends so that when drawn over the sand it leaves the surface the thickness of the paver, minus ⅜ in (9 mm), below the top of the sides.

4. Place the pavers on the sand in the desired pattern (see page 60).

5. Compact the pavers by placing a flat piece of wood on the surface and repeatedly tapping it with a club hammer.

6. Brush coarse sand over the surface, then again compact the pavers. Repeat this, then water the surface with a fine-rosed watering can.

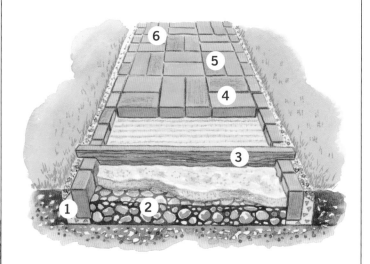

CONSTRUCTING A GRAVEL PATH

Gravel paths have a relaxing ambience, yet can be either formal or informal depending on the edging. Strong side constraints are essential. Provide these with concrete slabs or strong wood.

1. Dig out the area of the path, 4 in (10 cm) deep and 3–4 ft (90 cm–1.2 m) wide. Ensure that the path is dug out to an even depth, especially along its edges.

2. Position concrete side constraints, 3 ft (90 cm) long, 2 in (5 cm) thick and 6 in (15 cm) deep. Use a spirit level to check that the sides are level. Cement them in place.

3. When the side constraints are firm and cannot be moved, use a sledge hammer or club hammer to break up large bricks to form an even base. Do not dislodge the side constraints.

4. Spread gravel over the rubble, so that its surface is about 1 in (2.5 cm) below the side constraints. Use a short piece of stout wood or a metal garden rake.

Stepping trunks!

Gravel paths can be made more attractive by letting sections of wide tree trunks into them. A piece of wire netting secured on top of each slice prevents them becoming slippery.

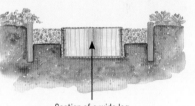

Section of a wide log

CONTRUCTING A CRAZY-PAVING PATH

1. Use strings to mark the position and width of the path. Dig out topsoil to 6 in (15 cm) deep; install side constraints.

2. Form a 2 in (5 cm) thick layer of compacted filler; then 1½ in (36 mm) of coarse sand.

3. Spread mortar over the sand and lay straight-edged pieces of crazy-paving along the sides, about 3½ ft (1 m) at a time.

4. Fill the center with irregularly shaped pieces

5. Fill cracks with mortar.

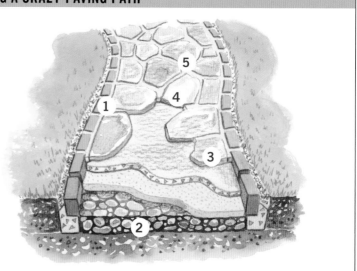

LAYING A NATURAL STONE PATH

Natural stone forms attractive paths. Use strings to mark the path's area and dig out topsoil. Add filler, then 2 in (5 cm) of coarse sand. Because of its uneven thickness, natural stone is more difficult to lay than crazy paving. Lay the stones on blobs of mortar. Dig out sand and filler from some of the larger joints, and fill with soil-based compost. Later, small, prostrate plants can be put in them.

PATTERNS FOR PAVERS

Complex patterns are best left to professional constructors. Several bonds are simple to create, including running and basketweave.

Before deciding the path's width, lay out pavers on a flat surface to the desired pattern. The width of the path can then be tailored to suit this measurement, thereby avoiding any unnecessary cutting of pavers.

Basketweave bond

Running bond (crosswise)

Running bond (lengthwise)

Herringbone bond

Squared bond

Simple bond with cross pavers

LIGHTING

Garden illumination – whether on patios, in borders, among trees or around ornamental ponds as well as submerged – has gained in popularity, and in return for the initial cost and subsequent maintenance makes a garden and patio more attractive and usable over a longer period each day. Additionally, autumn-colored deciduous trees and frost-covered stems during winter can be highlighted. For barbecue enthusiasts, patio lighting is essential.

Are garden lights worth installing?

Ornamental lights are ideal for patios and terraces.

Safety first

Electricity and water are not happy partners and all electrical installations need to be checked over or installed by a competent electrician. Where voltage is reduced through a transformer the risk to yourself and family is less than when the power comes directly from the household power supply.

DO NOT TAKE ANY RISKS – THINK SAFETY FIRST WITH ELECTRICITY AT ALL TIMES.

ON PATIOS

The edges of patios and terraces can be transformed by low spotlights as well as column types. Also, where a table is present a light that illuminates it is useful for late-evening relaxation. Avoid having cables suspended randomly over a patio.

IN BORDERS

Throughout summer and into autumn, borders of all types – packed solely with herbaceous perennials or a medley of types – benefit from illumination. Flowers and colored leaves can be given added qualities by lights positioned looking down on plants. Additionally, a few lights within a border create attractive shadows.

AROUND PONDS

Whether a garden pond is integrated with a patio or featured in a lawn setting, it will be enhanced by a few strategically placed lights. If a waterfall or cascade feeds water into it, these too can be illuminated. Fountains, with their wide and varying range of spray patterns, are also enhanced.

IN PONDS

Submerged lighting – sometimes colored in red, green, amber or blue – adds a fresh and often novel quality to ornamental ponds. Some lighting equipment creates a rainbow of changing light. Ensure that the equipment is safely installed.

FLOODLIGHTING TREES AND SHRUBS

Wall- and post-mounted lights create light over a large area, while low-powered colored lights in a continuous line of up to 40 lamps are possible for stringing between trees. For many gardens, however, a few white spotlights focused upwards and into branches have more appeal.

TYPES OF LIGHTING

The quality and intensity of light is influenced by the source of power – household power, battery or solar.

- **Household power:** this creates the strongest and most penetrating light and is suitable for large installations and powerful spotlights. It also requires the most careful and thorough installation.

- **Battery power:** the size and quality of the battery determines the power of the light, which slowly diminishes as the battery becomes exhausted. Nevertheless, it is a safe way to have light on a patio or terrace.

- **Solar power:** the penetrative quality of the light is poor, but is useful for highlighting the edges of features, from patios to paths and around ponds. It has the bonus of being powered by the sun and inexpensive to operate.

Spotlights are ideal for highlighting specific plants, as well as on patios during summer evenings

Low-intensity lights on short, supporting stems are good for positioning around either a patio or a garden pond

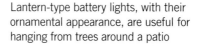

Lantern-type battery lights, with their ornamental appearance, are useful for hanging from trees around a patio

LAWNS AND EDGING

awns not only help to define and unify spaces, they also lead the eye from one area to another. If you want to increase the apparent size of your garden, run the lawns through and around the beds; if you want to chop the space into "rooms," have individual areas of lawn. A lawn is a great, low-cost, easy-maintenance, hardwearing but soft, self-renewing, multi-purpose surface for all the family. Remember to choose a grass type to suit your particular needs.

LAWN DESIGN

A lawn can be used for physical activities such as playing games, as a design feature, such as in a formal garden where the lawn is seen as a visual pattern-making device that links beds and paths, or as a functional path-like form that leads from one area of the garden to another. From a practical mowing point of view, the ideal lawn has a smooth-curved outline, with the edge set slightly higher than the surrounds so that the lawnmower can be run over the edge.

PREPARING THE SITE

Till to a depth of 3–4 in (7–10 cm). Remove stones and perennial weeds, break up large clods, and pick up debris. On a day when the ground feels dry, rake over the plot. Work systematically and firm the soil with a rented roller designed for this purpose.

MAINTENANCE

At regular intervals throughout the growing season, you need to mow the lawn, water it in dry spells, trim the edges, aerate, rake up dead grass, and topdress to fill hollows and improve vigor. Feeding with fertilizer should only be done if and when the need arises.

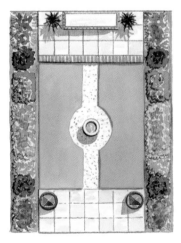

The lawn edging can be anything from a row of bricks hidden away just below the surface of the ground through to a trench full of pea gravel, a nicely cut edge where the lawn meets a flower bed, or a line of fancy tiles set on edge. There are many options.

Wooden boards fixed to stakes

Ready-made logroll

Round-nose tiles on edge

Soldier bricks set on end

Fancy rope-edge tiles

Bricks set at an angle

Sowing seed

- Buy a seed mixture that suits your needs.

- Pick a day when the soil is dry underfoot – either in the autumn or spring – and go over the whole site, gently raking the surface.

- Seeding in fall is the best option largely because grass can continue to grow at slightly lower temperatures than most weeds. So a lawn started in early fall gives the grass an edge over competing plants.

- Kill any existing lawn or weeds with a herbicide recommended by a local garden center or with black plastic sheeting.

- Watering grass seed and newly sprouted grass is critical to its survival and thriving growth.

- Try to stay off of newly sprouted grass and keep pets and children away.

Laying turf

- Use string and a couple of stakes to set a straight guideline along one edge of the site.

- Make sure that the weather is going to stay fine, check the size of the sod rolls with the supplier – mostly they measure about 1 ft (30 cm) wide and 3 ft (90 cm) long – and then order slightly more turf than you think you will need.

- Starting from the guideline, lay the first row of turf and gently ease and tamp them into place.

- When you come to the second row, cut the first piece into half and then continue butting the second row hard against the first – so that the end joints are staggered from row to row, like a brick pattern.

- Continue working across the site, standing on a plank on the turf that has just been put down, and always looking towards the next line of turf that needs to be put down.

- When the turf has been down for about a week, use a half-moon edging iron or an old bread knife to trim and shape curved edges.

- Watering newly lain sod is critical to its survival. The deeper roots that grass develops have been cut off, so the grass needs daily watering for several weeks depending on your soil and the weather.

BORDERS

How do I design a border?

In garden design, a border can be regarded both as an area for planting and as a three-dimensional element. Most modern gardens consist of four elements – lawns, paving, borders and water – so borders figure very highly in the scheme of things. When it comes to designing a border, there are three aspects to consider: the shape as seen on the ground, the character of the structure (the edgings, retaining wall and so on) and the type of planting it will support.

BORDER DESIGNS IN PLAN VIEW

Informal edge-strip borders	Formal, geometrical borders	Informal island border in lawn	Informal peninsular border

There are only six basic types of border.
- The edge-strip border that uses the boundary fence as a backdrop.
- The geometrical border that relates to some sort of formal design.
- The island border that is set within a sea of lawns.
- The peninsular border that runs out from a boundary fence.
- The border that runs hard up against the wall of the house.
- The border that relates to some sort of functional scheme – it looks to the sun, is just the right width away from the wall for the wheelbarrow, or whatever it might be.

When you come to design a border, you have to decide how you want it to figure in the scheme of things. For example, do you just want to break up an area of lawn, put distance between you and your neighbors, or create the illusion that your garden is, for example, wider or shorter?

PLANTING SCHEMES

(Above) A mixed border in summer is usually packed with color, texture and form. This example includes climbers on tripods, shrubs and herbaceous perennials in a variety of flower colors.

(Above) Mixed borders have an exciting, dynamic nature – they are invariably colorful and vibrant.

EDGINGS

Edgings function on two levels: they physically prevent the earth of the border running over the path or lawn next to it, and they are a design feature in their own right – such as a wall, a row of tiles or a railroad tie.

Raised borders

Ready-made rustic log rolls are an easy option.

A double-thickness wall is a good choice for a small garden.

Red brick is a good traditional choice.

MULCH

A mulch has many functions. For example, while a mulch such as a layer of manure or tree bark prevents the soil from drying out, holds back the growth of weeds and rots down to enrich the soil, a mulch such as pea gravel or crushed rock holds in moisture, holds back the weeds and functions as a design feature in its own right.

PERGOLAS, ARCHES AND TRELLISES

If your idea of heaven is a mix of woodwork and gardening, you are going to enjoy building features such as pergolas and arches. Just think about it – a nice bit of woodwork followed by lazing under your beautifully crafted garden pergola, with a drink and a good book just within reach, all perfectly enclosed with an impressive trellises, with fragrant plants and dappled sunlight all around. Pergolas, arches and trellises can all be used to create instant features.

Are these features easy to create?

A pergola weighed down with a vine creates an eye-catching feature as well as a very private area.

A ready-made arch is good for creating instant height, but plants will take time to grow over it.

Plant-covered trellises are a good option if you want privacy. Use a variety of different climbers to add interest.

PERGOLAS

If you want to create an instant architectural feature in your garden – a place to snooze and play in the shade, a structure for growing climbing plants over, and an eye-catching focal point – then a pergola is an exciting option. The visual impact of a pergola clothed with a wisteria, a grapevine or a honeysuckle can be absolutely stunning. If you are wondering if there is enough room in your garden, a pergola can easily be shaped to suit your needs. It can be anything from four uprights topped with a handful of cross-beams – just large enough to sit under – or a lean-to structure made from rustic poles, through to a substantial brick and wooden walkway that runs the length of the garden.

A lean-to pergola is a traditional option that is a very good choice for a patio area, especially in a small garden.

Radial-topped pergolas provide distinctive points of interest.

Climbing plants can be used to transform an old, ugly pergola into a striking feature.

A traditional pergola bedecked with wisteria is a beautiful, inspiring sight.

A porch-type pergola complete with lattice screens.

This simple pergola has been constructed using rustic poles.

ARCHES

Arches are functional in the sense that they can provide a support for plants, and of course they add architectural style, but a small, well-placed arch can also be beckoning and mysterious – an inviting route or gateway for your feet, eyes and mind to pass through. At the practical level, a wooden arch over a gate is a really good way of strengthening and bracing the gateposts. All you do is have posts that are slightly higher than head height, and top them off with a pergola-like cross-beam. If you have plans to create a romantic garden and like the notion of holding hands under a leafy arbor, then an arch in a hedge or an arch-like tunnel covered with a scented climber such as a honeysuckle is a good feature to go for.

This arch-pergola leads the eye to a focal point.

Here a flower-covered arch creates a secluded bower.

A rose-covered arch is perfect for a country garden.

An arch has been used to transform this plain doorway.

The trellis arch makes more of this simple door.

ARCHES IN HEDGES

Arches in hedges can be used to create sudden and surprising entrances into other parts of the garden. Unusual shapes will create talking points for visitors, and can be used as design features to complement the overall style of the garden.

TRELLISES

While, at the practical level, trellises are no more than a structure or pattern of slender wooden strips used for supporting plants – as with free-standing trellises, or a trellis fence, or a trellis fixed to the wall of a house – a piece of trellises can also be an imposing and eye-catching architectural feature in its own right. In the 18th and 19th centuries in England and Europe, it was a much-favored way of embellishing the house and garden. One such design involved covering the whole outside of the house with a pattern of trellises, with the effect that the house looked delicate – like wedding-cake decoration. With this in mind, perhaps a trellis is the answer to the problem of hiding an ugly garage or a neighbor's unsightly concrete wall.

False-perspective trellis

Trellis with "window"

Open-character screen

Integral seat

Greenwood trellises

This pretty little trellis feature is characteristic of the spidery rustic woodwork that was favored in the 19th century by gardeners who were trying to achieve a romantic cottage garden – a mix of an 18th-century French romantic garden and a pastoral sheep-and-shepherdess garden.

Fixing trellises to walls

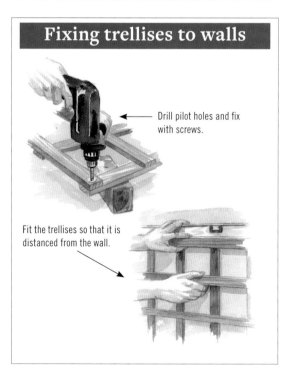

Drill pilot holes and fix with screws.

Fit the trellises so that it is distanced from the wall.

GARDEN BUILDINGS

What are the possibilities?

There is a long tradition of householders making all manner of garden structures from greenhouses, sheds, porches and gazebos to log cabins and summerhouses. If you enjoy basic "do-it-yourself," are good with a saw, hammer and drill, and are keen and enthusiastic, then there is no reason at all why you cannot build just about any garden shelter that strikes your fancy. Don't forget, however, that the key words here are "keen" and "enthusiastic"!

SHEDS

SITING A SHED

Walk around your garden and try to visualize the perfect setting for a shed. Of course, much depends on what sort of shed you are looking to build, but ideally it needs to be positioned on dry, high ground, in a quiet spot, with the doors and windows looking towards a nice view. If you can imagine yourself sitting in the shed – dry, warm, with no noise, and sheltered – then you will probably have got it just about right.

A small, apex-roofed, free-standing shed.

A medium-sized, slope-roofed shed.

Shed foundations

A shed needs to be built on a solid foundation. A good foundation is made up from compacted gravel topped with concrete. Foundations should be built according to your local building code.

This shed has double doors for easy storage.

This small shed will fit snugly into a corner.

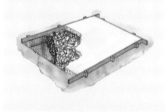

GREENHOUSES

Traditional apex design

Modern apex design

Large lean-to

Octagonal design

Mini lean-to

Combination shed/greenhouse

SITING

A greenhouse should be set on dry ground away from anything that is likely to cast shadows or scatter debris, meaning buildings and trees. If you have no choice other than to site it near a fence or a hedge, then try to place it so that it is on the sunny, sheltered side.

Foundations

The average, small, rectangular greenhouse can be set on concrete blocks – one at each corner, with a row of blocks running in through the doorway.

Screening

In mid-summer the interior of a greenhouse can get hot enough to kill the plants within. You can mitigate that heat with automatic vents and by using netting or fabric to create shade.

Mini plastic greenhouses

While a small plastic greenhouse is usually fine for growing a few tomatoes – but even then it can swiftly overheat – it is not a very attractive option from a design point of view.

Barn design formed of sheet glass.

Modern design made of plastic sheeting.

Cloche

Traditional bell jar design made out of blown glass.

SUMMERHOUSES

SITING

A summerhouse can be a magical place – for children sleeping over, for a quiet drink, or for a doze and a read – if it is well sited. It needs to be positioned on dry ground, away from dank corners, with the doors and windows facing the afternoon sun.

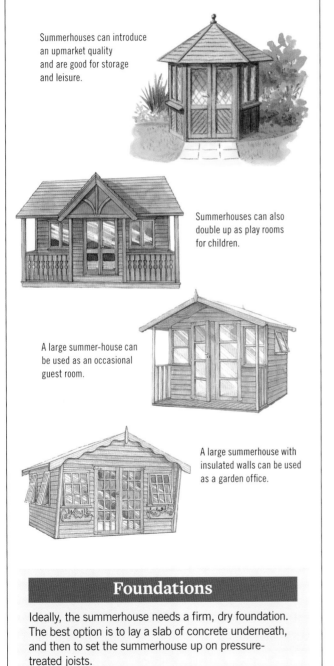

Summerhouses can introduce an upmarket quality and are good for storage and leisure.

Summerhouses can also double up as play rooms for children.

A large summer-house can be used as an occasional guest room.

A large summerhouse with insulated walls can be used as a garden office.

Foundations

Ideally, the summerhouse needs a firm, dry foundation. The best option is to lay a slab of concrete underneath, and then to set the summerhouse up on pressure-treated joists.

ARBORS

SITING

In the sense that an arbor is designed to be an eye-catching feature, it needs to be sited where it fits into your overall scheme of things – for example, in a corner with climbing plants scrambling over it, or looking out over a pond. If you know that you are most likely to use the arbor in the late afternoon, make sure it takes best advantage of the sun at that time.

A traditional arbor complete with trellises sides and back and roses growing over it to provide color and scent.

Foundations

Although much depends on the design of your particular arbor, just make sure that its base is high and dry. Foundations made from wooden lumber (posts, beams or joists) shold be made from lumber that has been treated with a presrvative that is designed for "ground contact."

Play houses

While a play house needs to be sited on dry ground, away from dank corners, and in the sun – just as with a summerhouse – it also needs to be near the house and in full view. It is vital that you can see and hear the children at play. Better yet, join the fun and take part in their imaginative play.

Kids will enjoy the exciting bright colors.

A "Wendy" house gets its name from the Peter Pan story.

CHOOSING THE STYLE

Which style is right for me?

Informality in gardens appeals to many home gardeners and especially to devotees of a relaxed, casual and Bohemian way of life. Traditionally, cottage gardens had this feel, where plants of all types jostled side by side in the same bed. Fortunately, even in small gardens this ambience can be recreated through informal plants and features, as well as decorative and relaxed paths, fences and hedges. Remember, also, to choose rustic benches.

Planned informality is the key to achieving a successful look with relaxed and informal gardens.

SOOTHING SOUNDS?

As well as demure colors and irregular shapes, soothing sounds have a relaxing nature. These range from the rustling of leaves to the reassuring pitter-patter of water splashing and tumbling from fountains and waterfalls.

A few bamboos are ideal for planting in a small garden and these are described on page 91, as well as their use in Mediterranean and Japanese gardens on pages 84 and 90. Their leaves rustle in even the slightest breeze, creating a soothing and irregular sound. Additionally, some can be grown in containers, and these are ideal for bringing both color and sound closer to a house.

Garden wind chimes suspended from trees and close to a house create gentle and comforting sounds, but do not position them where they are easily bumped into.

RELAXED LAYOUT AND INFORMAL PLANTS

Several examples of informal designs are featured on the left of this page. Remember to ensure that paths, lawn edges and borders do not create straight lines, and check that garden furniture completes the informality. Rustic benches and thin-framed metal chairs have a relaxed nature.

INFORMAL LAYOUT EXAMPLES

Brick paths crossing an area of gravel create texture variations

Irregularly positioned paving slabs create an unusual, attractive path

Natural stone paths epitomize a relaxed and informal garden

Meandering, maze-like paths have eye appeal, especially for children

Curved patios and paths create a unified, informal garden

A meandering path, combined with shrubs, creates mystery in a garden

Wisteria sinensis 'Alba,' with its clusters of attractive white flowers, contrasts well with the old brick wall behind it.

DESIGN FOR AN INFORMAL GARDEN

Although small and informal, a garden must have a focal point. There are several to consider, including:

- Benches constructed with a framework of thin, rustic poles but with a flat sitting area.

- Wrought-iron chairs and tables, perhaps with the benefit of lighting.

- Bird baths and feeders positioned on an informally paved area – but always make sure uneaten food does not attract squirrels.

- Armillary spheres and informal statues – use these to create relaxed focal points.

- Grass benches surrounded by clipped Box – these are simple to construct and ideal for a relaxed area at the end of an informal path.

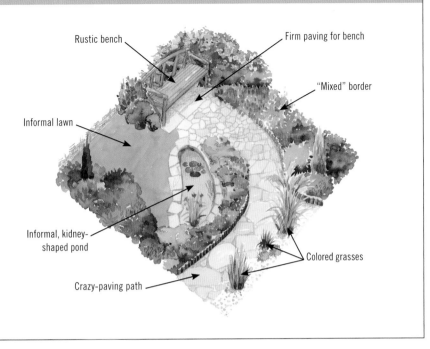

Rustic bench

Firm paving for bench

"Mixed" border

Informal lawn

Informal, kidney-shaped pond

Crazy-paving path

Colored grasses

INFORMAL PATHS

Ideas for informal paths include well-weathered bricks (not concrete pavers), sections of logs, reconstituted stone, and circular pavers (see above) that can be laid to create an attractive and unusual meandering path.

Natural stone with small, prostrate plants positioned between them creates a cottage-garden ambience. An alternative is crazy paving, which is not quite so informal.

INFORMAL BACKGROUNDS

Natural stone walls are informal in appearance, but are available to only a few home gardeners. There are some other relaxed, and much cheaper, backgrounds, including the following.

- **Wattle panels:** ideal for a "countrified" fence, but they do not create a strong barrier against animals.

- **Interwoven panels:** these create a solid screen, usually in panels 6 ft (1.8 m) long and in several heights.

- **Horizontal lap panels:** overlapping horizontal strips are attached to a framework, and are sold in panels 6 ft (1.8 m) wide and in several heights.

GAZEBOS AND ORNAMENTAL WELLS

Gazebos are distinctive features and certain to gain attention, as well as forming leisure areas. By definition, they allow people to "gaze out" onto a garden. They have a long history, originating in early Persian gardens, and generally have a wooden framework, with wooden lattice-work at the back and an ornate roof. An ornamental well is sure to attract glances; but you must ensure that it has a firm surround.

Rustic gazebos have an informal nature

Ornamental wells need strong construction

FORMAL GARDENS

Regimented gardens must be kept neat and tidy, otherwise they will lose their distinctive character. Neatly outlined edges of *Buxus sempervirens* 'Suffruticosa' (Dwarf Edging Box) need to be maintained throughout the year, while edgings of formal summer-flowering bedding plants require attention to ensure that they do not invade each other or become dominated by weeds. Lawns require regular mowing and edge trimming.

CLASSICAL HERITAGE

Creating patterns and shapes has long captivated gardeners, usually by using plants such as trees and shrubs to produce permanent designs. Seasonal patterns in gardens have also been created, mainly using summer-flowering annuals in neat designs popularized through "carpet bedding" (also known as tapestry, mosaic and jewel bedding) in the 1800s. It gained an enthusiastic following, with motifs and intricate patterns created in local and national competitions.

Formal bedding schemes – earlier and still widely known as carpet bedding.

Shapes and patterns are claimed to influence our lives and to have curative values. However, not everyone is sensitive to the auras created by pattern therapy, described in writings dating back several thousand years. Nevertheless, plants in attractive patterns seldom fail to attract attention.

FORMAL LAYOUTS AND PLANTING EXAMPLES

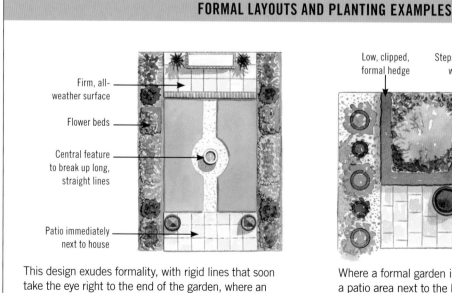

Firm, all-weather surface

Flower beds

Central feature to break up long, straight lines

Patio immediately next to house

Low, clipped, formal hedge

Steps that harmonize with the patio

Patio immediately next to house

This design exudes formality, with rigid lines that soon take the eye right to the end of the garden, where an additional leisure area has been created.

Where a formal garden is to be on a slope, first construct a patio area next to the house and then create a series of steps. A small hedge will help to unify the design.

Plants for formal summer bedding

Here are a few of the most popular plants used in summer bedding.

- *Begonia semperflorens* (Fibrous-rooted Begonia/Wax Begonia): tender perennial invariably grown as a half-hardy annual. Glossy green or purple leaves are surmounted from early to late summer by red, pink or white flowers. Height: 6–9 in (15–23 cm) Spread: 8–10 in (20–25 cm)

- *Lobelia erinus* (Edging Lobelia): half-hardy perennial invariably grown as a half-hardy annual. Masses of blue, white or red flowers throughout summer. Some forms have trailing stems and are best used in hanging baskets. Height: 4–9 in (10–23 cm) Spread: 4–6 in (10–15 cm)

- *Lobularia maritima* (Sweet Alyssum; also known as *Alyssum maritimum*): hardy annual usually grown as a half-hardy annual. Densely covered with rounded clusters of white, violet-purple, rose-carmine or deep purple flowers throughout summer. Height: 3–6 in (7.5–15 cm) Spread: 8–12 in (20–30 cm)

- *Salvia splendens* (Scarlet Salvia): tender perennial invariably grown as a half-hardy annual. Glossy green leaves are surmounted from early to late summer by red, pink or white flowers. Height: 12–15 in (30–38 cm) Spread: 9–15 in (23–38 cm)

- *Tanacetum parthenium* 'Aureum' (Edging Chrysanthemum; also known as *Chrysanthemum parthenium* 'Aureum'): short-lived perennial raised as a half-hardy annual. It produces aromatic, light green leaves and white flowers from mid-summer to early autumn. Height: 9–12 in (23–30 cm) Spread: 8–10 in (20–25 cm)

SPECIMEN PLANTS FOR SUMMER FLOWERING

- *Abutilon pictum* **'Thompsonii'** (Flowering Maple; also known as *Abutilon striatum* 'Thompsonii'): half-hardy perennial with maple-like, dark green leaves splashed and spotted in bright yellow. Height: 3–4 ft (90 cm–1.2 m) Spread: 15–18 in (38–45 cm)

- *Bassia scoparia* **'Childsii'** (also known as *Kochia scoparia* 'Childsii'): half-hardy annual. Light green foliage. Height: 1¹⁄₂ ft (45 cm) Spread: 9–12 in (23–30 cm)

- *Canna x generalis* (Indian Shot): half-hardy perennial. There are two main types – green-leaved and purple- or brown-leaved. Height: 2¹⁄₂–3¹⁄₂ ft (75 cm–1 m) Spread: 12–15 in (30–38 cm)

- *Cordyline australis* (Cabbage Palm): slow-growing and tender evergreen. Height: 3–4 ft (60–90 cm) Spread: 1¹⁄₂ ft (45 cm)

FORMAL FEATURES

PATHS AND STEPS

Straight paths and steps, perhaps formed of clinically arranged paving slabs or concrete pavers, epitomize the nature of a formal path.

DECORATIVE SCREENS

Ornamental screens and entrances have an attractive yet functional nature, helping to create distinctive and separate parts in a garden.

PORCHES

Porches constructed from planed lumber and with a tiled or boarded roof create formality. They can be attached to a formal-style fence.

PERGOLAS

Pergola-type structures need not be solely positioned over a path. A small, hard-surfaced area is enhanced by overhead screening.

LAWN CENTERPIECES

Clinically outlined lawn features, such as bird baths and sundials. On a small lawn, keep their size in proportion to the area, ensuring they are not dominant.

WATER FEATURES

Several types of water features can be integrated into a small garden. Try a small fountain against a wall, or create a pebble pond.

FLOWER GARDENS

Is a flood of color possible?

Even in small gardens it is possible to create a miniature, English-style flowering garden, with masses of color provided mainly by herbaceous plants with help from summer-flowering bedding plants. Herbaceous perennials create superb displays for 3–4 years before needing to be lifted and divided, while summer-flowering bedding plants are planted fresh each year.

INFORMAL MEDLEYS OF FLOWERING PLANTS

Informal medleys of herbaceous perennials, summer-flowering bedding plants, shrubs, small trees, biennials and summer-flowering bulbs are especially popular in small gardens where, perhaps, only one border is possible. These "mixed" borders create color

Integrate garden ornaments into flower borders.

over a long period and often enable the inclusion of your most diverse and favorite plants. In a small garden, rely mainly on herbaceous perennials, with just a few shrubs that have a dual quality of flowers and colorful leaves. If some of these plants have fragrant flowers, that is a bonus.

Where bulbs are used in mixed borders, choose mainly summer-flowering types, such as lilies. If spring-flowering bulbs are used, this prevents soil cultivation in early summer. Also, when their leaves have died down there is a risk of damaging the hidden bulbs.

"Mixed" borders have a colorful and vibrant nature.

Floral entrances with climbers and containers

English-style entrances become awash with color and fragrance from scented flowering climbers, with a variety of container-grown plants adding to the riot of color.

For formal entrances: large-flowered Clematis: wide range, with a deciduous nature and mainly single flowers, in many colors and often throughout summer.

For semi-formal entrances: Clematis macropetala: bushy and deciduous, with light and dark blue, bell-shaped and nodding flowers during late spring and early summer.

For rustic settings: *Lonicera periclymenum* (Woodbine/ Honeysuckle): popular cottage-garden climber – the cultivar 'Belgica' (Early Dutch Honeysuckle) flowers during late spring and early summer, and 'Serotina' (Late Dutch Honeysuckle) from mid-summer to autumn.

Raised beds enable a variety of plants to be seen easily, as well as making gardening more comfortable for people who are confined to wheelchairs or who cannot easily bend down.

HOW TO CREATE A MINIATURE FLOWER GARDEN

Whatever a garden's size, the desire to create masses of color is paramount, as well as replicating a traditional English-style flower garden with its homely and reassuring nature. In earlier years and on a grand scale, borders were sometimes color-themed – perhaps mainly white, gold-and-yellow, green or blue – now this is seldom attempted.

Traditionally, herbaceous perennials were grown in double borders, facing each other, separated by a broad grass path and backed by hedges that created shelter and harmonized with color-themed borders. Nowadays, and on a small scale, this can be replicated by creating borders with small-garden herbaceous perennials, a central path and two small lawns on either side of it. Path edgings of summer-flowering bedding plants can be used to introduce further color.

Adding a paved or bricked surface at the far end of these borders and lawns creates a focal point, as well as a leisure area for an attractive bench.

Ornate bench, creating an area of rest as well as a focal point

Colorful herbaceous border

Well-manicured formal lawn

Range of colorful summer-flowering bedding plants

Firm, all-weather surface formed of paving slabs

Second herbaceous border complementing the other

Lawn and bedding plants mirroring the opposite side

Central brick path

Range of plants

Using a wide range of plants creates greater interest.

- **Hardy annuals:** these are sown in their flowering position outdoors in spring; they die in autumn.

- **Half-hardy annuals:** these are sown in gentle warmth in late winter or early spring and planted in early summer; they die in autumn.

- **Herbaceous perennials:** these grow and flower for 3–4 years before being lifted and divided. Each year, plants die down to ground level in autumn and develop fresh shoots in spring.

- **Bulbs, corms and tubers:** there is a wide range of types, but all are powerhouses of stored energy. Some flower in winter or spring, others in summer or autumn.

- **Climbers:** a few of these are hardy annuals, while others are perennial and will grow happily from one year to another with very little attention.

- **Shrubs:** these are woody-natured, with several stems growing from ground level. Most live for ten years or more. They can be deciduous or evergreen.

- **Small trees:** these are woody-natured, with a single stem (trunk) connecting the branches to the roots. Most live for 20 or more years, and they can be deciduous or evergreen.

Honeysuckle arbor

As well as clothing porches and rustic arches alongside boundary hedges and over garden paths, consider creating a Honeysuckle-covered arbor in a secluded part of your garden. Such a feature has a relaxed character and is best used in an informal setting. Choose a semi-rustic bench.

INITIAL COST

- With shrubs, the initial cost is high, but remember that this will be spread over ten years or more.
- Herbaceous perennials are less expensive than shrubs, and they can be lifted and divided after 3–4 years before being replanted, thus creating more plants for free.
- Summer-flowering bedding plants have a summer-only value, but displays can be changed each season.

MAINTENANCE TIME

Keeping a herbaceous border tidy throughout summer requires more attention than just a border full of shrubs and underplanted with bulbs. Summer-flowering bedding plants also need regular care, including pulling out weeds, watering and removing dead flowers and invasive stems.

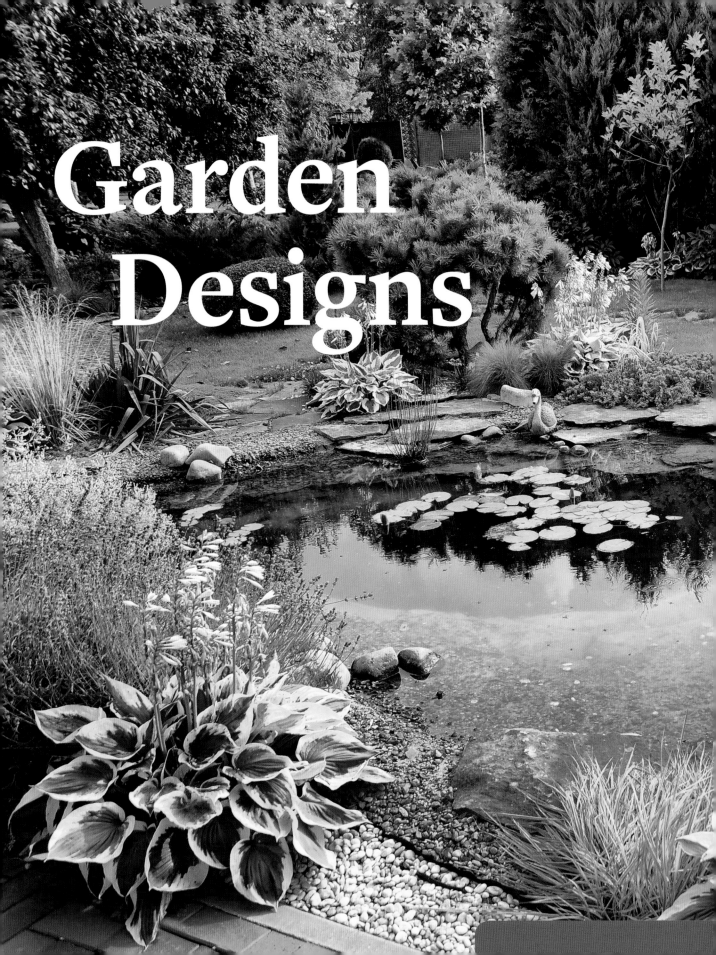

Garden Designs

TRADITIONAL COTTAGE KITCHEN GARDEN

What elements should be included?

A cottage kitchen garden is a romantic coming-together of traditional ideas and notions that have their roots in the agricultural, pre-industrial past when subsistence gardens were made up of vegetable beds, chicken runs, apple trees and compost heaps, with lots of meandering paths, herbs and wildflowers all included in the mix. If you include a lovers' arbor, a kissing gate, a water fountain, or a natural pond, you will be heading in the right direction.

Every cottage garden needs a water pump barrel feature.

Plant fruit, vegetables amd flowering plants together for the perfect cottage garden – then both enjoy the flowers and eat the produce.

A meandering cottage kitchen garden, consisting of a rich mix of flowers and vegetables, can be a visual delight in summer.

Design guidelines for success

- A small garden at about 100 x 35 ft (30 x 10.5 m) is ideal.
- Keep the lawn as small as possible.
- Give half of the total space over to the fruit and vegetables.
- Mix the fruit, vegetables and flowers.
- Include meandering paths.
- Use natural materials – best if they are salvaged.
- Use local materials.
- Stay away from modern paints – no blues.
- Try to have a feature like a well or an oak water barrel.
- Use traditional cottage flowers – no exotics.
- Include a pond if there is space – otherwise have a well.
- Include apple and plum trees.

LOOKING AT THE PROJECT

If we take it that our cottage kitchen garden design (see opposite) draws its inspiration from the small, higgledy-piggledy and somewhat humble country cottages that were once commonplace in England, for example, it will help if your garden is already small with lots of salvaged materials and meandering paths. Have a look at your space and make decisions about what to keep. A good overall size is about 100 ft (30 m) long and 35 ft (10.5 m) wide.

CONSIDERING THE IMPLICATIONS

Traditional cottage kitchen gardens could be described as a bit "folksy." Will this "needs-must-and-mend" mix of fantasy and function suit all the members of your household?

VARIATIONS TO CONSIDER

If you like the overall notion of a loosely defined mix of fruit, vegetables and flowers, but want to nudge the emphasis so there are more vegetables than flowers, or vice versa, then just go your own way.

HOW TO CREATE A TRADITIONAL COTTAGE KITCHEN GARDEN

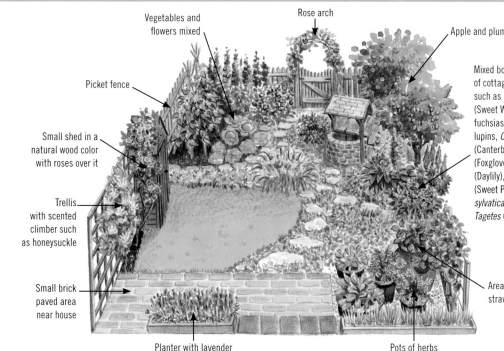

Vegetables and flowers mixed

Rose arch

Apple and plum trees

Picket fence

Mixed border consisting of cottage-garden plants such as *Dianthus barbatus* (Sweet William), hardy fuchsias, delphiniums, lupins, *Campanula medium* (Canterbury Bells), *Digitalis* (Foxglove), *Hemerocallis* (Daylily), *Lathyrus odoratus* (Sweet Pea), *Myosotis sylvatica* (Forget-me-not) and *Tagetes* (Marigold)

Small shed in a natural wood color with roses over it

Trellis with scented climber such as honeysuckle

Small brick paved area near house

Area of fruit and strawberries in pot

Planter with lavender at the side of door

Pots of herbs by doorstep

Order of work

- Draw up your designs so that they take into account the house, the boundaries, immovable structures and large trees.

- Keep choice plants – either leave them in place or move them to other sites within the garden – and give unwanted plants away or dispose of them.

- Build structures like the pond.

- Put down the paths, and prepare the soil for the various beds.

Planting

Start by making sure that all your existing plants are thriving. Don't be in too much of a hurry with the new planting, other than to set out new shrubs and trees. Plant all the other flowers, herbs, fruit and vegetables in the appropriate seasons.

1. Dig a hole deep enough for a heavy-duty plastic garbage can, so that the rim ends up at ground level.

2. Dig a 1 ft (30 cm) trench around the outside of the garbage can rim, and fill it with concrete.

3. Build a circular brick wall off this foundation, with all the bricks set on edge, so that the face of the wall is made of header ends.

4. Use reclaimed wood to build a post-and pitch roof. Pivot the winding beam between the two posts.

5. Cover the roof with reclaimed shingles or old red roofing tiles.

Building a cottage well.

Care and maintenance

A good cottage kitchen garden is never tidy or finished, but always in a busy, continuous state of change. The vegetable beds are always going to look scruffy – because you will either be harvesting or preparing for the next crop – and the flowers will always be coming in or going out of season.

Development

You will find that you are constantly making modifications. One moment such and such a bed will be right, and the next moment you may need to reshape it to accommodate another shrub, for example.

WATER GARDEN

How can I incorporate water?

Water gardening provides countless opportunities for the garden designer – all of them exciting. Themes for water gardens include modern city, Japanese, lakeside, forest, formal, seaside and many more. Alternatively, you could choose a style that has its roots in historic buildings, canals, climate, materials, planting or color, for example. Having a water garden, however large or small, will also enable you to grow some different and fascinating plants.

This formal pond has been designed as part of a large brick patio, with container plants all around it creating instant interest.

If you have a very large garden, you could include a "natural" pond, surrounded by a wildflower area, that will attract wildlife.

Marginal plants add character to this "lakeside" pond, providing height, texture and color as well as shelter for wildlife.

Design guidelines for success

- A medium-sized garden, about 100 x 50 ft (30 x 15 m), is ideal.
- The brick patio needs to take best advantage of sun, shade and shelter.
- The paths must be both functional and decorative – strong and wide enough to accommodate a wheelbarrow and the mower, and good on the eye.
- The wild pond needs to be as large as possible.
- Include a lush abundance of plants, so that the pond and the bog garden are seen as one element.
- A rock garden needs to be on high ground.
- Include a formal water feature somewhere on the patio.
- The patio needs to be embellished with sweet-smelling climbing plants.
- Plant a lawn in the rest of the garden.
- Include trees and shrubs as a backdrop.

LOOKING AT THE PROJECT

If you look at the design opposite, you will see that there are four basic elements: a wild pond, a bog garden fed by the rainwater run-off from the pond, a large patio that looks down over both the pond and the bog garden, and a formal spouting mask feature on the patio. The whole area is set against a backdrop of trees. Look at your space and make modifications to suit.

CONSIDERING THE IMPLICATIONS

Consider how the design works for you. If you want to have the wild pond slightly bigger and the patio smaller, or the whole design bigger and more formal, then that is fine.

VARIATIONS TO CONSIDER

If you like the overall design but are not so keen on the bog garden, you could have a cascade running off from the main pond into a secondary, smaller pond. Alternatively, you could have small, self-contained bog gardens.

A small, self-contained bog garden with its own water-feed pipe that will keep the soil moist at all times.

This ornate water-spout feature would suit a traditional patio or courtyard area. It can be fixed to stone, brick or block walls.

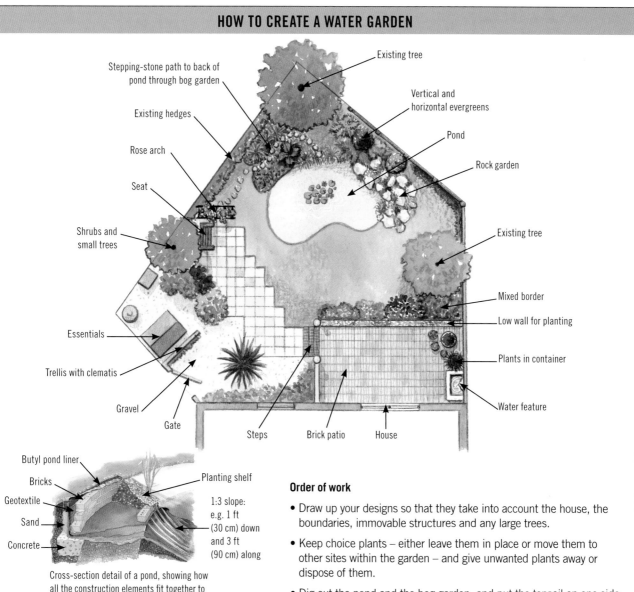

- Stepping-stone path to back of pond through bog garden
- Existing hedges
- Rose arch
- Seat
- Shrubs and small trees
- Essentials
- Trellis with clematis
- Gravel
- Gate
- Steps
- Brick patio
- House
- Existing tree
- Vertical and horizontal evergreens
- Pond
- Rock garden
- Existing tree
- Mixed border
- Low wall for planting
- Plants in container
- Water feature

- Butyl pond liner
- Bricks
- Geotextile
- Sand
- Concrete
- Planting shelf
- 1:3 slope: e.g. 1 ft (30 cm) down and 3 ft (90 cm) along

Cross-section detail of a pond, showing how all the construction elements fit together to create a successful feature.

Care and maintenance

Other than removing leaves and sludge, and dividing up plants, a good wild pond will, to a great extent, look after itself. You will have to clean it up about once a year.

Development

Within two years, there will probably be frogs, toads, snakes, newts, more birds, and many other creatures – all attracted by the pond.

Order of work

- Draw up your designs so that they take into account the house, the boundaries, immovable structures and any large trees.
- Keep choice plants – either leave them in place or move them to other sites within the garden – and give unwanted plants away or dispose of them.
- Dig out the pond and the bog garden, and put the topsoil on one side. Use the subsoil to build up the patio area.
- Build the brick patio and retaining double-wall beds.
- Build the pergola and the patio water feature.
- Build the mini-wall around the pond, lay the butyl liner, and use the scraps of butyl left over from the pond to line the bog garden.
- Use the topsoil to model the edges of the pond and to fill the bog garden.
- Complete the rock garden.

Planting

Make sure your existing plants are thriving. Work from the center to the sides when planting the pond and the bog garden. Plant the lawn. Plant the vines, shrubs and trees, and the flowers, in the appropriate seasons.

MODERN MEDITERRANEAN GARDEN

What is a Mediterranean garden?

A Mediterranean garden is a mixture of different styles that evoke memories of Mediterranean holidays. There are glazed, tiled patios with pools that feel slightly Spanish, terracotta tiles, pottery and statuary fountains that are sort of Italian, enclosed courtyards that look a bit Moroccan, and so on. The overall feeling is one of bright sunlight and color – flat, plastered walls painted in white, blue, or orange – with dry-climate plants, and crystal-clear water.

Choose a combination of plants and containers that suggest a warm climate through shape and color.

In this garden, the Moorish arch, the tiles and the palms speak immediately of North Africa or southern Spain.

LOOKING AT THE PROJECT

The design opposite is based on a small courtyard garden. There is a back door leading to a yard, high walls at the sides, and steps leading up or down to a patch of lawn (not shown here), with the total space measuring about 20 ft (6 m) wide and 50 ft (15 m) long. There are four elements: a small, circular, raised pond with a mosaic design and a fountain, a level paved area, plastered walls that have been painted a restful blue, and lots of plants in containers.

CONSIDERING THE IMPLICATIONS

The success of a garden of this character hinges on everything being cool and unruffled – no children's toys, bicycles or garbage cans on view. Is this going to work for you? A garden of this character must be kept clean and tidy.

VARIATIONS TO CONSIDER

If you have in mind a more modern, minimalist garden, you can leave out the pots and the color – the paint and mosaics – and opt for white ceramic pots and white paint instead.

A Mediterranean-style garden can be created just about anywhere merely by growing the right type of plants.

Design guidelines for success

- You need a medium-sized yard, about 20 x 50 ft (6 x 15 m).
- You need high walls at the sides.
- All walls should be plastered – there should be no large areas of red brick.
- Walls must be painted flat white, or in a color like blue or orange ochre.
- You could top the walls off with Spanish-style clay tiles.
- The pond should be raised and either round or square, made from decorative brick or tiles.
- You need lots of terracotta pots or simple raised borders.
- Include lots of easy-care plants, such as yuccas, palms and bamboos.
- Choose good-quality designer furniture – no deck chairs or plastic fold-up chairs.

HOW TO CREATE A MEDITERRANEAN GARDEN

- Pots hung on wall brackets
- Terracotta tile capping to wall
- Tile picture
- Circular raised pond and fountain
- Pots and plants on steps
- Level paved area
- Brightly painted door
- Fig tree
- Pelargoniums in pots
- Yucca
- *Echinops ritro* (Globe Thistle)
- *Sedum* (Stonecrop)
- Large terracotta pots with palms and grasses

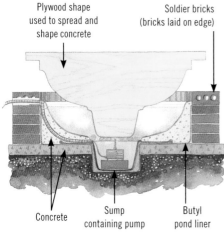

- Plywood shape used to spread and shape concrete
- Soldier bricks (bricks laid on edge)
- Concrete
- Sump containing pump
- Butyl pond liner

Cross-section detail showing how to make a small circular concrete and brick pond.

Order of work

- Draw up your designs so that they take into account the house, the boundaries, immovable structures, drains and large trees.

- Keep choice plants – either leave them in place or move them to other sites within the garden – and give unwanted plants away or dispose of them.

- Plaster all the side walls, and paint them the color of your choice – white, orange ochre or pale blue.

- Pave the yard with tiles – either terracotta or matt white.

- Build the raised pond and decorate the inside and/or the outside with a mosaic design.

- Fit a pump with a simple fountain spray.

- Get as many large terracotta pots as you can afford.

Planting

Make sure your existing plants are thriving. Fill the containers with dry-garden plants such as *Agave* (Century Plant), *Cortaderia* (Pampas Grass), *Sedum* (Stonecrop), *Eryngium* (Sea Holly) and *Echinops* (Globe Thistle). Spread a mulch consisting of crushed stone or pebbles over the soil.

Care and maintenance

Mediterranean gardens need to be kept clean. At the beginning and end of each season, clean up dead leaves, remove damp mold and renew paintwork.

Development

You could add landscape lighting and a small, discreet barbecue for evening entertaining.

FORMAL ENGLISH GARDEN

What does this style entail?

The term "formal English garden" has come to describe a rather restrained garden, one with such features as a small, formal pond, steps, dwarf box hedges, a knot garden, a lawn, a pergola, a terrace, red-brick paths, roses and trelliswork. The emphasis should be on small and symmetrical, with the total form drawing inspiration from the late English Tudor period. The key words are English, red bricks, roses and symmetrical.

The red bricks, pergola and close-cropped lawns speak of England.

It has been said that English gardeners are obsessed by symmetry, and perhaps the formal English garden bears out this theory.

Design guidelines for success

- You need a medium space about 50 ft (15 m) wide and 100 ft (30 m) long.

- The overall design must be symmetrical and geometrical, with the central circle cutting into the lawns.

- You need to have a red-brick path running centrally down the length of the garden.

- You need crisp-edged lawns and flower beds, all mirror-imaged on each side of the main path.

- There should be a pond, flower bed or sculpture right at the center of the design.

- While the ideal is to have hedges all around, you might have to start off by having fence panels covered with climbing plants.

LOOKING AT THE PROJECT

This design can be modified to suit the size of your garden. There are six primary elements: a level area close to the house, steps leading up or down to the garden, a centrally placed red-brick path, a symmetrical, knot-inspired formation of beds and lawns, dwarf *Buxus sempervirens* (Box) hedges, and lots of roses. While you might not want, or be able, to include all these elements, you do need to keep the knot-like design, the symmetry, the red bricks and the roses.

CONSIDERING THE IMPLICATIONS

There is a lot of work in a garden of this character – topiary hedges to trim, roses to prune and so on. Will this fit into your lifestyle?

VARIATIONS TO CONSIDER

If you have a very small garden, you can create the effect of an English garden by having decorative red-brick paths set within a simple pattern of lawns and beds.

Square herringbone bond is a very decorative style.

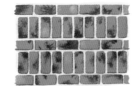

Running and stack bond is good for paths.

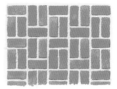

Double basket weave minimizes the need to cut bricks.

The quintessential English garden look – a red brick path, a rose-covered pergola, low box hedging and a formal seat as a focal point.

HOW TO CREATE A FORMAL ENGLISH GARDEN

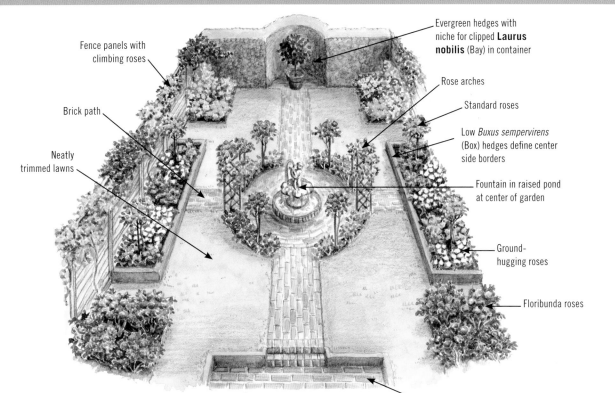

Fence panels with climbing roses

Brick path

Neatly trimmed lawns

Evergreen hedges with niche for clipped **Laurus nobilis** (Bay) in container

Rose arches

Standard roses

Low *Buxus sempervirens* (Box) hedges define center side borders

Fountain in raised pond at center of garden

Ground-hugging roses

Floribunda roses

Small sunken patio with a clipped **Buxus sempervirens** (Box) hedge and steps to brick path

Order of work

- Draw up your designs so that they take into account the house, the boundaries, immovable structures and large trees.

- Keep any choice plants – either leave them in place or move them to other sites within the garden – and give unwanted plants away or dispose of them.

- Level the space.

- Use a tape measure, stakes and string to mark out the size and shape of the pond, paths, beds and lawns.

- Build the pond.

- Build the red-brick paths and lay the turf.

Planting

Make sure your existing plants are thriving. Plant the various roses – ramblers, climbing roses, dwarf or bush roses, standards and shrubs. Plant the *Buxus sempervirens* (Box) hedging and the main *Ligustrum* (Privet) hedging. Set out all the other flowers in the appropriate seasons.

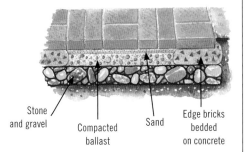

Stone and gravel

Compacted ballast

Sand

Edge bricks bedded on concrete

Development

Wait until the main structure is in place, and then build the other items little by little – things like a pergola, a terrace and an herb garden.

Care and maintenance

A formal garden of this character involves a lot of care and maintenance. It does not look too difficult on the face of it – straight lines and unchanging patterns of planting – but of course the unchanging character can only be achieved by hard work. Lawns need to be cut and rolled, the roses are a lifetime's work, and care of the hedges is ongoing.

SECLUDED CITY GARDEN

How can I get some privacy?

Nobody likes to be watched by neighbors when they are trying to relax in the garden, whatever its size. Seclusion is not about how much space you have got, but about being private. It could be a whole garden, or just a little hideaway in a corner of a large garden. The main thing is to create an area that is screened off with walls or fences, shrubs, climbing plants and small trees.

(Above) Rooftop garden with grasses, palms and bamboos growing in decorative containers.

(Left) A private arbor with sweetly scented climbers, lavender and other herbs all around to provide calming fragrance.

Packing the space full of container plants will help create an oasis of seclusion and quiet, as the foliage and flowers will muffle any unwanted sounds.

LOOKING AT THE PROJECT

This design is for a very small city garden, not much more than 20 ft (6 m) wide and 30 ft (9 m) long. It is, in effect, just an area of ground with high walls all around. The garden is composed of four elements: a patch of lawn as you step out of the house, a small gravel area just big enough for a seat or table, a minute pool, and a pitched-roof pergola with an unrestrained jungle of climbing plants growing over it.

CONSIDERING THE IMPLICATIONS

The pergola with the climbing plants will drip during and after rain. Do you want to replace it with, say, a shed with an old armchair, so that you can enjoy the seclusion even when it is raining?

VARIATIONS TO CONSIDER

While this hideaway is made from a pergola with climbing plants on it, you could have anything that takes your fancy – a hut, a huge sun umbrella, an awning. Style it to suit your activities.

Design guidelines for success

- You need a yard at about 20 x 30 ft (6 x 9 m).
- You need high walls on three sides.
- All walls should be left in their rough, as-found state.
- If the walls are plastered, cover them with trellis.
- The pool should be silent – just a pool with fish and plants.
- You need lots of terracotta pots.
- You need lots of climbing plants such as *Vitis vinifera* (Grapevine), *Clematis, Passiflora* (Passionflower), *Wisteria* – no roses or plants with thorns or unpleasant smells.

HOW TO CREATE A SECLUDED GARDEN

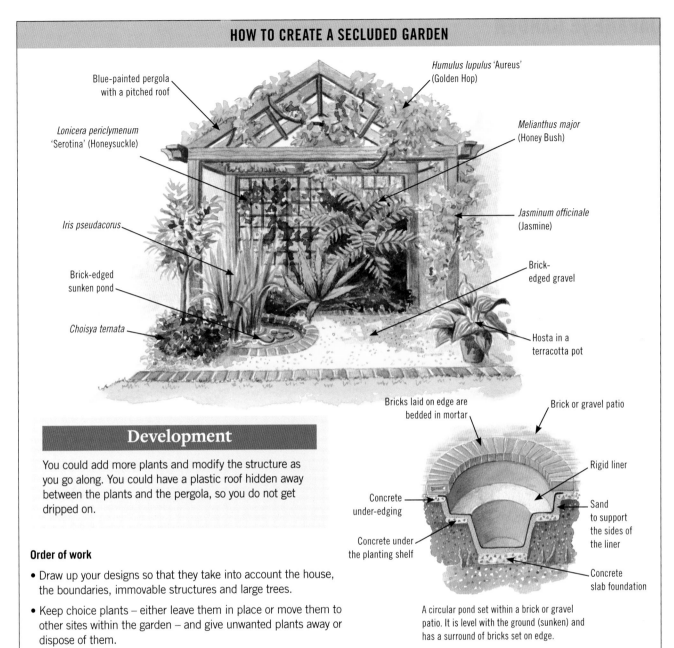

Blue-painted pergola with a pitched roof

Humulus lupulus 'Aureus' (Golden Hop)

Lonicera periclymenum 'Serotina' (Honeysuckle)

Melianthus major (Honey Bush)

Iris pseudacorus

Jasminum officinale (Jasmine)

Brick-edged sunken pond

Brick-edged gravel

Choisya ternata

Hosta in a terracotta pot

Bricks laid on edge are bedded in mortar

Brick or gravel patio

Concrete under-edging

Rigid liner

Concrete under the planting shelf

Sand to support the sides of the liner

Concrete slab foundation

A circular pond set within a brick or gravel patio. It is level with the ground (sunken) and has a surround of bricks set on edge.

Development

You could add more plants and modify the structure as you go along. You could have a plastic roof hidden away between the plants and the pergola, so you do not get dripped on.

Order of work

- Draw up your designs so that they take into account the house, the boundaries, immovable structures and large trees.

- Keep choice plants – either leave them in place or move them to other sites within the garden – and give unwanted plants away or dispose of them.

- If necessary, build the walls higher.

- Build the pergola.

- Build the pond.

- Pave the yard with a mix of gravel and salvaged bricks.

- Prepare the small beds at the side.

Planting

Make sure your existing plants are thriving. Plant climbers like *Clematis*, *Vitis* (Grapevines), *Humulus* (Hops), *Passiflora* (Passionflower), *Fallopia baldschuanica* (Mile-a-minute Vine), *Lonicera* (Honeysuckle) and *Wisteria*. Spread a mulch of pea gravel or bark over the soil.

Care and maintenance

At the beginning and end of each growing season, you need to sweep up dead leaves, clean out the pond and remove debris. Check that your hideaway – shed, shelter or pergola – is in good order.

JAPANESE GARDEN

Is this suitable for a small space?

A good part of the Japanese tradition has to do with smallness, privacy and silence. Japanese gardeners have formalized what is needed in the way of elements, features and plants. You should try to include in your design some of the following: a small water feature, stepping stones, boulders, raked gravel, Japanese stone lantern, a small *Acer* (Japanese Maple), a dwarf pine and perhaps a bamboo. Stay away from paint, stained wood and brightly colored pots.

LOOKING AT THE PROJECT

This design is for a very small yard, with green foliage plants as a backdrop – bamboos and *Acers* and dwarf pines – and includes a stone lantern, boulders and rocks, stepping stones, raked gravel and a deer scarer – a decorative Japanese bamboo water feature.

CONSIDERING THE IMPLICATIONS

Will a cool, calm, quiet, unchanging Japanese garden suit the rest of the family? Will you perhaps need additional areas for the children to play in?

VARIATIONS TO CONSIDER

While this design features a deer scarer, you might prefer to go for something a bit more statuesque, such as a Japanese stone basin, which looks a bit like a bird bath.

A traditional Japanese garden with *Acers*, feature rocks and raked pea gravel.

Design guidelines for success

- You need a yard about 20 x 20 ft (6 x 6 m).
- You need trees, fences or walls at the sides.
- You need a stone basin to catch rainwater, or perhaps a deer scarer.
- You need one or more green or attractive plants in containers – bamboos, dwarf pines and grasses.
- If there is room, include a small tree, something like a small *Acer* (Japanese Maple). Note that the *Acer* will eventually need to be root-pruned to stop it growing into a full-sized tree.
- You need raked gravel.
- You need a stone lantern.
- You need selected pieces of feature stone and stepping stones.

HOW TO CREATE A JAPANESE GARDEN

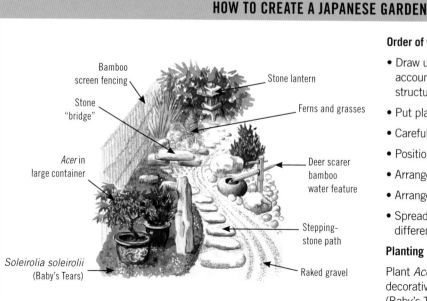

Bamboo screen fencing

Stone "bridge"

Acer in large container

Soleirolia soleirolii (Baby's Tears)

Stone lantern

Ferns and grasses

Deer scarer bamboo water feature

Stepping-stone path

Raked gravel

Order of work

- Draw up your designs so that they take into account the house, the boundaries, immovable structures and large trees.
- Put plants that you want to save to one side.
- Carefully arrange the lantern.
- Position the deer scarer.
- Arrange the feature stones for best effect.
- Arrange the stepping stones.
- Spread and rake the gravel around the various different features.

Planting

Plant *Acers*, bamboos and dwarf pines in decorative containers. Plant *Soleirolia soleirolii* (Baby's Tears) to spread over the ground.

JAPANESE INFLUENCES

Japanese gardens exude peace, serenity and contemplation and have a distinctive, uncluttered character that encourages meditation and a desire to know oneself. The design of Japanese gardens is an expression of appreciation and delight in the beauty of nature, which must be respected. Water features and decorated bridges, plants in containers and a gravel base combine to produce a distinctive garden that creates interest throughout the year.

Areas of gravel, incorporating a stepping-stone path, create a perfect base for a Japanese garden.

Feng shui

Originally in Chinese mythology but known in Japanese culture, feng shui is a concept of spirit influences – good and evil – which inhabit natural features in landscapes. By orientating plants and entrances, spirits are given the opportunity to enter and depart.

SERENITY

Years ago countryside noises were clearly heard, and the loudest sound was often the ringing of church bells. Nowadays the intrusion of general noise has almost removed this cherished, life-calming quality, something which a Japanese garden attempts to recapture.

MINIMALISM

A Japanese garden is one that is in balance with nature, where neither plants nor structural introductions dominate each other. An uncluttered background is essential and this can be achieved by erecting a bamboo-like screen.

GRAVEL

Few parts of a Japanese garden are as restful to the eye as gravel, which can be given extra interest by laying a stepping stone path across it, but avoid splitting it up and producing two unrelated areas. Raking the surface of gravel creates the impression of water and waves.

Tea garden

A garden is an essential part of a tea ceremony. In a tranquil setting, those taking part first assemble to cast off worldly cares. Trees, shrubs and ferns, with their perennial nature, create a timeless aura. Ephemeral flowers, however, are not allowed, as they express the passing of time.

BAMBOOS FOR CONTAINERS

Bamboos, with their distinctive quality, are essential parts of Japanese gardens and several are suitable for growing in containers, including:

- *Fargesia nitida:* a hardy and evergreen bamboo, with bright green leaves and light purple canes.
- *Phyllostachys nigra:* dark green leaves and canes first green, later jet-black.
- *Pleioblastus viridistriatus:* purple-green canes and golden-yellow leaves with pea-green stripes.

OTHER PLANTS FOR CONTAINERS

- *Acer palmatum* var. *dissectum* 'Atropurpureum': hardy, slow-growing, deciduous, dome-headed tree with finely dissected, bronze-red leaves.
- *Acer palmatum* var. *dissectum:* as above, but with all-green leaves.
- *Fatsia japonica:* this is the False Castor Oil Plant, evergreen and slightly tender with large, glossy, hand-like leaves.

Outdoor bonsai

Bonsai has a natural affinity with Japanese gardens, where the art of growing diminutive trees and shrubs in shallow containers was refined. Today, the art of bonsai has spread to many other countries. Bonsai can be displayed on staging, as well as on "monkey poles," which have flat tops and are available at different heights so that a bonsai can be easily admired by everyone.

CONTAINER GARDEN

Is it easy in a small garden?

Growing plants in containers has never been more popular, and many home gardeners find it an ideal way to grow plants in a small garden, especially when courtyard, patio and balcony gardening are the only opportunities. A wide range of containers — from hanging baskets to tubs and pots — is described below. Additionally, some gardeners rely on containers such as wall baskets, troughs, window boxes and wall-secured pots to create color.

Short, bushy, summer-flowering bedding plants are superb for bringing eye-catching color to containers.

Wall baskets can be used to drench walls with welcome color, especially in combination with hanging baskets.

Hanging baskets create color at about head height. Ensure, however, that they cannot be bumped into.

CONTAINERS CREATE MORE SPACE

Containers suspended from wall-secured brackets or supported on windowsills leave more space at ground level for larger and often more permanent plants in tubs and pots, where a firm base is essential. To get the best displays, however, try permutations of them all.

CONTAINERS BECOME PART OF THE INFRASTRUCTURE

In small gardens, tubs and large pots planted with shrubs, trees and conifers become permanent parts of a garden. These containers can be displayed in many positions – near to doors, either side of a window or in a corner on a patio. Ephemeral plants in pots and troughs can be temporarily placed around them during summer, where they gain protection from wind and strong sunlight. Alpines and miniature rock-garden plants in old stone sinks last several years.

RANGE OF CONTAINERS

POTS AND TUBS

From wooden tubs to terracotta pots. Make sure that they harmonize with their surroundings.

OLD STONE SINKS

Old stone sinks can be used as miniature water gardens, as well as for rock-garden plants.

WINDOW BOXES

These are ideal for clothing both sash and casement windows in color.

HANGING BASKETS

Position these at head height, between windows or either side of a doorway.

WALL BASKETS AND TROUGHS

These help bare walls between windows, and around entrances, to become awash with color.

OLD ARTIFACTS

You will be surprised at how many old pieces of "jumble" can be used to create unusual plant holders.

DECORATING SMALL PATIOS AND COURTYARDS

It is best to choose a combination of floor-positioned pots and tubs and hanging baskets and window boxes.

- Where space is severely limited, use mainly wall-mounted displays as well as window boxes.
- Try to direct foot traffic away from open casement windows by using tubs and large pots of shrubs and upright conifers in appropriate positions. Sink gardens will also guide foot traffic.
- Position troughs packed with culinary herbs near a kitchen door.

DOORWAY AND STEP DISPLAYS

Brightly decorated entrances and steps give immediate vitality and interest to houses and apartments. Position a series of color-packed pots alongside stepped entrances – and, if space allows, on the steps.

LOOKING AFTER CONTAINER PLANTS

Accessibility is the main consideration when you are looking after container-grown plants in a courtyard, basement, entrance or on a patio. Always use a reliable stepladder when watering plants that are raised up high. Alternatively, use a watering device that enables watering to be carried out from ground level. There is also the possibility of making a home-made watering device; to do this, tie the end of a hose to a long bamboo cane.

Roof gardens and balconies

Weather-resistant displays are essential for roof gardens. Balconies create a more plant-friendly environment, although even they can be blustery and cold if facing away from the sun.

USING A WALL AS A GARDEN

At first sight, an old wall in a small courtyard or basement entrance may appear to be inhospitable, but it is amazing how wall gardening can transform it. Tiered troughs, wall baskets and window boxes all create attractive homes for plants.

Troughs

Large troughs positioned at ground level become homes for many plants, including small or slow-growing conifers. Choose conifers with different colors and shapes. These displays can be left in position for several years.

Planting pockets

Recessed areas in walls are novel places for small pots packed with upright or trailing plants. Where recesses are alongside a flight of steps, make sure pots cannot be knocked and toppled. They will require frequent watering during hot weather.

Choosing plants for different containers

Suitable plants for container gardening in a small area depends on the nature of the container. Here are some clues to their success.

Pots ~ choose from summer-flowering annuals to scented-leaved Geraniums (botanically, *Pelargoniums*). Ensure that pots cannot be toppled, especially if they have a large proportion of foliage.

Tubs ~ these are ideal for woody perennials such as shrubs, trees and conifers. They will need a permanent position on a patio, terrace or courtyard.

Window boxes ~ these never fail to create interest, with displays specially selected for spring, summer, and winter. Those that create summer displays rely mainly on summer-flowering bedding plants; displays in winter are frequently devoted to dwarf conifers and small, hardy, bushy and trailing evergreen shrubs; spring displays are packed with spring-flowering bulbs and hardy, bushy and trailing evergreen shrubs.

Hanging baskets ~ these are ideal for creating color at head height, and with their summer-only display are packed with bushy, trailing and cascading, summer-flowering bedding plants. Trailing and cascading plants such as Fuchsias are also used.

Wall baskets ~ these resemble hanging baskets cut in half and secured to a wall. During summer they become awash with bushy and trailing summer-flowering bedding plants, and in spring with bulbs and biennials.

Free-standing metal basket ~ these are similar to wall baskets, but are made with thicker and more substantial metal, and are usually wider, creating dominant features. Plant in the same way as for wall baskets.

WILD GARDENS

Are they possible in a small area?

Wild gardens are not a contradiction in terms, but a planned and fascinating way of introducing wild landscape features into a garden, whatever its size. Additionally, this approach is good for the environment. Too often, fields are intensively cultivated, hedges removed and long grass and native plants cut down. Yet even a small wildlife area in a garden, perhaps with a diminutive pond, helps redress this negative attitude towards the environment.

WILDFLOWER GARDENS

After many years of plant breeding and creating new varieties, many gardeners realize that native plants have a grace, charm and delicacy not present in human-created forms. Native wildflowers usually have an annual or perennial nature; both create magnificent displays. Wildflowers also attract a wide range of insects, including butterflies. Many seed companies sell individual wildflower species, as well as mixtures. They are best sown in spring and, while annuals reseed themselves each year, perennials become permanently established – although even they produce seed that germinates in suitable conditions.

HOW TO SOW

During early winter, fork or dig the soil, loosening the surface to about 8 in (20 cm) deep. Leave the surface uneven but approximately level; in late winter or early spring, rake the area and systematically shuffle over it to create a moderately firm surface. In mid- and late spring, thinly scatter seeds over the surface and lightly cover them by using a rake. Gently but thoroughly water the area, taking care not to wash away the seeds by mistake.

WILDLIFE GARDEN

These are best given a quiet, out-of-the-way position, but one where the feature and activities of its residents can be readily seen. Such tranquillity brings pleasure to many gardeners and can be cathartic. A light, overhead canopy provided by deciduous trees helps to create shade for ground-level plants, birds and small mammals. It also keeps the soil damp and cool during summer, a benefit to many insects as well as small mammals. Where a pond is part of the feature, in autumn you will need to scoop out dead leaves that have fallen from trees.

Wildlife areas introduce a new dimension to gardening.

WILDLIFE PONDS

Unlike ornamental garden ponds, wildlife types are meant to be havens for birds, amphibians, insects and small mammals, as well as fish. Aquatic plants, together with those along the edges, create retreats for insects.

BOG GARDENS

These are often linked with water features, and are where moisture-loving plants can be grown. Because of their leafy and informal nature they also attract insects and small mammals.

Watering device

Fragrant flowers

Some seed companies sell mixtures of fragrant annuals. These are not necessarily wildflowers, but can still be raised in the same way as suggested for wildflowers (see left). Mixtures of fragrant perennials are also available.

Protecting garden wildlife

When encouraging wildlife into your garden, do not use insecticides or weedkillers. Contaminated flowers and leaves are deadly to fish, amphibians, insects and small mammals.

All you need is a small patch of water for toads, frogs, newts and fish, nesting-boxes and pole-houses for birds, piles of mossy logs and leaf litter for bugs, and a carefully considered mix of just the right plants. The real fun starts when small birds come in for the bugs, the pond life starts emerging, reptiles come in for the pond life, and bigger birds and mammals come in for the reptiles. Children, cats and dogs all like wildlife gardens.

Frogs and toads are beneficial in gardens

Dragonflies are attracted by water

Newts are attractive creatures in ponds

LOOKING AT THE PROJECT

In this design, the space is about 50 ft (15 m) wide and 100 ft (30 m) long. The design is based on a woodland glade. Just imagine that you are walking through a wood and you come across the perfect picnic area. There is a pond, a broad, meandering path of close-cropped grass running down the center of the plot, woodland trees with shrubs underneath them at the sides, and fallen wood or piles of logs left to rot and decay.

Color- and size-dominant plants will always help to frame a garden pond.

Design guidelines for success

- You need a space no smaller than about 50 ft (15 m) wide and 100 ft (30 m) long. A square plot is better than a long, thin one.
- Include a pond, pool or stream.
- You need a glade of grass or woodchip with trees around it.
- A seat is essential.
- Include one or more bird feeders and houses.
- You need trees as a backdrop.
- Plant some shrubs underneath the trees.

CONSIDERING THE IMPLICATIONS

By the very nature of things, this is going to be a shady garden with lots of leaves and bits and pieces underfoot. It is a good idea to be aware from the start that a wildlife garden is not necessarily a comfortable garden – you will have birds, but they will be coming in for "unpleasant" things like gnats and bugs.

VARIATIONS TO CONSIDER

If you like the overall notion of the design but do not want the grass, you could replace it with thick mulch of woodchip and leaf mold.

HOW TO CREATE A WILDLIFE GARDEN

Order of work

- Draw up your designs so that they take into account the house, the boundaries, drains, immovable structures and large trees.
- Dig out and build the pond. A butyl liner is the best option for a natural-looking pond.
- Include an area of bog garden that will take the overflow from the pond.
- Plant the primary trees – these are species that can be found growing wild in your area.
- Underplant the trees with shrubs and ground-cover plants.

Planting

Visit local gardens and see what grows best in your soil. The easiest option is to plant container-grown trees, such as *Betula pendula* (Silver Birch), *Sorbus aucuparia* (Mountain Ash) and *Acers* (Japanese Maples). If you have a small garden, remember to choose compact varieties. Plant the shrubs and ground-cover plants only when the trees are in place. (Note that the seedpods of some species are poisonous.)

WILD MEADOW ORCHARD GARDEN

This garden draws inspiration from the traditional orchard. The important ingredients are standard or half-standard apple and plum trees (Cox and Bramley apples, and Victoria plums), long meadow grass that is scythed twice a year, wild meadow flowers, perhaps a fallen tree and a pile of hay, and maybe a small, natural pond, all ringed with a hawthorn hedge interwoven with wild woodbine. If you can have chickens and geese, so much the better.

LOOKING AT THE PROJECT

The design involves a garden as big as you like, planted out with fruit trees and meadow flowers, with hedges all around, and a natural pond if there is enough room. The paths and level areas are mown at regular intervals.

CONSIDERING THE IMPLICATIONS

Will the notion that your garden is wild upset your neighbors?

VARIATIONS TO CONSIDER

You could simplify the design by replacing the mown paths with woodchip or bracken.

An old orchard makes a perfect patio – the table is ideal for informal meals.

Old wooden benches are always useful and look good, blending into the scene with ease

Crushed bark

Woven plastic weed-stop sheet over rolled gravel

Tree-stump seating

Design guidelines for success

- You need a space that is no smaller than 30 ft (9 m) wide and 50 ft (15 m) long.

- You need apple or plum trees – half-standards for a big garden, bush apples for a small space.

- You need hedges or rustic fences all around.

- Shape the pond to suit your space.

- Try to include a selection of "found" items like logs and tree stumps.

HOW TO CREATE AN ORCHARD MEADOW GARDEN

Order of work

- Draw up your designs so that they take into account the house, the boundaries, immovable structures and large trees.

- Keep choice plants.

- Dig a pond and fit a butyl liner.

- Plant a hedge of *Crataegus monogyna* (Common Hawthorn) all around.

Planting

Plant choice plum and apple trees. Plant the whole area with meadow grass and wildflowers. Mow paths through the grass. Plant the pond with native wild species.

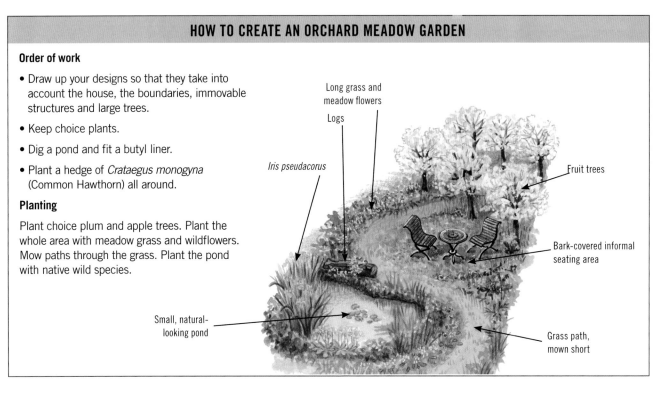

Long grass and meadow flowers

Logs

Iris pseudacorus

Fruit trees

Bark-covered informal seating area

Small, natural-looking pond

Grass path, mown short

SMALL PATIO GARDEN

In much the same way as you can create a wonderfully relaxing, comfortable space in the smallest of rooms, so you can build a small patio. Do not worry in the first instance about style or even materials, but focus on your basic needs. Do you want a small quiet space to read, a place with a table and a couple of comfortable chairs, a place for a barbecue, a place in the sun or shade, or the sound of running water? Let the overall design evolve around your needs.

Can I build a small patio?

MAKING THE MOST OF A SMALL SPACE

A dull or ugly area of garden can be dramatically improved by laying a decorative patio design like this one.

A patio can be anything you want it to be. This calm, ordered look draws inspiration from a formal Japanese garden.

A pergola can turn a small patio into an exciting area – it makes the patio feel more defined and solid, as well as private.

LOOKING AT THE PROJECT

Have a good look at your garden. Assess its size in relation to your needs. If you are working in a very small space close to the house, decide how you are going to cover up existing items like drainpipes and disguise sewer covers.

CONSIDERING THE IMPLICATIONS

Just like when you are revamping a room in your house – where you might, for example, draw inspiration from Victorian imagery and then go on to decorate the room so that everything corresponds to the original inspiration – you must remember to design the patio with materials and items that relate to your main idea or theme.

VARIATIONS TO CONSIDER

For patios, there are hundreds of styles, forms and materials to choose from. There are decking patios, brick patios and patios made from bark and gravel. There are patios made from real cut stone and reconstituted stone. There are patios that draw inspiration from all sorts of cultural styles – Mediterranean, Moorish, Japanese, modern. No matter the size of your garden, it is guaranteed that there will be an exciting option just waiting for you.

Although real cut stone pavers are expensive and difficult to fit, they are an exciting option.

Brick and stone look good together, and are perfect if you want to create a low-cost patio.

A formal pattern of bricks, with an infill of cobblestones, gravel and plants, is an eye-catching option.

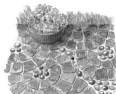

Crazy (cleft stone) paving is a good choice if you want a relatively cheap patio; the stone is bedded on blobs of mortar.

This unusual patio has been embellished with an infill of cobbles pressed into concrete.

Paving stones come in many types and sizes; salvaged paving stones from city roads may be obtainable from local authorities.

HOW TO CREATE A SMALL PATIO GARDEN

TRELLIS

A good-quality trellis makes an interesting backdrop, perfect for a dreary wall

CLIMBING PLANT

Rosa 'Aloha,' a very fragrant, large-flowered climbing rose

COLOR

Pelargoniums flower for a long season and look best in a single-color theme

TERRACOTTA POTS

Large pots are good for semi-hardy plants that need to be brought in for the winter

CLIMBING PLANT

Clematis 'Huldine'

Trained "standard" plants make a good feature

Choisya ternata

Hosta crispula

RAISED BED

Raised beds make for easy planting with no bending or stooping, which is often helpful for the older gardener

PATIO SLABS

Dampen each slab and set it level on five blobs of mortar, one at each corner and one in the center

Modify the project according to your unique situation and preferred materials. This project uses a layer of gravel to stabilize the ground; if you are building on, for example, an existing concrete base, there is no need for the gravel.

ORDER OF WORK

Mark out the patio area and clear the topsoil down to a depth of 8 in (20 cm). Dig a 1 ft (30 cm) deep trench for the low wall. Put 4 in (10 cm) of compacted gravel in the trench, followed by 8 in (20 cm) of concrete. Spread 4 in (10 cm) of compacted gravel over the patio area followed by 2 in (5 cm) of sharp sand. Set and level the slabs on blobs of mortar. Build the wall up to about six courses. Paint the walls and fix the trellis.

PLANTING

Go for plants like hardy fuchsias and Pelargoniums in the pots, a mix of climbing roses and Clematis up the trellis, and small shrubs of your choice in the raised border. Plant the container-grown shrubs as soon as possible, and the other less hardy plants in due season. Water them, and carefully monitor their progress.

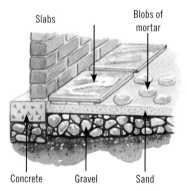

Slabs   Blobs of mortar

Concrete   Gravel   Sand

A cross-section through the project, showing how the various components relate to each other to create a stable, long-lasting patio.

Care and maintenance

Care and maintenance needs to be ongoing. You must remove weeds and moss, prune back vigorous plants, replace any broken pavers, fill gaps with sand mixed with dry concrete by sweeping it into the gaps when wetting it, sweep up the debris, and occasionally scrub with bleach or spray with a high-pressure jet.

Development

Just as you might add to a room inside your house, so you can add to your patio. If, when you are sitting there, you have a fancy for more comfortable chairs, a heater, subtle lights or anything else, then why not just go for it?

BALCONY AND ROOF GARDENS

It is surprising how much color can be created on a balcony or roof, whatever its aspect. Pots, troughs and hanging baskets packed with summer-flowering bedding plants are ideal during summer, while from autumn to spring reliance is mainly on small, evergreen shrubs and dwarf conifers. When tender plants are grown, these may have to be taken indoors during winter. Alternatively, a friend with a frost-proof greenhouse might be able to offer them sanctuary.

Roof gardens are idyllic throughout summer; perennial plants in containers can be removed during winter to a less exposed position.

ON TOP OF THE WORLD

Roof gardens are popular where the climate allows more than half the year to be spent on it. In other places, despite initial enthusiasm, the reality of a seasonal garden becomes apparent when icy winds roar across the site. Conversely, during summer the area may be exposed to strong, scorching sunlight, which may be ideal when attempting to gain an attractive sun tan but will shrivel plants which are not regularly watered. Nevertheless, the ability to garden "on top of the world" has unmatched eye appeal.

ROOF-GARDEN IDEAS

Construct screens to create privacy as well as giving you protection from strong wind. In summer, temporary privacy screens may be all that is needed. Privacy screens are also essential to reassure neighbors they are not being spied upon; before problems arise, tell them about your plans.

In windy positions, it is best to rely on summer-flowering plants in troughs and tubs to create color.

Construct a series of strong railings along the outer edges of the roof garden and then train small-leaved, variegated Ivies to grow over them.

Roof-garden caution

Check that the infrastructure is suitable and there is an easily accessible source of water. A combination of strong sunlight and breezes soon causes soil to become dry.

Balcony key features

In cold and exposed areas rely mainly on summer displays from summer-flowering bedding plants. Use trailing, small-leaved, variegated Ivies to create more permanent color.

MAKING THE MOST OF A BALCONY

- For a color contrast, secure pots of red or scarlet Geraniums (*Pelargoniums*) to the tops of white railings. At floor level, use a combination of trailing *Lysimachia nummularia* 'Aurea' (yellow flowers and leaves) and red Petunias. Let the *Lysimachia* trail through the railings.
- Fragrant displays in spring can be created from troughs or large pots of *Hyacinthus orientalis* (Hyacinths), in colors including white, rose-pink and soft blue. Plant them in autumn and await a magnificent, superbly fragrant display the following year.
- Several Lilies can be grown in pots on warm and wind-sheltered balconies.

Leisure balconies

In addition to growing plants on balconies, don't forget that they are leisure areas:

- Where the view allows and the balcony's size is suitable, consider having a deck-chair and small table that can both be easily stored indoors when not in use.
- Low-intensity and unobtrusive lights provide another opportunity for making the best of a balcony after the sun has gone down.

DRIVEWAY GARDEN

How can I accommodate my car?

If your front garden is big enough for parking, there is no reason why it cannot be an attractive space. Think carefully about how the car is to be parked in relation to the house and the road, and how the passengers are going to move to and from the car, and then design using smooth curves, attractive paving, plants in brightly colored containers, small enclosed borders, hanging baskets and climbing plants. Avoid having all-over surfaces like concrete or asphalt.

LOOKING AT THE PROJECT

In the design, the front garden is about 15 ft (4.5 m) square, the area to the right of the door is paved with bricks, and there is easy-care planting in the bed.

CONSIDERING THE IMPLICATIONS

If you need to turn the car slightly to get in or out of the space, will this upset the neighbors? Will the lights shine into their windows? Will the car doors bang into their fence? Will you be driving over sewer covers?

VARIATIONS TO CONSIDER

You could have raised beds, so that people cannot easily walk on the plants.

This design cleverly blurs the edge of the paved parking area, and is a good option for a small front garden.

Design guidelines for success

- You need a space no smaller than about 15 ft (4.5 m) square.
- You need good-quality brick paving with a solid foundation.
- Edge the drive with decorative bricks or tiles.
- Include dwarf shrubs and rock-garden plants in the border.
- Mulch around the plants with something like crushed stone or pea gravel.
- Try to blur the edges between the planting and the pavement.
- Allow for drainage.

HOW TO CREATE A PARKING GARDEN

Order of work

- Draw up your designs so that they take into account the house, the boundaries, drains, immovable structures and any large trees.
- Mark out the parking area.
- Dig the area out to a depth of 1 ft (30 cm).
- Set a level edge of concrete.
- Put down well-compacted gravel and top it off with bricks bedded in sand – or concrete if the ground is soft.

Planting

Include plants like dwarf conifers and slow-growing alpines – the type of plant that you would grow in a rock garden or alpine garden (see pages 160–162). Place hanging baskets or containers at the side of the door.

LOW-MAINTENANCE GARDEN

There are subtle differences between "low" and "easy" maintenance, although the reasoning is often blurred. An easy-maintenance garden is a lawn – and little else. All that is needed is to cut the grass weekly, from spring to autumn. This design is ideal for young families, where ball games and bicycles take priority. A low-maintenance garden is one where the area is planned to have desirable features and plants, yet require minimal maintenance.

> *Low maintenance or easy maintenance?*

LOW-MAINTENANCE PLANTS

Once established, many plants create magnificent displays and with minimal attention. Here are some to consider:

- **Herbaceous perennials:** some are self-supporting and trouble-free.
- **Ground-cover plants:** plants that smother the soil's surface with attractive leaves and flowers that prevent the growth of weeds.

- **Naturalized bulbs:** large-faced Daffodils planted in out-of-the-way grassy areas will produce magnificent displays in spring. Once flowering is over, leave the foliage to wither and die naturally.
- **Shrubs and small trees:** both deciduous and evergreen types are low-maintenance plants. Apart from a little (or no) pruning, shrubs and small trees need minimal attention once established.

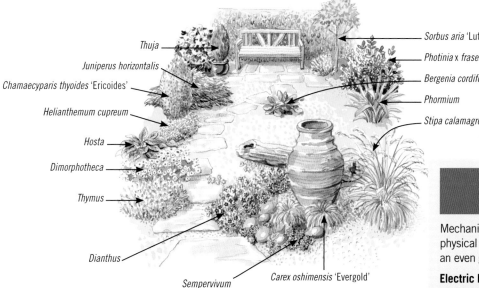

Thuja
Juniperus horizontalis
Chamaecyparis thyoides 'Ericoides'
Helianthemum cupreum
Hosta
Dimorphotheca
Thymus
Dianthus
Sempervivum
Carex oshimensis 'Evergold'
Sorbus aria 'Lutescens'
Photinia x fraseri
Bergenia cordifolia
Phormium
Stipa calamagrostis

Equipment for easy gardening

Mechanical equipment has taken the physical toil out of gardening and made it an even greater pleasure.

Electric lawn mowers: ideal for gardeners who need to have regular rests when mowing (the machine can be easily stopped and it is then silent).

Gas-powered lawn mowers: excellent for large lawns or where a safe electrical supply is not available.

String trimmers: suitable for cutting long grass or clearing undergrowth. Some models convert to trim lawn edges.

Hedge trimmers: make hedge cutting less arduous than with manual shears.

Lawn rakes: take the strain out of raking, sweeping and scarifying lawns.

Compost shredders: used to convert woody garden waste into invaluable mulch to protect the garden soil.

Design factors for easy gardening

When designing garden features, think about the mechanical equipment used with them.

Alongside border edges, and especially where herbaceous perennials spread over the edge of a lawn and create bare areas, install a row of 18 in (45 cm) square paving slabs. Plants can then be allowed to spread and soften unattractive border edges, while a power mower can be used to cut up to and slightly over the edging.

Where stepping stones are inset into lawns, check that they are set fractionally below the lawn surface so that, without damage, a power mower can be used to cut the grass.

Where lawns abut walls, install a cutting strip to enable edges to be cut without damaging the mower or grazing hands against the brickwork.

Where lawn edges are alongside borders, use a half-moon edging knife to cut each edge or long-arm edging shears to trim them.

ROCK AND WATER GARDEN

Is this easy to construct?

From a practical viewpoint, it is a good idea to start with a pond and rocky cascade – the largest you can manage – and then extend it over time to include rock pools and rivulets, a fountain, rocky grottoes, a bog garden, a rock garden, an alpine garden, side pools, and so on. Working in this way, you will gradually be able to landscape the whole garden, until it is one big rock and water feature. This is a good option if you are short of time or money, or both.

This exquisite little garden features just the right mix of cascading water, weathered rock and lush green foliage.

LOOKING AT THE PROJECT

In the design below, the whole garden has been given over to a mix of rock and water. If it is not water tumbling over rock, then it is a rock garden or an alpine garden.

CONSIDERING THE IMPLICATIONS

Look carefully at your garden and consider how the design is going to affect the way you use the overall space. Are there going to be problems with children or pets, perhaps?

VARIATIONS TO CONSIDER

You could theme the garden so that it becomes a beach or Japanese garden, or so that it uses a particular type of stone.

Design guidelines for success

- Decide how much space you want to give over to the project.
- Create the biggest pond that you think you can manage.
- A butyl liner is the best option.
- You need the biggest pump possible.
- Buy local stone in bulk – even if you are not going to use it all for the first stage – because large loads are more cost-effective.
- Work with existing slopes and levels.

HOW TO CREATE A ROCK AND WATER GARDEN

Order of work

- Draw up your designs so that they take into account the house, the boundaries, immovable structures and any large trees.
- Dig out the pond and use the dirt to create a stepped mound that leads into the pond.
- Line the hole and the stepped mound with a sheet of butyl.
- Run a water pipe from the pump in the pond to the top of the mound.
- Build the rock steps and sculpt the remaining area with soil and stone.

Planting

When you come to planting, start at the center of the pond and work along the edges of the stream, finishing with the rock garden and the bog garden. Include items like alpines and dwarf conifers in the rock garden, and **Acers** (Japanese Maples) by the waterfall.

HERB GARDEN

Herb gardens come in many forms. You could have a courtyard garden dedicated to growing herbs, herbs in containers placed within a dry garden, herbs as the main planting in and around a patio, herbs grown within the vegetable garden, or an old-fashioned cottage garden planted with herbs – no grass, just lots of little meandering paths with herbs growing in the borders. Some people favor herbs in containers, arranged just outside the back door.

Design guidelines for success

- You need a space no smaller than about 6 ft (2 m) deep and 9 ft (2.7 m) wide, with a wall as a backdrop.
- Edge the border with bricks.
- The wall needs to be on the cold side, so that the border is facing the sun.
- Arrange the plants so that the tall ones are at the back.

LOOKING AT THE PROJECT

In this design, the space – about 6 ft (2 m) from front to back and 8–9 ft (2.5–2.7 m) in width – is completely given over to a cottage herb garden, meaning that the herbs are all suitable for the kitchen. All you have, in effect, is a deep bed edged with red brick, with a brick wall as a backdrop, to keep off cold winds.

Herbs arranged by the patio, so that they can be easily appreciated.

CONSIDERING THE IMPLICATIONS

Because beginners are sometimes worried about using unsuitable herbs – perhaps even herbs that are potentially dangerous – this garden only features culinary herbs. Everything can be safely used in the kitchen. If you have doubts, question your supplier.

VARIATIONS TO CONSIDER

This design can easily be modified to suit your garden. It can be stretched in length, mirror-imaged either side of a central path, changed into a raised border, or set within a pattern of lawns and paths – there are countless options.

HOW TO CREATE A COTTAGE HERB GARDEN

Horseradish · Rosemary · Bay · Fennel · Angelica · Parsley · Thyme · Mint · Marigold · Chives · Bergamot · Sage

Order of work

- Draw up your designs so that they take into account the house, the boundaries, drains, immovable structures and large trees.
- Choose an area in full sun, with a wall on the windward side.
- Mark out the area.
- Double-dig the area to a depth of 12–18 in (30–45 cm).
- Set the brick edging in concrete.
- Improve the soil with an abundance of well-rotted compost and leaf mold.

Planting

Container-grown plants can be planted at any time that suits. Sow or plant new herbs in the spring. Work from the back of the bed to the front. Make sure you can reach the plants.

FOOD-PRODUCING GARDEN

Is this possible in a small garden?

Whatever the size of a small garden, it is possible to grow vegetables and fruit. Fertile patches in gardens create opportunities for rows of salad vegetables, while pots, tubs and grow bags offer space-saving homes for many others, including culinary herbs. Apples can be grown in tubs and large pots on a patio. Strawberries are suitable for planters and hanging baskets; tomatoes can also be planted in hanging baskets.

WHAT TO EXPECT FROM A SMALL GARDEN

Small vegetable patches are ideal for salad-type crops, such as lettuces, carrots, spring onions, beets and tomatoes. French beans, with their low, bush-type habit, are another possibility. Vegetables with a perennial nature, such as asparagus and globe artichokes, are best left for larger gardens.

Potatoes in small gardens are usually treated as a novelty crop and grown in tubs, large pots or potato-growing containers. Additionally, they can be grown in peat-based compost in black plastic bags.

Apples grown as cordons or espaliers against walls make full use of space; in tubs and large pots they have a shorter life-span.

VEGETABLES IN WINDOW BOXES

Regular watering is essential to stop plants wilting and the crops being damaged.
- **Cucumbers:** plant compact varieties as soon as plants are available and all risk of frost has passed. Pinch out the growing point when the plant has 6–7 leaves.
- **Sweet peppers:** when all risk of frost has passed, put 2–3 young plants in a window box. Harvest then when the fruits are swollen and glossy.
- **Tomatoes:** plant two bush-type tomato plants as soon as all risk of frost has passed. It is not necessary to remove side shoots.

Teepees made of bamboo canes soon become drenched in leaves and beans.

VEGETABLE GARDEN DESIGN

Small-garden vegetable plots need not be formal, with plants growing in clinical rows at right-angles to paths. Climbing beans are ideal for scaling trellises and bamboo teepees, while a half-standard Bay tree creates distinction in a herb area.

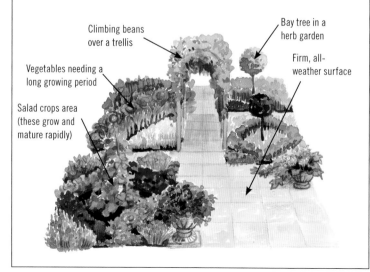

Climbing beans over a trellis

Bay tree in a herb garden

Vegetables needing a long growing period

Firm, all-weather surface

Salad crops area (these grow and mature rapidly)

Vegetables for grow bags

Here are four popular vegetables to try.

Bush French beans ~ grow six plants in each bag.

Zucchini ~ two plants in a bag.

Lettuces ~ eight lettuces in a bag.

Tomatoes ~ see above.

Tomatoes in small greenhouses

Even the smallest greenhouse offers gardening opportunities, especially for tomatoes. Plant a standard-sized growing-bag with 3–4 cordon-type plants; support them either with canes pushed through the bag and into the soil, or with a proprietary supporting frame.

HERBS IN TINY PLACES

Where space is limited, try growing herbs in a cartwheel pattern – it is both decorative and practical.

- Prepare soil in winter, digging and removing perennial weeds. Rake the soil level in spring.
- Use large pebbles to form a circle 5–6 ft (1.5–1.8 m) wide. Add a central circle and spokes.
- Plant a dominant herb in the center (perhaps a Bay tree).
- Plant different herbs in the areas between the spokes.
- Spread gravel or colored gravel around the plants and between the spokes. This helps to conserve moisture in the soil.

Strawberries in containers

Containers to try:

Planters with cupped holes in their sides ~ leave plants in the container for 2–3 years.

Hanging baskets ~ use three plants in a large basket.

Window boxes and wall baskets ~ space plants about 20 cm (8 in) apart.

Barrels with holes cut in their sides ~ put one plant in each hole, as well as several in the top.

TREE FRUITS

The three tree fruits most popular with home gardeners for growing against walls or alongside paths are:

- **Apples:** use dwarfing rootstocks such as M27 and M9, and choose a space-saving form (see below). Additionally, choose varieties not readily available in shops.
- **Pears:** use the Quince A rootstock, and train trees as espaliers or cordons. Pears need pollination partners, so grow three different varieties as cordons, such as 'Conference,' 'Doyenne du Comice' and 'Williams' Bon Chrétien.'
- **Peaches and nectarines:** use St Julien A rootstock, and grow as a fan.

SPACE-SAVING FRUIT TREES

Espalier, fan- and cordon-trained fruit trees need secure support from tiers of strong, galvanized wires. Fan-trained trees are best planted against a warm wall, while espaliers and cordons are ideal for growing as wall-trained trees and alongside paths, where they can be used to separate different parts of a garden.

ESPALIER

Lateral branches on two sides are trained in equally spaced tiers. Ideal for apples and pears.

FAN-SHAPED

Distinctive and ideal for planting against a wall. Not widely used for apples and pears; better for peaches and nectarines.

CORDONS

Single-stemmed trees growing at an angle of 45°. Ideal for apples and pears.

GROWING FOOD IN CONTAINERS

VEGETABLES ON PATIOS

Grow bags are ideal for a wide range of vegetables (see details opposite for bush French beans, zucchini, lettuces and tomatoes). Additionally, cordon tomatoes can be grown in pots and placed against a warm wall. Grow bush tomatoes in a hanging basket.

APPLE TREES IN POTS AND TUBS

There are three essential factors.

- Select wooden tubs or large terracotta pots, at least 15 in (38 cm) wide.
- Use dwarfing rootstocks, such as M27 or M9. Without their use, growing apples in containers is not practical.
- Buy a two-year-old tree, stake it firmly and train as a pyramid.

HERBS IN CONTAINERS

Many herbs are small and ideal for growing in containers on a patio, balcony or just in a window box.

- **Herb planters:** these resemble large pots, but with cupped, planting holes around their sides into which herbs can be put. Also, put herbs in the planter's top.
- **Grow bags:** these are superb for mints (wide range).
- **Pots:** groups of herbs in individual pots look fine. They include chives, mint, parsley and thyme.
- **Window boxes:** leave plants in their individual pots and pack moist peat around them.

No-Dig
Gardening

BENEFITS OF THE NO-DIG METHOD

What is no-dig gardening?

No-dig gardening is an organic system that allows you to grow vegetables and other plants in raised beds without the need for any back-breaking digging, and without having to "improve" the underlying natural soil in your garden. You can control the quality and depth of the growing medium in the raised beds and reduce the amount of work required to keep them free of weeds, pests and diseases.

NO DIGGING

The no-dig system allows and encourages worms and other soil life to carry out the cultivation operations. Mulches of garden compost, farm manure, leaf mold and other organic materials are layered up in raised beds in such a way that there is a reduction in pests, diseases and weeds, and an increase in beneficial soil fungi, worms, insects and microbes. This system might sound a bit too clever, but it is exactly how nature works: vegetation falls to the ground, worms and other soil organisms drag the organic matter down into the soil thereby enriching it, new plants grow, and so on.

HARDLY ANY WEEDING

There is an old adage that says "one year's weed seeds means seven years' digging" – if you allow weeds to seed, you will be shackled by seven years of back-breaking digging and weeding. The no-dig system, however, sidesteps the whole problem of weeding by burying the seeds under layers of mulch. The undisturbed weed seeds are never given the chance to germinate.

SAVING EFFORT

In traditional vegetable cultivation you spend a huge amount of effort digging the whole plot, and then waste a good part of your efforts by walking over and compacting at least a third of the ground that you have painstakingly dug. With the no-dig raised bed system, the layout of paths and beds is permanent. Once the infrastructure is in place, you only need to expend effort on the growing areas within the beds.

PERFECT BALANCE

The no-dig system allows the population of beneficial soil life – worms, insects, microbes and fungi – to build up in such a way that a natural undisturbed environment is created in the important upper soil layers, with the effect of achieving a positive balance.

More benefits of the no-dig system

- The height of the beds and the width of the paths can be tailored to suit your unique physical needs – for example, if you are in a wheelchair or are unable to bend.
- Higher crop yields are produced on a smaller ground area.
- The underlying soil and the layered growing medium within the beds remain undisturbed.
- More water and organic matter are retained in the growing medium.
- The structure and make-up of the growing medium within each bed can be targeted to suit specific plants.
- Beds can be designed to be hot, cool or deep.
- The narrow width of the beds means that you never have to walk on the planted area, and never have too far to stretch.
- The structure of the beds more easily allows the use of nets, windbreaks, plastic sheeting and garden fabric.

The no-dig system of raised beds and paths enables easy access to your crops.

RAISED-BED OPTIONS

Raised beds are essential in this system because they define and separate the growing and walking areas, and enable the gardener to control the quality of the growing medium by layering up organic matter within the beds. The height of the beds can also be modified to increase or decrease the depth of the growing medium, as required for different crops. The beds can be made from a variety of different materials.

What is the best material for raised beds?

THE POSSIBILITIES

Although there are many options – you could build raised beds in metal, wood, plastic, brick, stone, woven willow, straw bales, old tires or whatever else you can find (some of these are easier on the eye than others) – the two key thoughts here are that the structure of the beds should be long-lasting, and the design should be adaptable so that the beds can be stacked and/or moved. Woven willow looks good, but it is fragile and not easily adapted. Brick beds, on the other hand, certainly look good and they are long-lasting, but they are so fixed in form that they cannot be modified. While large tires last for ever and they can be stacked, they fail because the cavities hold too much water and give home to pests such as ants and mice. Look at the materials available in your area, and design the beds accordingly.

A bed made from readily available planed and treated softwood is a swift but expensive option.

You must think very long and hard before opting to build a long-lasting but inflexible brick bed.

Above: A long, deep bed made from thick-section treated softwood.

Left: Beds made from railroad ties are long-lasting, flexible and good on the eye.

An extra-long bed made from treated thick-section softwood – it is not very attractive, but is wonderfully practical.

A runner bean bed with a removable top section and a fixed central pole.

A builders' waste bag makes a swift and efficient temporary bed.

This bed has been made from the top section of a salvaged galvanized water barrel.

The various photographs here will show you that there are indeed many possibilities, but you still must be mindful that if you really want to get the best out of a no-dig raised bed garden – maximum crops for minimum effort – then function is all-important. For this reason, a pattern of stackable wooden raised beds, as shown on page 13, with the addition of recycled trash cans and builders' waste bags to be used as fill-in standbys, works extremely well. For example, if you decide to trial a new crop in a little-used marginal area of your plot, you could use a mix of waste bags and salvaged metal trash cans before going to the effort and expense of building a more permanent wooden bed.

BUILDINGS AND EQUIPMENT

A water barrel and a shed for your gardening tools are both essential. There is no reason why you cannot manage without extras such as greenhouses and hoop houses, but if you have room for them they will make life easier in your no-dig garden. It is a pleasure to work in a warm, cozy greenhouse or hoop house, especially when the weather is wet and windy, and they will allow you to extend the growing season.

What equipment will I need?

SOME BASIC EQUIPMENT

A selection of tools and materials you are likely to need is illustrated below. Buckets, old metal trash cans and more nets may be a useful addition to this list, and, if you can afford it, a large woodchipping machine would be a good option.

GARDEN SHED

No doubt you could leave your tools and materials in various corners of the garage or house, but in practice a dedicated garden shed is best. The ideal shed will have a bench on one side, an old armchair, natural light, plenty of hooks and shelves to hold and contain your tools and materials, a radio, an electrical outlet so that you can make tea or coffee, a calendar, a pad and a pencil, and so on. Remember that a shed is more than just a place to store your things – it is also a place where you can just sit and contemplate.

GREENHOUSES AND HOOP HOUSES

Every no-dig grower of vegetables, no matter how small their plot, needs some means of raising, sprouting and hardening off plants so that they are ready for planting out in the open. This is even more important if you want to extend the growing season. Plastic-covered frames, hotbeds with some sort of frame over them, cloches, fabrics, nets and so on are all good options – but, when you really get down to it, the ideal is to have a greenhouse or, better still, a hoop house.

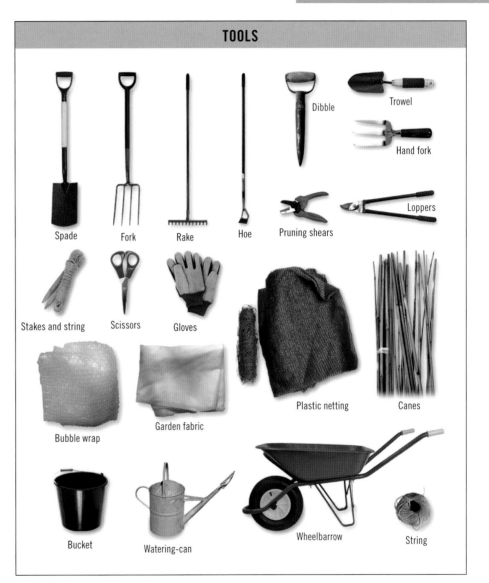

TOOLS

Dibble · Trowel · Hand fork · Loppers · Spade · Fork · Rake · Hoe · Pruning shears · Stakes and string · Scissors · Gloves · Plastic netting · Canes · Bubble wrap · Garden fabric · Bucket · Watering-can · Wheelbarrow · String

GREENHOUSES

While any greenhouse is better than nothing, the ultimate is to have a traditional cedarwood greenhouse set on a low brick wall. Wood can easily be mended and modified, and the bricks hold in the warmth of the sun. Such a greenhouse will also need an area of slatted staging at table level, and a selection of shelves. Most greenhouses are limited in size and shape, however, so they are really only good for sowing, potting on, and growing pot-grown crops.

HOOP HOUSES

A hoop house can be used – because of its size and shape and the way the ends can be opened up to the air – for sowing seeds, potting, growing various plants prior to planting them out, growing crops like tomatoes, sweet peppers and cucumbers, and growing a whole range of salad leaf crops directly in beds. This versatility gives them the advantage over a greenhouse. They allow you to work in wet and windy weather, and to plant early and harvest late.

A hoop house is a great option if you have the space and the money.

Collecting rainwater

If you have a shed, or your no-dig plot is close to the house, then one or more water barrels, old tin baths, tanks or other receptacles to catch the rainwater are vital. There is no doubt that an ugly mix of barrels, baths and buckets looks a bit of a mess, but they are a wonderful way of saving water, and they really come into their own when you want to water in seedlings without going to all the bother of turning on the garden hose. Before setting out rain barrels, make sure they are allowed by your local codes.

A good part of the pleasure of designing, building and working a no-dig raised bed garden is figuring out just how to use found and salvaged materials to combat and beat the weather – to protect against wind, to shelter from frost, to capture the heat from the sun, and generally to create the best environment for the plants. If you enjoy recycling and salvaging materials, and generally playing around with hammers, nails and string, then you will have a great time.

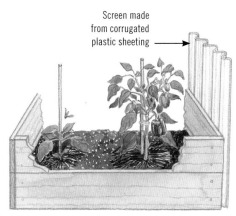

Screen made from corrugated plastic sheeting

A bed designed specifically to nurture delicate plants. The deep sides protect from blustery winds and the screen makes the most of the sun.

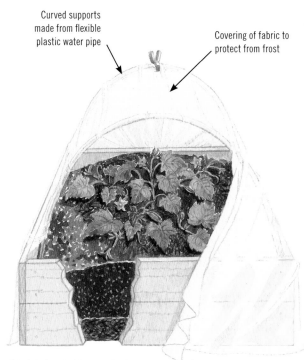

Curved supports made from flexible plastic water pipe

Covering of fabric to protect from frost

A bed designed with removable frames that allow for extra deep mulches. The idea is that you can sit an extra frame in place, add more mulch, fit another frame, and so on, to suit the growing depth of the plant.

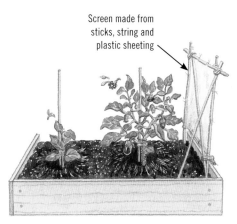

Screen made from sticks, string and plastic sheeting

A small bed with a screen made and positioned to suit – either to keep off the wind or to focus the rays of the sun onto the growing crop.

THE PERFECT PLOT

What makes the perfect plot?

The wonderful thing about no-dig raised bed vegetable gardening is that you can, to a great extent, ignore the make-up of the basic natural soil. Certainly, you would need to drain a wet site, and you still have to think about how the plot relates to the sun and to large trees or other obstructions such as outbuildings, but at least you do not have to think about the quality of the soil and/or digging it.

Checklist

- The ideal is to have either a level or a gently sloping site that faces the sun at midday.

- It is best if the plot is protected to the windward side – with trees or rising ground to mitigate the prevailing winds.

- Good free drainage is important – avoid a site that looks in any way damp, or smells sour.

- You need one or more standpipes – so that you can rig up a sprinkler watering system.

- Make sure if you aim to have a greenhouse and/or hoop house that there is enough room to site them at the back of the plot – so that they get the sun without casting a shadow over the rest of the plot.

- Make sure there is enough room for a shed – so that you can put it well away from the beds and it will not cast a shadow over them.

- If you have a long, narrow garden with high walls to the sunny side, site the beds on the side away from the walls so they make the most of the sun.

- If you have a very large garden in the country, so that you can more or less design the garden to suit, have two gates so that you can push carts, trolleys or wheelbarrows in through one gate and out through the other.

- Try to avoid trees or large shrubs that might suck water out of the ground and/or shed leaves over the beds.

- If you have a large garden and intend keeping chickens, ducks or geese to give you manure, try to arrange the set-up so that you keep the distance between the poultry shed and the vegetable garden to the minimum.

A plot in its early stages – note the netting to protect from frost, the recycled galvanized water barrels, and the black plastic sheet that will eventually be covered in wood chips.

TOWN PLOT

A town garden is fine, as long as you dedicate the whole area to the no-dig system, because a no-dig raised bed system works best when all the elements are shaped and positioned for the common no-dig good. For example, imagine a small town garden scenario where the family – mother, dad and two children – have six raised beds in the front garden, and a dozen or so beds and four chickens in a coop in the back garden. There is not much lawn, but the kids are so involved with the fun of it all that they do not really need a big play area.

VILLAGE PLOT

A village plot is a good option in that, to a great extent, the whole rural community set-up tends to be in tune with nature. Imagine a village scenario where mother, dad and four children live in a large end-terrace house where they have a huge corner plot plus a strip of unused land at the far end of the garden. They have a massive system of beds that covers just about the whole garden. They have chickens, an old greenhouse and a very long hoop house. Their plot is so productive that they also sell produce at the gate. Villagers pop in and buy fresh eggs, vegetables and fruit – anything that is in season.

COUNTRY PLOT

The very best option is a virgin plot in the country. Right from the start you can stake out what you think is the perfect arrangement of beds and take it from there. There may be overhanging trees, slopes and other problems, but if you are starting from scratch you can easily work round these. You may subsequently need to make changes to the height of the beds, the position of gates and other items, but that is all part of the fun.

THE IDEAL NO-DIG PLOT

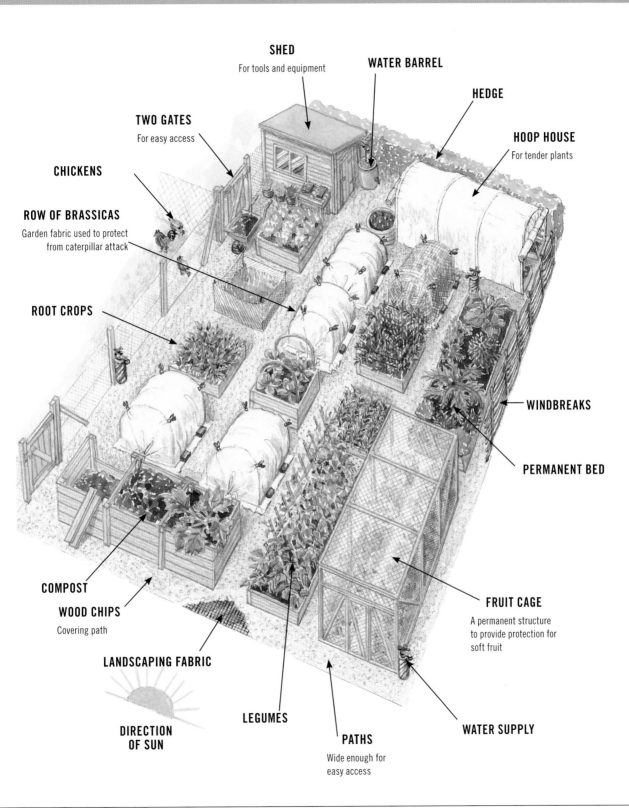

SHED
For tools and equipment

WATER BARREL

HEDGE

HOOP HOUSE
For tender plants

TWO GATES
For easy access

CHICKENS

ROW OF BRASSICAS
Garden fabric used to protect
from caterpillar attack

ROOT CROPS

WINDBREAKS

PERMANENT BED

COMPOST

WOOD CHIPS
Covering path

FRUIT CAGE
A permanent structure
to provide protection for
soft fruit

LANDSCAPING FABRIC

LEGUMES

**DIRECTION
OF SUN**

PATHS
Wide enough for
easy access

WATER SUPPLY

SMALL NO-DIG GARDEN

> *Is no-dig possible in a small garden?*

There are examples of communal no-dig gardens on the flat roofs of high-rise blocks, productive set-ups in minute front gardens, beautifully inventive beds made of corrugated sheet, and gardens built and stepped like a Mayan ruin – all designed to make the most of limited space. If you are keen and inventive, there are endless possibilities for creating a no-dig system in your small garden. Here are a few ideas.

CONCRETE GARDEN

A couple moved into a property where the garden was full of concrete slabs and corrugated steel Quonset hut-type buildings that had been used as chicken sheds. They simply dismantled the buildings, rebolted the corrugated sections together to make raised beds, set the beds in place on the concrete slabs, filled them up with the well-rotted chicken manure that littered the site, and began planting.

HOOP HOUSE GARDEN

Another couple moved into a village property where the long, thin garden was mostly taken up by a huge hoop house (probably part of some long-gone nursery). They built an arrangement of raised beds in the hoop house, rigged up as many shelves and hanging baskets as the structure would hold, and gave the rest of the garden over to chickens. It is intensive and a bit smelly, but it works for them.

JUNKYARD GARDEN

An old couple moved into a country property where the garden was packed full of large wooden packing cases, pallets and stacks of old truck tires. It was a complete junkyard. They stacked the tires three deep to make raised beds, turned the pallet and packing cases into more beds and a couple of chicken sheds, begged horse manure from the local stables, and then got on with rearing chickens and planting the raised beds. It is not very pretty, but its productivity and order make the garden special.

PLANNING A SMALL NO-DIG RAISED BED GARDEN

Walk around your garden at various times, at sunrise and sunset and in various weather conditions, and consider carefully how the season of the year, time of day and weather conditions all affect the space. Look at the width and length of the garden, the height of boundary walls and fences, the shape of the plot in relation to tall trees and neighboring buildings, and think it all through. Do you want to turn the whole space into a no-dig garden with a range of raised beds and a poultry run, or do you simply want to set a single small area aside? Consider how friends and family use the space. Take everything into account, then draw up a design.

Railroad ties have been used to build a mix of steps, beds, walls and patios.

Small garden solutions

- You could be single-minded, clear out everything and dedicate the whole plot and all your spare energy to using every bit of available space.

- You could approach the local community council and see if they have any available funds, or perhaps even a patch of vacant ground.

- You could double your space by building stepped beds, meaning that you grow some crops such as salad leaves, herbs and tomatoes on special frames, wall boxes and racks.

- You could join forces with a neighbor and divide the whole project into tasks – building beds, keeping poultry, sowing, planting – and then split the work according to your needs and pleasures.

- You could join forces with several neighbors to create a mini cooperative with lots of chickens and a large hoop house. In this way you could maximize your output and completely use up extra produce.

- You could join forces with an aged neighbor – you take over their plot and in exchange you give them as much produce as they need.

- You could join forces with a physically disabled neighbor – you take over their garden and build beds that are wheelchair accessible, and in return you divide the produce.

- You could join forces with a neighbor who hates gardening but enjoys indoor activities such as cooking – you take over their plot, you split the produce and they turn some of the produce into jams, preserves, frozen vegetables and so on.

SMALL GARDEN DESIGNS

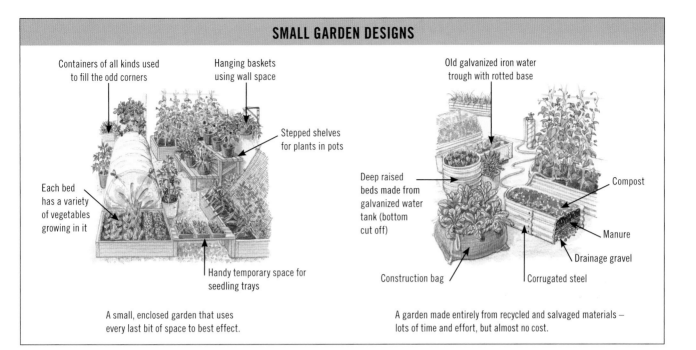

Containers of all kinds used to fill the odd corners

Hanging baskets using wall space

Stepped shelves for plants in pots

Each bed has a variety of vegetables growing in it

Handy temporary space for seedling trays

A small, enclosed garden that uses every last bit of space to best effect.

Old galvanized iron water trough with rotted base

Deep raised beds made from galvanized water tank (bottom cut off)

Compost

Manure

Drainage gravel

Construction bag

Corrugated steel

A garden made entirely from recycled and salvaged materials — lots of time and effort, but almost no cost.

HOW TO MAKE A SMALL NO-DIG GARDEN

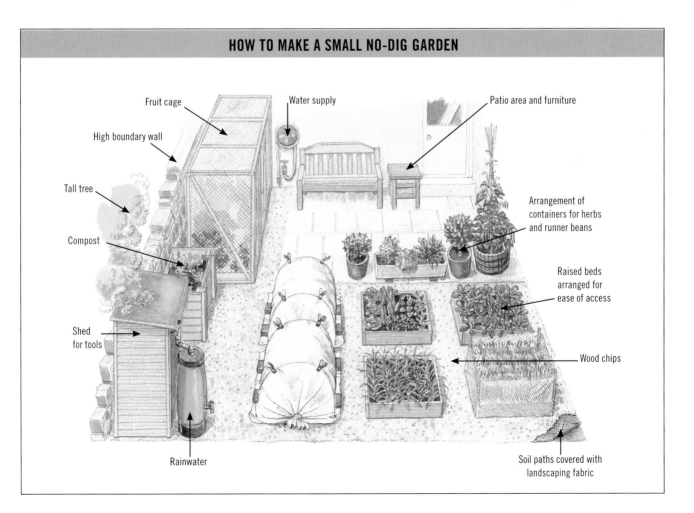

Fruit cage

Water supply

Patio area and furniture

High boundary wall

Tall tree

Compost

Arrangement of containers for herbs and runner beans

Raised beds arranged for ease of access

Shed for tools

Wood chips

Rainwater

Soil paths covered with landscaping fabric

RAISED-BED CONSTRUCTION

Are raised beds necessary?

Raised beds are an essential element of no-dig gardening. They contain and define the growing area and allow you swiftly to create an ideal growing medium. The decomposing layers of various organic materials within the bed mirror nature and reduce the need for watering and weeding. The width of the bed means that you can work without compacting the growing area, and the height of the bed can be adjusted.

RAISED BEDS FROM FOUND ITEMS

An attractive raised bed made from an old cast-iron bath.

A raised bed made from a builders' construction bag is good for runner beans.

Raised beds can be created from various materials ranging from old bricks and salvaged timber through to found containers such as tin baths, trash cans, wooden boats, wheelbarrows, water tanks, apple orchard bins and builders' construction bags (used for delivering sand and gravel). Containers that are at least 2 ft (60 cm) in width or diameter are most useful. Old railroad ties (large beams of preserved timber) make excellent beds but are very heavy. Containers must allow for drainage – if there are no holes in the bottom, is it possible to make some? Thin metal containers offer less protection in frosty weather so are not ideal. Before using construction bags and pallets, check that they are non-returnable.

MAKING A RAISED BED FROM A CONSTRUCTION BAG

1. Cut 1 in (2.5 cm) diameter plastic water pipe to length so that it makes a hoop that is a snug fit within the neck of your found construction bag.

2. Trim a piece of found wood to size (so that it is a tight fit in the tube) and use it to link the two ends of the pipe to make a hoop.

3. Sit the construction bag on the ground, or better still on a found wooden pallet, and half-fill it with layers of manure and organic materials that will compost.

4. Put the hoop over the outside of the bag and fold the top of the bag over-and-out so that the hoop is contained. Use a bodkin and nylon string to sew the neck of the bag so that the hoop stays put.

5. Add more layers of compost and manure, and materials that will compost, until the bag bulges to clinch the hoop in place.

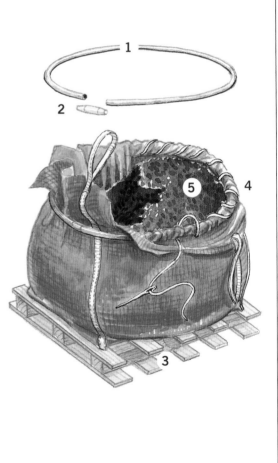

BUILDING A RAISED BED USING TREATED WOOD

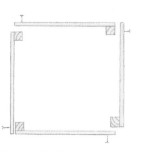

1. You will need: four planks that are roughly 9 in (23 cm) wide, 2 in (5 cm) thick and 3 ft (90 cm) long; and four posts that are 9 in (23 cm) long and 3 in (7.5 cm) square.

2. Screw a post to the end of a plank as shown above so that it is aligned to the end but offset by 1 in (2.5 cm). The protruding post facilitates stacking. Repeat for the other planks and posts.

3. Assemble the pieces to make a square frame.

4. Set the frame stub side down on the levelled ground, scrape off any weeds, and then fill it up in layers in the following order: newspaper and brown cardboard, 2 in (5 cm) compost, 2 in (5 cm) farmyard manure, and 3 in (7.5 cm) well-decomposed compost.

- The optimum width of a bed is around 3 ft (90 cm) – any wider and it is difficult to reach across (you need to avoid walking on the growing medium); any narrower and it will result in a less efficient use of materials. It can be square (as shown in the sequence above) or a rectangular shape (as long as you like), but always consider the site and your specific requirements.

- Frames assembled acording to the design below can be stacked one upon another, so that the overall depth can be adjusted for specific crops.

- Timber treated with preservative will make a long-lasting structure (lasting up to 20 years). It is worth using stainless-steel screws to avoid rust problems.

CONSIDERING THE LAYOUT

The arrangement of the beds must allow for paths that are wide enough for a wheelbarrow to be pushed along, and for locations that take best advantage of the sun.

A long grid layout with beds 3 ft (90 cm) wide and at various lengths to suit the plot.

A layout composed of a mix of purpose-made beds and salvaged containers.

A square grid layout with 3 ft (90 cm) square beds set 30 in (75 cm) apart.

PREPARING THE GROUND

Beds need to be positioned on fairly level ground. If your site is sloping, consider levelling areas for a terraced effect. Brick or stone-built beds will require foundations which are slightly larger than the beds themselves. Mark out areas using stakes, string and a large tape measure.

Cover the ground with weed-suppressing landscape fabric followed by a 2 in (5 cm) layer of wood chips.

CONSTRUCTING THE PATHS AROUND THE BEDS

Paths are essential and can be constructed quickly using landscape fabric and wood chippings as shown below. The advantage of wood chip paths is that they are easily rebuilt or re-routed to accommodate any changes in layout that you may find necessary over time. Paths made from gravel, concrete, paving slabs or bricks are more permanent.

Alternatively, cover the ground with found materials such as old carpet and plastic sheeting. Make holes in any plastic to allow for drainage.

RAISED BED LAYOUTS

A layout for a basic rectangular plot with a shed and a three-section compost bin.

A layout for a difficult corner plot with house and garden walls to one side.

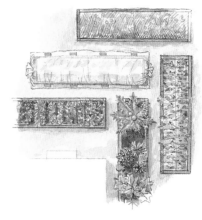

A layout for a corner plot where function is more important than decoration.

BUILDING RAISED BEDS USING RAILROAD TIES

If you are looking to build a permanent no-dig raised bed garden that checks off all the form and function boxes – meaning the garden must be a joy to the eye as well as functionally sound – then building the beds from used railroad ties is a good option. The ties are expensive, difficult to move, and tricky to joint and put together, and the whole task will require a lot of sweat and effort – it takes two strong people to lift a tie into place – but once the beds are built they will be there for a lifetime. The other bit of good news is that, while ties are undoubtedly heavy, the weight and structure of the

beds is such that they can be placed with little or no ground work. If you are keen to make the beds from railroad ties, a good starting point is to look at the shape of your garden and take measurements. Note that the ideal bed needs to be about 3 ft (90 cm) wide – so that you can work the bed from both sides without standing on the growing medium – and then start phoning around for facts and figures. Once you know the type of ties – their age and dimensions, and how much they cost to be delivered – you can start drawing up designs.

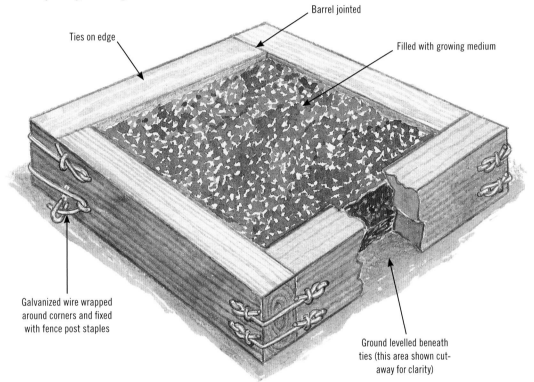

Barrel jointed

Ties on edge

Filled with growing medium

Galvanized wire wrapped around corners and fixed with fence post staples

Ground levelled beneath ties (this area shown cut-away for clarity)

Designing bed modules

Salvaged railroad ties tipically measure 5–6 in (13–15 cm) in depth and can be up to 10–12 in (25–30 cm) in width. They come in a variety of lengths, from 6 ft (1.8 m) up to 14 ft (4.3 m). With ties weighing in at 100–240 lb (45–110 kg), they are difficult to cut and handle. It is vital to decide up front an overall design for the beds. Considering that the ideal bed width is 3 ft (90 cm), you need to measure the size of your plot, take into account that the paths need to be wide enough to take a wheelbarrow and then decide on a bed size that makes the best use of tie lengths. You must do all this before you ever put tool to wood. A good way forward is to measure your plot, see what ties are available in your area, and then make a small working model.

Cutting

Salvaged railroad ties are heavy, difficult to manhandle, and more often than not bristling with bent nails, rusty bolts, bits of wire and all sorts of foreign bodies, so you must always handle them with extreme care and caution – all the more so if you plan to use a chainsaw to cut them into lengths. There are three sawing options: you could cut them with a heavy-duty cross-cut handsaw, or with a chainsaw, or you could get them cut by the supplier. The important thing here is that the cuts must be true and square to the face and edge. If you have any doubts about your woodworking skills, then it is best to pay the extra and get the supplier to do the cutting. Make sure that you provide a precise cutting list.

Railroad ties can be positioned on edge or on face. For example a 6 x 10 in (15 x 25 cm) section tie can be positioned on edge to make a bed wall that is 6 in (15 cm) wide and 10 in (25 cm) high, or on face to make a wall 10 in (25 cm) wide and 6 in (15 cm) high. There are two basic options for jointing corners: they can be barrel-jointed (cut straight through at right angles to the face and edge, and fitted end to side-end), or they can be cut at the ends to make simple half laps.

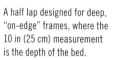

A half lap designed for deep, "on-edge" frames, where the 10 in (25 cm) measurement is the depth of the bed.

A half lap designed for shallow, "on-face" frames, where the 6 in (15 cm) measurement is the depth of the bed.

Maintaining beds and paths

- Beds made from railroad ties and treated wood have a tendency to pull apart at the corners. A swift and easy repair is to clench the timbers together with sash clamps and bind the beds around with high-tensile heavy-duty fencing wire.

- Every two years scoop the rotted woodchip up off the paths, put it to one side to use on the beds as mulch and replace it with fresh.

- Avoid having a non-rot option on the paths, such as stones, gravel or crushed shells, because, when the path eventually gets fouled up with growing medium, leaves and so on, they are difficult to wash.

- If you feel that some beds will later require a greater depth of growing medium to accommodate deep-rooted crops and/or crops that need to be earthed up as they grow, design the beds so that they can be built up with additional frames. (On page 119 we show how we have solved the extra height dilemma by developing a system of frames that notch together. This system could be modified to suit just about any bed material from brick to railroad ties.)

- The depth of beds can be increased to suit gardeners who are in some way physically restricted, so that the gardener can work on a bed without bending or leaving the wheelchair.

GROWING MEDIUM

The quality and fertility of any growing medium is all-important, and in times past a keen gardener would spend a lifetime trying to improve their soil. The no-dig method sidesteps the slog involved by swiftly layering up manure, leaf mold and compost to create the ideal medium. Once the basic mix of purchased material is in place in the bed, you can top it up with mulches of organic manure and garden compost.

How important is the growing medium?

LEAF MOLD

Leaf mold is a mix of fallen leaves from deciduous shrubs and trees that has been collected and encouraged to decompose rapidly. The leaves can be added in small amounts to existing compost bins, or stored in well-aerated purpose-made bins. Once decayed, the leaf mold can be added to the raised beds as a mulch.

GARDEN COMPOST

Compost is a well-rotted mix of kitchen and garden plant waste – peelings and leftovers from the kitchen, and leaves and vegetable matter from the garden. A good option in the context of no-dig gardening is to have several compost heaps or bins on the go, so that leaves, stalks and general vegetable waste can be constantly recycled. While most weeds can be composted directly, weeds like thistles and nettles are best burnt – you can then use the resultant ash as a thin mulch or as a slug repellent.

SPENT MUSHROOM COMPOST

This is a waste product from mushroom farms that is relatively inexpensive, smells good, and is easy to handle. Never buy it by the bag, as it is far too expensive – it is much better to purchase it by the truckload. It is a very good starter option when you are looking for bulk material to top up your first beds.

Garden compost

Leaf mold

Spent mushroom compost

HOW TO MAKE A THREE-PART COMPOST BIN

A home-made compost bin is a good option, especially one like this three-part design. It is less expensive to make than three separate bins. In practice, while the first bin is being filled, the second has already been filled and is decomposing, and the third is full of compost that is ready to use. When the third bin is empty it becomes the first, and so on in a continuous cycle. Use reclaimed materials or buy treated timber and assemble using galvanized nails or screws.

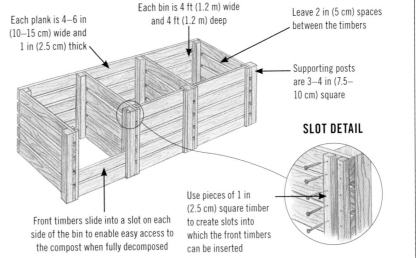

Each plank is 4–6 in (10–15 cm) wide and 1 in (2.5 cm) thick

Each bin is 4 ft (1.2 m) wide and 4 ft (1.2 m) deep

Leave 2 in (5 cm) spaces between the timbers

Supporting posts are 3–4 in (7.5–10 cm) square

SLOT DETAIL

Front timbers slide into a slot on each side of the bin to enable easy access to the compost when fully decomposed

Use pieces of 1 in (2.5 cm) square timber to create slots into which the front timbers can be inserted

MANURE

What is well-rotted organic manure?

Organic manure is the excrement from domesticated livestock such as cows, horses, poultry, pigs, goats, rabbits and sheep that have been fed on organically grown fodder. It usually comes as bedding, that is mixed with straw, chopped newspaper, sawdust or wood chips. Cow, horse and poultry manures are best, since they are stiff-textured, sweet-smelling, relatively free from harmful organisms, and readily available.

TYPES OF ANIMAL MANURE

The only surefire way of ensuring that your manure is free from chemicals is to keep your own livestock.

Horse manure At about 0.6 per cent nitrogen, horse manure is easy to handle, low in cost, sweet-smelling and readily available from farms and stables.

Cow manure At about 0.4 per cent nitrogen, cow manure is a good option if it is mixed with lots of absorbent straw.

Chicken manure At about 1.8 per cent nitrogen, chicken manure can be a bit messy to handle; it is especially smelly when it is fresh and wet. The best method is to use poultry house bedding. Chickens are a good choice if you want to keep your own animals.

Goose manure At about 0.5 per cent nitrogen, goose manure is also a good option if you want to keep your own livestock. The main difficulty is that farmyard geese tend to spread their manure. It is advisable to cover their sleeping and watering area with straw or sawdust bedding, and then collect the bedding when it is in a mess.

Rabbit manure High in nitrogen, rabbit manure is very good if you can get enough of it; some gardeners reckon that it is the best ever. It is available as a mix of manure and sawdust, and is very convenient and easy to handle. It has a sweet, strong, nutty smell.

Sheep manure High in nutrients, sheep manure is a difficult option because, as the sheep live most of their lives outside, the manure has to be collected by hand. It is an inexpensive, easy-to-handle choice when mixed with straw or hay.

Chinese geese like these will produce plenty of top-quality organic manure that is ideal for using in the no-dig system.

KEEPING CHICKENS AND USING THE MANURE

Chickens have long been the traditional choice of livestock for home-makers, keen gardeners and homesteaders. They will recycle most of your kitchen scraps, help keep rough grass and weeds down, eat lots of garden bugs and pests, and, best of all, give you eggs, meat and unlimited manure. The first step is to decide on your needs (do you want big fat birds, hardy birds, large white eggs, or some other feature?) and then pick the most suitable breed. Chickens can be fed on leftover kitchen scraps and garden greens, but they also need grit, to help with their digestion, and a ready supply of either organic meal or layers pellets.

For managing the manure, you need to house them in a large, walk-in, shed-type chicken house with plenty of floor space and a good wide door for wheelbarrow access. Cover the floor with a bedding of straw, chopped newspaper or sawdust. When the bedding is in a mess, you have chicken manure that can be wheelbarrowed out and either added to the compost heap or rotted down and sprinkled on the raised beds as a thin mulch.

Points to note

- Some farms are awash with chemicals – so you do have to make sure that your manure comes from a good, reliable, accredited, organic source.

- Your chosen manure might contain a lot of harmful but naturally occurring organisms – so make sure that you always wash your hands after contact.

- Fresh manures are too rich and strong for most growing plants – so it is best to let them sit and rot before use.

BED AND PLANT ROTATION

Different crops take different nutrients from the soil or growing medium. If, for example, you repeatedly plant brassicas in the same bed, the growing medium will become depleted in nitrogen and the plants will become sick. The traditional rule of thumb is that you have a three-year rotation — meaning that you grow, say, brassicas in year one, root vegetables in year two, legumes and salad leaves in year three, and then go back to brassicas in year four.

Why is rotation necessary?

Permanent

The following crops are defined as "permanent" in the sense that they can remain in or near the same bed for a number of years:

- Globe artichoke
- Asparagus • Bay
- Borage • Chervil
- Chives • Dill

Brassicas (rotated)

Brassicas and other plants that enjoy the same soil conditions:

- Broccoli
- Brussels sprouts
- Cabbages
- Cauliflowers
- Kale
- Kohl rabi
- Radishes

Legumes and salad crops (rotated)

- Broad beans
- French beans
- Runner beans
- Beet leaf
- Celeriac
- Endives
- Lettuces
- Onions and shallots
- Peas

Root vegetables (rotated)

Root vegetables and other plants that enjoy the same conditions:

- Beets • Carrots
- Celery • Chicory
- Leeks • Parsnips
- Potatoes • Salsify
- Spinach • Rutabagas
- Sweetcorn • Turnips

YEAR 1

PERMANENT   BRASSICAS   ROOT   LEGUMES AND SALADS

Radishes

Asparagus

Cabbages

Herbs

Kale

Globe artichoke

Beets

Onions

Leeks

Lettuces

Celery

Runner beans

Rhubarb   Cauliflowers   Rutabagas   Peas

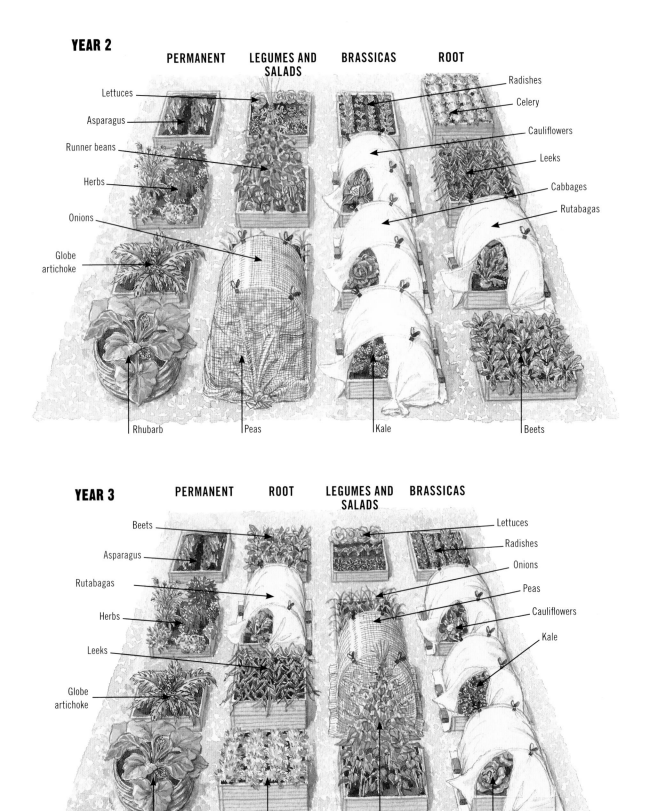

YEAR 2

PERMANENT   LEGUMES AND SALADS   BRASSICAS   ROOT

Lettuces
Asparagus
Runner beans
Herbs
Onions
Globe artichoke
Rhubarb
Peas
Kale
Beets

Radishes
Celery
Cauliflowers
Leeks
Cabbages
Rutabagas

YEAR 3

PERMANENT   ROOT   LEGUMES AND SALADS   BRASSICAS

Beets
Asparagus
Rutabagas
Herbs
Leeks
Globe artichoke
Rhubarb
Celery
Runner beans
Cabbages

Lettuces
Radishes
Onions
Peas
Cauliflowers
Kale

CATCH CROPS AND INTERCROPPING

Catch cropping and intercropping allow you to take full advantage of the growing potential of a bed. Catch cropping involves planting swift-growing vegetables in a vacant bed; intercropping involves planting swift-growing crops among slow-growing ones. For example, fast-growing salad leaves can be planted alongside celery, and radishes alongside beans. The disadvantage of both is that the closeness of the planting increases the risk of pests and diseases.

What is the difference?

Swift-growing onions planted, or "intercropped," each side of a row of slow-growing raspberries.

ARE THESE TECHNIQUES COMPLICATED?

While it is easy enough to plant a fast-growing crop in a vacant bed or between slow-growing plants, the complexity comes when the planting is so close that you have to monitor the beds constantly to ensure that the close-packed plants have enough light and air. It might seem a lot of fuss, but if you only have room for a small number of beds and you are prepared to put in the time and effort then it is no bad thing. That said, some plants seem to flourish when they are grown in a tight, companionable environment.

THE BENEFITS

The main benefit is that these methods allow you to swiftly take advantage of what you see happening on the ground. For example, if you see that a bed is empty or there is a lot of space between slow-growing crops, or a line of crops has failed, then you can swoop in and plant something that takes best advantage of the situation. The systems let you spontaneously make good use of what would otherwise be a "lose-lose" situation.

COMPANION PLANTING

Companion, or beneficial, planting describes a situation where different types of plants are brought together for their mutual benefit. French marigolds and cabbages are a good example – the marigolds flourish while they protect the cabbages against whitefly by repelling the insects. Onions and carrots also work well together because the onions ward off carrot fly.

French marigolds can be grown alongside a range of crops to deter whitefly. They also look very pretty.

BROCCOLI AND RADISHES

Step 1 MID-AUTUMN – plant Romaine lettuce 12 in (30 cm) apart

Step 2 LATE WINTER TO EARLY SPRING – sow dwarf peas between alternate rows of lettuces

Step 3 EARLY TO MID-SUMMER – pick peas and plant broccoli 18 in (45 cm) apart; sow cabbage lettuces between the broccoli plants

Step 4 LATE SPRING – clear the ground, mulch with manure and plant pot-grown cucumbers

Step 5 LATE SUMMER – plant cauliflowers between the cucumbers

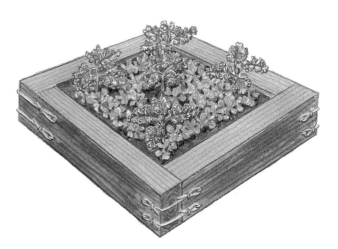

CABBAGE AND RADISHES

Step 1 EARLY SPRING – plant second early potatoes

Step 2 LATE SUMMER – lift potatoes and plant large and small varieties of cabbages 18 in (45 cm) apart

Step 3 MID-AUTUMN – plant cabbage lettuces 8 in (20 cm) apart in a row between the cabbages

Step 4 EARLY WINTER – lift the small cabbages

Step 5 LATE WINTER – clear the last of the small cabbages and plant broad beans in their place

Step 6 MID-SPRING – lift the last of the lettuces and sow a row of runner beans to fill the space

Step 7 MID-WINTER – lift all the beans, remulch and plant shallots

Step 8 EARLY SUMMER – lift all the shallots, mulch with manure and plant with celery 12 in (30 cm) apart; sow radishes between the rows

PARSNIPS AND LETTUCES

Step 1 LATE WINTER – plant two rows of cabbage lettuces 12 in (30 cm) apart

Step 2 EARLY SPRING – plant cauliflowers between alternate lettuces; sow carrots between the two rows

Step 3 LATE SPRING – clear the lettuces and set pot-grown dwarf beans between the cauliflowers

Step 4 EARLY SUMMER – lift the cauliflowers, beans and carrots

Step 5 MID-SUMMER – plant celery in two trenches; plant spinach or lettuces between the celery plants; follow the celery with parsnips, carrots and beets

ORGANIC PROTECTION

There is no need for chemicals in this system. You can use mouse traps, physical barriers (such as nets, garden fabric, plastic sheeting and wooden screens), beneficial insects and predatory bugs. Traditional home-made insect and disease controls are made from ordinary household foods and products like garlic, vegetable oil and water. You can also buy organic dusts and sprays, sprays made from milk, and washes made from water and soft soap.

Can I protect my crops without using chemicals?

GARDEN NETS

Depending upon the mesh size, configuration and set-up, a carefully chosen net will protect your plants from cabbage white butterflies that lay eggs that result in caterpillars, birds that chomp away at buds and foliage, small animals like mice, rats, rabbits and squirrels that dig up seeds and eat pods and fruits, bad weather such as severe frosts and lashing winds, and so on. For example, we protect our pea beds from mice and birds with barriers of fine net, mouse traps and little tin cans that tinkle in the wind, and our newly planted broccoli with garden fabric and nets to keep off birds and a sheet of corrugated steel to protect from the wind. Of course, many of these organic controls and barriers are a good deal less than beautiful – there is nothing pretty about a bent and rusty sheet of tin – but they work. If you can protect your plants with nets, old net curtains, sheets of tin or whatever you can find, without poisoning yourself and the environment, that is ideal. If it works for you, and is safe and non-toxic, then it has to be a good idea.

Builders' scaffold nets are very practical – they are strong, long-lasting and low-cost, and they will keep off a wide range of birds, animals and other pests.

A net-covered frame made from bamboo poles is ideal for tall-growing plants.

A draped net provides swift and easy protection in the early growing stages.

A frame built from steel fencing posts and plastic water pipe can be used to support a net.

A tightly stretched net over a water pipe frame is good for protecting strawberries.

Agriculture fabric is a non-woven fabric – think of a combination of fine fluffy gauze, a bed duvet, a super-thin sheet of cotton wool and extremely fine netting. Sold in a whole range of grades and thicknesses, agricultural fabric has rapidly transformed gardening practices. It can be used like a net, to keep away pests such as butterflies, slugs, snails, flea beetles, spiders and birds. It can protect plants by cocooning them, to keep heat in and cold out. It can be put down on the ground to warm the soil and control weeds. It is so light that it can be draped directly over plants, and it is so strong that it can be fixed up on a framework to create a sort of fabric hoop house.

When the plants are more mature, they should be strong enough to take the weight of the fabric themselves without the need for any other support.

For seedlings and young plants, use sticks to provide just enough support to take the weight of the fabric.

PHYSICAL PEST DETERRENTS

Simple, old-fashioned, home-made pest deterrents include trailing cotton streamers to deter pigeons from eating greens, crushed eggshells, soot, animal hair and bits of trailed knitting wool to make things difficult for slugs, snails and cutworms, spinning compact discs to scare off birds and squirrels, tinkling tin cans to frighten off rabbits and foxes, and copper wire stapled around the top of beds to keep off slugs. There is no proof that these actually work, but they recycle products that would otherwise go to waste, they are fun to make and set up, and there are many folk tales and stories that vouch for their efficiency.

Old, unwanted compact discs are good for scaring off birds and squirrels, which do not like the movement and "glitter."

SOWING SEEDS

The best way really depends upon the type of seed, the time of year, the location, whether or not you are trying to achieve an early crop, and your experiences with the last sowing. For example, to avoid trouble with mice eating expensive pea seeds planted directly in the raised bed, you could plant the seeds in plastic gutters full of growing compost in the greenhouse, and then slide them into place in the beds when they are well rooted.

> *What is the best way of sowing seeds?*

SOWING SEEDS IN RAISED NO-DIG BEDS

We used to sow seeds variously in shallow dibbled holes, V-section furrows and trays, and then pinch out or plant. However, the cost of seeds is now so high, the raised bed method so intensive and the end crop so valued, that we now sow either a single seed or tiny pinch of seeds – depending upon the size – in shallow dibbled holes or spaced in furrows, then either carefully thin out to leave a single best plant at each station or lift and replant; or we sow in individual pots or peat pots in the greenhouse or hoop house, and then plant out. This way of working keeps costs down, saves effort, advances the crop and generally results in better germination and better yield. We still sow some root crops in furrows and some small low-cost seeds in trays.

Sowing seeds in pots ensures that the seedlings are well protected in the vulnerable initial stages.

Seeds to sow in pots or trays

- Eggplants (see page 217).
- Beans, runner (see page 199).
- Broccoli (see page 189).
- Brussel sprouts (see page 193).
- Capsicums (sweet peppers) (see page 218).
- Cauliflowers (see page 191).
- Celeriac (see page 213).
- Celery (see page 195).
- Cucumbers (see page 216).
- Kale (curly) (see page 192).
- Leeks (see page 203).
- Summer squash and zucchini (see page 215).
- Onions (see page 202).
- Peas (see page 197).
- Sweetcorn (see page 201).
- Tomatoes (see page 214).

Seeds to sow in dibbled holes in the bed

- Beans, runner (see page 199).
- Chicory (see page 186).
- Garlic (see page 204).
- Land cress and salad leaves (see page 184).
- Lettuces (see page 185).
- Parsnips (see page 207).
- Potatoes (see page 205).
- Spinach (see page 188).
- Rutabagas (see page 209).
- Turnips (see page 210).

Seeds to sow into furrows in the bed

- Beet greens (see page 187).
- Beets (see page 208).
- Broccoli (see page 189).
- Brussel sprouts (see page 193).
- Cabbages (see page 190).
- Carrots (see page 206).
- Cauliflowers (see page 191).
- Kale (curly) (see page 192).
- Peas (see page 197).
- Radishes (see page 211).

TRAYS

1. Cover the drainage holes with bits of broken clay pots, fill the tray with moist growing potting soil, and use a wooden board to press it down firmly.

2. Use your palm or a folded piece of paper and the gently tapping action of your fingertips to distribute the seeds gently.

3. Use a sieve to cover the seeds with a sprinkling of potting soil so that the depth of the layer suits the type of seed.

SOWING IN THE GROUND

POTATOES

Dig a shallow hole and position the seed potato.

ONIONS

Make a shallow hole with a round-ended dibbler and gently put the onion sets into place.

TRENCH FURROW

Make a wide shallow furrow – a trench – and place each seed by hand.

V-SECTION FURROW

Make a shallow V-section furrow and dribble or trail the seed into it.

GUTTER

Cut plastic gutter to lengths to suit the width of your raised bed – say 3 ft (90 cm). Tape the ends up with plastic duct/gaffer tape. Fill the resulting long trays up with growing potting soil and sow your seeds as for trays. This option is especially good for sowing peas to stop them being eaten by mice. When the plants are well established, slide the plants with the growing medium into place in the prepared bed and water generously.

POTTING ON AND PLANTING OUT

Some seeds, like those of zucchinis, are sown in the greenhouse and then transplanted into the beds as seedlings, while others, like those of carrots, are often sown directly into the beds. Those that are sown under cover usually undergo various stages of "potting on" — meaning they are moved into a slightly larger pot — before the young plants are strong enough to be planted out, or transplanted, into their permanent places in the raised bed.

Why are these stages necessary?

Sowing seeds in "cell" trays allows for much easier management of the seedlings when it is time to pot them on.

Delicate seedlings need to be transferred from seed trays and cells into larger pots to "harden off" before being planted out.

Some medium-hardy plants, like these celery seedlings, can be planted directly out into the bed without being potted on.

Some plants, like these strawberries, can be propagated by staking their "runners" directly into pots, where new plants will form.

POTTING ON

When tray-sown seedlings are just large enough to handle, they are sometimes lifted, thinned out and transferred (this is also known as "pricking off" and "thinning") into another tray or into pots, so that each seedling has more space and sometimes more depth of growing medium. Potting on can be fiddly and time-consuming, but this extra effort usually pays off in the quantity and quality of the resulting crop.

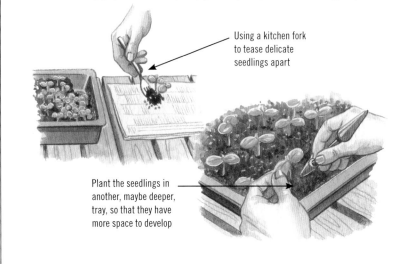

Using a kitchen fork to tease delicate seedlings apart

Plant the seedlings in another, maybe deeper, tray, so that they have more space to develop

Planting out

This is the end procedure of taking a seedling from a protected environment – the greenhouse, hoop house, or covered bed – and putting it into its final place in the bed. Some crops, like celery, might have been sown in trays in the greenhouse, transplanted to a pot, and potted on to a larger pot or even a peat pot, all before being planted out in the bed.

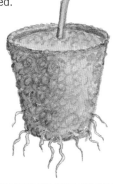

Thinning

This involves thinning out a mass of seedlings, such as might be found in a seed-tray in the greenhouse or a line in a seed bed – so that the spacing allows the plants to reach their potential. For example, you might sprinkle minute seeds like carrots in a V-section furrow in a bed and then, when the little seedlings are big enough to handle, pull up and remove some seedlings so that the remaining seedlings have space to develop.

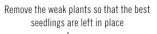

Remove the weak plants so that the best seedlings are left in place

Transplanting

Transplanting involves lifting fragile seedlings and setting them into their final growing space in the bed. Plants such as cabbages can be lifted by the trowel-full, teased apart and then transplanted. Plants such as tomatoes are best planted in pockets or peat pots so that the transplanting can be achieved with a minimum of root damage.

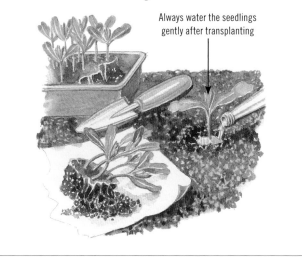

Always water the seedlings gently after transplanting

EXTENDING THE GROWING SEASON

Y̶ou can easily extend the growing season by 6–8 weeks in your no-dig raised bed garden by sowing a few weeks earlier, say in a greenhouse or hoop house, and finishing a few weeks later by protecting the growing plants with nets, fabric or clear plastic sheet. It is really worth considering this, as it will mean that you can enjoy your delicious home-grown produce over a much longer period for not much extra effort.

> *How can I maximize my crop yield?*

SOWING EARLIER

Looking at the recommended sowing times and temperature details on seed packets will show you that if you can increase local day and night temperatures by a just a few degrees – meaning temperature in and around the beds – and generally reduce the lowering of temperature by windchill effects, then it is possible to plant earlier. Just as our great-grandparents used cold frames, glass bell cloches, shields of calico and paper, straw mats and such devices for forcing, forwarding and protecting crops, you can use greenhouses, hoop houses, home-made shields, plastic nets and fabric to achieve the same effect.

HARVESTING LATER

Harvesting later is achieved by generally protecting the plants from the ravages of the weather. Of course, it is a bit tricky because once a plant's biological clock has started ticking there is a limit to how long you can extend its productive life. If, for example, you protect zucchinis with fabric at the end of the season then it is possible to squeeze out an extra few weeks of zucchinis on the plate.

These plastic cloches are good for getting strawberries off to a good start – they keep off pests and build up the heat.

Top ten methods

1 Cover the beds with fabric to keep out frosts.

2 Get off to an early start by growing crops in peat pots.

3 Start crops off in a greenhouse or hoop house.

4 Stack extra frames on beds so that you can heap mulches up around tender plants.

5 Apply a mulch of straw to protect plants from frost.

6 Drape tent-like nets over beds to break gusty winds and drafts.

7 Put up screens to keep off winds.

8 Cover beds with chopped straw topped with old carpet to keep in the heat.

9 Surround a bed with a mound of fresh horse manure to create a warm environment.

10 Build a bed on a mound of fresh horse manure to raise the temperature of the bed.

A good-sized hoop house will dramatically increase your yield, giving you an earlier start, a bigger crop and a longer season.

EXAMPLES FOR EXTENDING THE SEASON

Beans, runner

Normal season – sowing late spring; harvesting mid-summer through to early autumn.

No-dig raised bed season – sowing mid-spring in peat pots under glass for harvesting from mid-summer through to mid-autumn.

TIPS

You can extend the season by starting extra early by planting the seeds in peat pots under glass and by saving the roots from the previous year; once the seedlings are in the beds you must use nets and fabric to protect them from late frosts.

Zucchinis and summer squash

Normal season – sowing mid-spring; harvesting mid-summer through to mid-autumn.

No-dig raised bed season – sowing mid-spring; harvesting mid-summer through to mid-autumn.

TIPS

If you are prepared to create a bed on top of a deep-fill compost heap that has been well primed with a base of fresh horse manure, and to cover the bed with fabric the moment you have a frost warning, then you can bring sowing and planting out forward to the extent that you can advance the first harvesting date by about two weeks.

Broccoli

Normal season – sowing mid-spring; harvesting early autumn through to mid-autumn.

No-dig raised bed season – sowing mid-to late spring; harvesting mid-winter to late spring and mid-summer through to late autumn.

TIPS

By sowing early in a greenhouse, and sowing the full range of varieties – purple, white, perennial and calabrese – you can extend the harvesting period so that you will be picking for about two four-month periods.

Beets

Normal season – sowing early spring; harvesting mid-summer through to late autumn.

No-dig raised bed season – sowing early spring; harvesting late spring through to late autumn.

TIPS

The season is extended so that, by growing a full range of varieties and planting in succession, the first harvesting date merges with the last sowing.

Lettuces

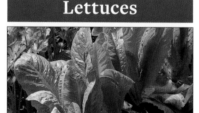

Normal season – sowing late spring through to early autumn; harvesting early summer around to the following late spring.

No-dig raised bed season – sowing early spring through to mid-autumn; harvesting for the best part of a year.

TIPS

To achieve a year-round supply, you must sow a whole range of varieties, always be ready with fabric, be vigilant with your watering, and sow in semi-hot frames in a hoop house.

Celery

Normal season – sowing early spring; harvesting late summer around to late autumn.

No-dig raised bed season – early spring; harvesting late summer to late winter.

TIPS

Sow early in the greenhouse.

SOWING TABLE

The following quick-reference sowing table gives the sowing times and the ideal distances between plants for a wide variety of vegetables. Remember that the intensive no-dig method allows you to maximize the growing area by growing in a much tighter grid pattern.

Quick-reference sowing table

CROP	SOWING TIME	DISTANCE APART
Artichokes, globe	sow mid-spring	18–36 in (45–90 cm) apart
Artichokes, Jerusalem	plant late winter to mid-spring	10 in (25 cm) apart
Asparagus	sow early to mid-spring	18 in (45 cm) apart
Eggplants	sow early spring	12–18 in (30–45 cm) apart
Beans, broad	sow late winter to mid-spring or late autumn	8–10 in (20–25 cm) apart
Beans, French	Sow mid-spring to early summer	5–6 in (13–15 cm) apart
Beans, runner	Sow late spring to early summer	6–8 in (15–20 cm) apart
Beet greens	sow mid- to late spring	8–10 in (20–25 cm) apart
Beets	sow early spring to late summer	4–5 in (10–13 cm) apart
Broccoli	sow mid- to late spring	12–18 in (30–45 cm) apart
Brussels sprouts	sow early to mid-spring	18–36 in (45–90 cm) apart
Cabbages	sow spring varieties mid- to late summer, summer varieties late winter to late spring, winter varieties early to late spring	all 12 in (30 cm) apart
Carrots	sow early spring to early summer	2–3 in (5–7.5 cm) apart
Cauliflowers	sow early to late spring	12–18 in (30–45 cm) apart
Celeriac	sow early to mid-spring, plant out late spring to early summer	10 in (25 cm) apart
Celery	sow early to mid-spring under glass, plant out late spring to early summer	9–12 in (23–30 cm) apart
Chicory	sow late spring to mid-summer	8 in (20 cm) apart
Cucumbers (outdoor ridge)	sow mid- to late spring	plant out 18 in (45 cm) apart
Garlic	plant out autumn to early spring	6–10 in (15–25 cm) apart
Kale	sow mid- to late spring, plant out early to late summer	15–18 in (38–45 cm) apart
Land cress	for autumn to spring crop sow mid- to late summer, for summer crop sow spring to early summer	8–10 in (20–25 cm) apart
Leeks	sow mid- to late winter or early to mid-spring, plant out mid-summer	6–8 in (15–20 cm) apart
Lettuces	sow spring varieties late summer to mid-autumn, summer varieties early spring to mid-summer	8–10 in (20–35 cm) apart
Onions	sow early spring to late summer	2–6 in (5–15 cm) apart
Parsnips	sow late winter to mid-spring	5–6 in (13–15 cm) apart
Peas	sow early spring to mid-summer	5–6 in (13–15 cm) apart
Radishes	sow mid-winter to early autumn	1–2 in (5–7.5 cm) apart
Rutabagas	sow mid-spring to mid-summer	6–9 in (15–23 cm) apart
Spinach, summer	sow late winter to late summer	9–12 in (23–30 cm) apart
Spinach, winter	sow mid-summer to early autumn	6 in (15 cm) apart
Summer squash and zucchinis	sow mid- to late spring	plant out late spring to early summer one plant to a 3 ft (90 cm) square box
Sweetcorn	sow mid-spring in peat pots	plant out in late spring 12–16 in (30–40 cm) apart
Sweet peppers (capsicums)	sow late winter to early spring	12–18 in (30–45 cm) apart
Tomatoes, indoors	sow late winter to early spring	2 ft (60 cm) apart
Tomatoes, outdoors	sow early spring to late spring	18 in (45 cm) apart
Turnips	sow mid-spring to late summer	6–9 in (15–23 cm) apart

Deciding What to Plant

CHOOSING PLANTS

What do I need to know?

Acommon problem with beginners to garden design is that, while they have a clear understanding of what they want in the way of structures – paths, patios, ponds, raised borders and so on – they know very little about plants. They then make matters worse by trying to cram their heads full of planting facts. Initially, it is best to focus all your energies on design, and tackle the planting on a need-to-know basis. Keep asking questions – until you know the answers.

WHAT DO YOU NEED TO KNOW?

At this stage, just concentrate on basic facts – things like what such and such a plant needs in the way of soil, shelter, shade and sunlight, how it will look at various times of the year, how big it will grow, and how long it will last. You will eventually want to know about pruning, propagation, diseases and so on, but you can find that out along the way. If you are a complete beginner, make a selection from the following pages of favorite or familiar plants, and then take it from there. Learning by reading is good, but learning by doing is usually much better.

TREES AND SHRUBS

Trees and shrubs are perfect for growing in all gardens; some grow low and broad while others grow very tall. Some are famed for their flowers while others have attractive leaves and berries in autumn and even winter.

HEDGES AND WALL SHRUBS

Hedges and wall shrubs are just the thing for creating boundaries and for camouflaging an ugly shed or wall. Many wall shrubs benefit from the warmth and protection provided by a wall.

CLIMBING PLANTS

There are climbing plants for every situation: from ones that cover everything with attractive leaves to those that produce distinctive flowers. Self-climbing and self-supporting climbers are a good option.

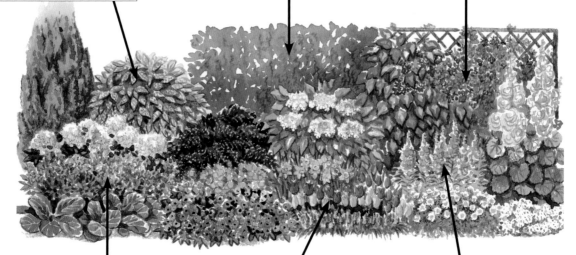

HERBACEOUS PERENNIALS

Herbaceous perennials usually live for 3–4 years before they need to be lifted and divided – perfect for flower borders. In the spring they send up new shoots, which die down to ground level again in the autumn.

BEDDING PLANTS AND BULBS

Most spring-flowering bedding plants are biennial – they have a two-year life cycle – and look good when grown alongside bulbous plants. Bulbs have an underground storage organ that sees them through dormant periods.

ANNUALS AND BIENNIALS

Annuals are raised from seed and grow to flower in the period of one year, while biennials are raised from seed one year and grown to flower the next. Some self-seeding annuals will reappear every year.

ROCK, ALPINE AND DESERT PLANTS

There is a huge range of plants that thrive in rocky, alpine and desert situations – everything from alpines and dwarf trees to hardy cacti and succulents.

WATER PLANTS

From the side of the pond to the center, there are bog plants, marginals, deep-water aquatics, and plants that spend their life either floating on the surface or submerged beneath it.

BAMBOOS AND GRASSES

Bamboos and grasses belong to the same plant family. There are bamboos and grasses for every situation – from small ones that can be grown in pots to ones that can fill a border.

CONTAINER PLANTS

Container plants are simply any plants that are small enough to be grown in containers. While pots can be grouped on the ground, hanging baskets are good for small areas where there is a shortage of floor space.

HERBS

While there is a huge range of herbs to choose from – ones to eat, ones to take as medicine, and ones that smell nice – it is best to grow ones that you can safely eat, meaning the culinary ones that can be used in the kitchen.

FRUIT AND VEGETABLES

We all know about fruit and vegetables. What better way to enjoy a garden than to watch the plants growing and then to eat the produce?

WHICH PLANTS SUIT MY GARDEN?

The best way of getting an answer to this question is to assess the size of your garden – it might be anything from minute to small, big, very big or positively huge – and then arm yourself with a pencil and notepad and visit the nearest show garden, followed by a whole range of local gardens, taking note of plants that are thriving.

HOW MANY PLANTS WILL I NEED?

Bearing in mind that plants not only grow in size but can also be increased by seed, cuttings, division and so on, there are two options. You can start off with a few architectural plants like trees, bushes and climbers, and then beg and buy the rest, or you can spend a lot of money instantly filling the garden to overflowing, knowing that very soon you will have to thin the plants out and give them away to friends and family.

Buying plants

Plants are best purchased from specialists. If you want apple trees, go to a nursery that specializes in apple trees, and so on. In this way, you will get the best product and the best advice. It is always a good idea to arm yourself with a list of questions to ask, so that you end up getting just the right plants.

Garden centers Garden centers are good for small "one-offs," but they are not good for initial stocking. You should always avoid anything that looks tired and neglected.

Nurseries A good nursery is the best option. Try to get your plants from long-established specialists. Call around for the best prices.

Mail order Mail order is fine for the occasional "one-off," or for some sort of special offer, but that is about it. Certainly be tempted by the pretty photographs, but make sure that you thoroughly research your purchases.

WHAT CAN I GROW FROM SEEDS?

If you are patient and likely to live to a ripe old age, you can grow just about everything from seeds, but they are normally used for annuals, lawns and a whole range of vegetable and salad crops. For some, growing plants from seeds can be a rewarding challenge.

CHOOSING HEALTHY CONTAINER PLANTS

If a plant looks tired, scraggy, dusty, too dry or too wet, or in any way uncared for, it is likely to be a bad buy. Ideally, the plant needs to look compact and clean-stemmed, with no dead or dying bits and no roots growing up from the pot. Don't be tempted by low cost.

IMMEDIATE PLANT CARE

Remove all the straggly bits. Wait for a mild day (not too hot, and not frosty), and then set the plant in position in the garden and give it a generous watering.

DESIGNING WITH PLANTS

If you liken the garden with its related structures to a room in your house, the plants are like the wallpaper. The only difference is that the plants are constantly changing in size, shape and color. Your task, therefore, is not only to select plants that you know will suit the various microclimates that you have around the garden, but also to have some idea of how the ever-changing plants are going to fill the space. Be aware that some plants will rapidly double in size.

What does this involve?

Points to consider

As you work around the garden choosing plants to fill the various spaces, you must make decisions about every plant's suitability. A good way to do this is to ask yourself the following questions.

Sun and shade Is there enough sun or shade? If conditions are not quite right, can you make small modifications by building walls or alpinens? It might be a sunny position, but are there trees, buildings and the like that will create shade?

Sheltered and exposed Is the plant going to be able to withstand the worst that is going to be thrown at it in the way of wind, rain and frost?

Soil type Is the soil going to suit the plant? If your soil is sandy, does the plant like sandy soil?

Size Is the plant big enough? If it takes time to reach its potential, are you patient enough to wait? If it will eventually be big enough, can you use other plants to fill in the gaps, and then take them out at a later stage?

Personal taste If you like tall and thin, or evergreen, or shrubs that flower for long periods, or whatever it might be, is your plant going to suit?

Cost The initial plant might be expensive, but is this expense going to be offset by the plant's characteristics – the fact that it grows to a huge size or lives a long time, for example?

Maintenance You might like the notion of the plant, but is it going to need a lot of maintenance?

Longevity Is the plant going to live long enough, or even too long, to suit your needs?

Color Is the plant going to give you plenty of color? For example, some hardy fuchsias have not only bright flowers and beautiful green foliage but also red berries and red stems.

Contrast and harmony You have chosen two plants – are they going to look good together? Is there enough contrast, or are you looking for plants that are in harmony with each other?

SUITABILITY

Each plant you choose needs to fit its purpose. If you want a plant for, say, a shady, slightly damp space behind a tall wall, then you need to ask yourself two basic questions. Is the plant going to thrive in that position, and, when it reaches maturity, is it going to live up to your design expectations? That is, will it be tall enough, wide enough, the right color, flower at the right time, be happy alongside your other chosen plants, and so on?

Elaeagnus pungens 'Maculata'

Aucuba japonica 'Variegata'

Euonymus fortunei 'Emerald 'n' Gold'

Brachyglottis 'Sunshine'

This group of shrubs will create color throughout the year. You could also underplant them with bulbs to enhance the effect even further.

HABIT

A plant's habit has to do with its appearance. Some plants want to grow straight up like a rocket; others want to creep along the ground. The clue to the habit is usually given in the name. For example, a "prostrate" plant is one that likes to stay very close to the ground, while a "fastigiate" plant (think of "fast up") is one that wants to grow upwards.

PRACTICALITIES

A plant cannot be *almost right* – it has got to be right in every respect. Sometimes there are so many impracticalities that get in the way – cost, size, sensitivity, unwanted prickles, poisonous berries, unpleasant smell, wrong height, and other disadvantages – that you just have to bite the bullet and choose something else.

EXAMPLES OF PLANTING SCHEMES

A "MIXED" BORDER

Rhododendrons have both eye-catching flowers and beautiful waxy leaves

Evergreens provide form all year round

Acer for brilliant color

This glorious summer border is made up of shrubs, climbers, small trees, herbaceous perennials, bulbs and bedding plants. A mixed border of this character is especially useful because it will display color and form throughout the year.

BAMBOOS AND GRASSES

Pseudosasa japonica

Sasa veitchii

Carex buchananii

Lagurus ovatus 'Nanus'

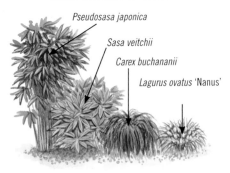

Bamboos and grasses are much favored for their form and their color, which changes with the seasons, and they also give useful protection to other plants.

CLIMBERS

Jasminum nudiflorum (Winter-flowering Jasmine) and *Cotoneaster horizontalis*

Tropaeolum speciosum and *Hedera helix* 'Goldheart'

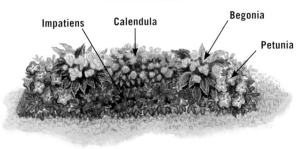

A well-chosen group of climbers gives exciting year-round form and color. The group on the right consists of *Actinidia kolomikta, Eccremocarpus scaber* and *Lonicera japonica* 'Halliana.'

BEDDING PLANTS

Impatiens   Calendula   Begonia

Petunia

Bedding plants give a blaze of color. They can be swiftly changed to suit your requirements, and are a very good standby if other things fall by the wayside, leaving unsightly gaps in the border.

Colored bark and stems

Brilliant foliage is good, and brightly colored flowers are great, but there is just as much to be said for startling stem or bark colors. In this context, it is a good idea to walk around a show garden in the autumn and winter, to see what is on offer. The dazzling white bark of *Betula pendula* (Silver Birch) and the brilliant red-pink stems of plants like hardy fuchsias and striped or peeling *Acers* (Maples) are wonderfully uplifting in winter, when the world can be a foggy blur of white and gray.

Salix (Willow) – there are many types, sizes and varieties of this popular tree with its colorful stems.

Betula utilis var. *jacquemontii* has a dazzling white trunk and characteristic peeling bark.

Acer griseum (Paperbark Maple) has dark bark that peels to reveal orange underbark.

Cornus (Dogwood) – commonly called "Red twig Dogwood" – is favored for the bright color of its young stems.

SHRUBS AND SMALL TREES

Many shrubs and trees are ideal for growing in small gardens; some have a ground-covering habit while others help to create height, but not excessively. Some shrubs are famed for their flowers, and others have attractive leaves or berries. Most of these shrubs are fully hardy and will survive winter weather in temperate areas. On these and the following two pages, a wide range of shrubs and small trees is described, with some illustrated.

Is there a wide choice for a small garden?

QUALITIES TO LOOK FOR

- **Naturally small:** although diminutive, a shrub or tree should reveal a natural and attractive appearance and not have to be radically pruned in an attempt to keep it small – which invariably does not work.
- **Slow-growing:** avoid shrubs and trees that grow rapidly and soon become too big for their allotted positions. Excessively vigorous plants are a waste of money, as too soon they have to be dug up and removed.
- **Varying interest:** wherever possible, select a shrub or tree that has at least two attractive qualities.
- **Easy to establish:** rapid and easy establishment are essential, so always buy a healthy plant. Do not buy an inferior plant just because it is cheap.
- **Non-invasive:** check that the plant is not invasive – meaning that it could soon dominate nearby plants.

Attractive combinations

- Plant yellow-flowered, trumpet-type Daffodils around *Amelanchier lamarckii* (Snowy Mespilus), a deciduous shrub or small tree with pure white flowers in spring and colored leaves in autumn.
- Plant groups of *Helleborus foetidus* (Stinking Hellebore), with yellow-green flowers in early spring, around *Chimonanthus praecox* (Winter Sweet), which produces sweetly scented yellow flowers during mid- and late winter – and sometimes later. For further color, add a few *Galanthus nivalis* (Snowdrops) to the picture.
- Plant *Lavandula angustifolia* (Old English Lavender) around a bed of pale pink bush roses.

Amelanchier lamarckii

June Berry (USA/UK)

Snowy Mespilus (UK)
Hardy, deciduous shrub or small tree with pure white flowers in mid-spring. Colorful leaves in autumn – shades of soft yellow and red.

Soil and situation: lime-free, moisture-retentive but well-drained soil in light shade or full sun.

Increasing plants: layer low-growing stems in late summer or early autumn. Alternatively, detach sucker-like shoots in spring and plant into a nursery bed.

↕ 10–15 ft (3–4.5 m)   ↔ 10–12 ft (3–3.6 m)

Brachyglottis 'Sunshine'

Also known as *Senecio* 'Sunshine,' this mound-forming, evergreen shrub has silvery-gray leaves and daisy-like, bright yellow flowers during early and mid-summer.

Soil and situation: deeply prepared, well-drained but moisture-retentive soil in full sun.

Increasing plants: layer low-growing stems in late summer. Rooting takes about a year. Alternatively, take 3–4 in (7.5–10 cm) long cuttings in late summer and insert in pots of equal parts moist peat and coarse sand. Place in a cold frame.

↕ 2–4 ft (60 cm–1.2 m)   ↔ 3–5 ft (90 cm–1.5 m)

Caryopteris x clandonensis

Bluebeard (USA/UK)
Bushy, deciduous shrub with gray-green leaves and clusters of blue flowers in late summer and autumn. Varieties include 'Arthur Simmonds' (bright blue) and 'Heavenly Blue' (deep blue).

Soil and situation: moderately fertile, well-drained soil in full sun and shelter from cold wind.

Increasing plants: take 3–4 in (7.5–10 cm) long cuttings in late summer and insert in pots of equal parts moist peat and coarse sand in a cold frame.

↕ 2–4 ft (60 cm–1.2 m)   ↔ 2–3 ft (60–90 cm)

Ceratostigma willmottianum

Chinese Plumbago (USA)

Hardy Plumbago (UK)
Half-hardy, deciduous shrub with dark green leaves that assume rich-red shades in autumn. During mid- and late summer it has terminal clusters of blue flowers.

Soil and situation: fertile, well-drained but moisture-retentive soil in light shade or full sun.

Increasing plants: take 3–4 in (7.5–10 cm) long cuttings in mid-summer and insert in pots of equal parts moist peat and coarse sand in gentle warmth.

↕ 2–3 ft (60–90 cm)   ↔ 2–3 ft (60—90 cm)

Choisya ternata

Mexican Orange Blossom (USA/UK)
Slightly tender evergreen shrub with a bushy nature and clusters of sweetly scented, orange-blossom-like white flowers mainly in mid- and late spring, and intermittently throughout summer.

Soil and situation: deeply prepared, fertile, well-drained soil in light shade or full sun.

Increasing plants: take 3 in (7.5 cm) long cuttings in mid-summer and insert in pots of equal parts moist peat and coarse sand in gentle warmth.

↕ 5–6 ft (1.5–1.8 m)   ↔ 5–7 ft (1.5–2.1 m)

Cistus x dansereaui

Rock Rose (USA/UK)

Sun Rose (UK)
Also known as *Cistus x lusitanicus*, this evergreen shrub has white flowers, 2 in (5 cm) wide and splashed with crimson, during early and mid-summer.

Soil and situation: poor, light, well-drained soil in full sun and shelter from cold wind.

Increasing plants: take 3 in (7.5 cm) long cuttings in mid-summer. Insert them in pots of equal parts moist peat and coarse sand in gentle warmth.

↕ 1–2 ft (30–60 cm)   ↔ 1½–2 ft (45–60 cm)

Euonymus fortunei
'Emerald 'n' Gold'

Hardy, dwarf, evergreen shrub with golden variegated leaves that in winter assume bronzy-pinks tones. Other forms include 'Emerald Gaiety' (creamy-white and green) and 'Harlequin' (spring leaves mottled white and green).

Soil and situation: moderately fertile garden soil in light shade or full sun (which gives the best leaf colors).

Increasing plants: layer low-growing stems in autumn. Rooting takes about a year.

↕ 1–1½ ft (30–45 cm)   ↔ 1½–2 ft (45–60 cm)

Forsythia x intermedia

Golden Bells (USA/UK)
Hardy, deciduous shrub with masses of golden-yellow flowers in early and mid-spring. The leaves start to appear as flowering finishes.

Soil and situation: fertile, deeply prepared, moisture-retentive soil in light shade or full sun.

Increasing plants: take 10 in (25 cm) long cuttings of the current season's shoots in early autumn and insert 4–6 in (10–15 cm) deep in a nursery bed. Sprinkle coarse sand around each cutting's base.

↕ 6–8 ft (1.8–2.4 m)   ↔ 5–7 ft (1.5–2.1 m)

Hebe 'Autumn Glory'

Shrubby Veronica (UK)
Hardy, evergreen shrub with glossy leaves and deep purplish-blue flowers from mid-summer to autumn. 'Midsummer Beauty' has lavender-purple flowers and grows to about 4 ft (1.2 m).

Soil and situation: moderately fertile, well-drained soil in full sun.

Increasing plants: take 3–4 in (7.5–10 cm) long cuttings from non-flowering shoots in mid-summer. Insert them in pots of equal parts moist peat and coarse sand in a cold frame.

↕ 2–2½ ft (60–75 cm)   ↔ 2–2½ ft (60–75 cm)

Helichrysum italicum

Curry Plant (UK)
Also known as *Helichrysum angustifolium*, an evergreen shrub with narrow, silvery-gray, needle-like leaves that reveal the bouquet of curry. Mustard-yellow flowers throughout much of summer.

Soil and situation: light, moderately poor, well-drained soil in full sun. Avoid wet and cold soils.

Increasing plants: take 3 in (7.5 cm) long cuttings from the current season's shoots in mid-summer; insert in sandy compost and place in a cold frame.

↕ 12–15 in (30–38 cm)   ↔ 15–24 in (38–60 cm)

Hypericum 'Hidcote'

Rose of Sharon (USA/UK)
Hardy, almost evergreen, bushy shrub. From mid-summer to autumn it bears 3 in (7.5 cm) wide, saucer-shaped, waxy, golden-yellow flowers.

Soil and situation: fertile, moisture-retentive but well-drained soil and full sun. Avoid positions in shade.

Increasing plants: take 4–5 in (10–13 cm) long cuttings from the current season's shoots in mid-summer. Insert in pots of equal parts moist peat and coarse sand and place in a cold frame.

↕ 3–5 ft (90 cm–1.5 m)   ↔ 5–7 ft (1.5–2.1 m)

Magnolia stellata

Star Magnolia (USA/UK)
Hardy, slow-growing deciduous shrub with a rounded nature and fragrant, star-shaped flowers up to 4 in (10 cm) wide during early and mid-spring. Several forms, including 'Waterlily' with petal-packed flowers.

Soil and situation: deeply prepared, well-drained but moisture-retentive soil in full sun and a wind-sheltered position.

Increasing plants: layer low-growing branches in early summer. Rooting takes up to two years.

↕ 8–10 ft (2.4–3 m)   ↔ 8–10 ft (2.4–3 m)

Philadelphus Hybrids

Mock Orange (USA/UK)
Hardy, deciduous shrubs with single or double, sweetly scented, white, cup-shaped flowers during early and mid-summer. Many hybrids are ideal for small gardens. 'Avalanche' is 3–5 ft (90 cm–1.5 m) high.

Soil and situation: moderately fertile, well-drained yet moisture-retentive soil in partial shade or full sun.

Increasing plants: take 10–12 in (25–30 cm) long hardwood cuttings in autumn and insert 6 in (15 cm) deep in a nursery bed.

↕ 3–10 ft (90 cm–3 m)   ↔ 3–12 ft (90 cm–3.6 m)

Potentilla fruticosa

Shrubby Cinquefoil (USA/UK)
Hardy, deciduous, bushy but compact shrub with masses of buttercup-yellow flowers from early to late summer – and sometimes into autumn. Several hybrids, in colors including soft yellow, glowing-red and tangerine-red.

Soil and situation: light, moisture-retentive but well-drained soil in full sun.

Increasing plants: take 3 in (7.5 cm) long cuttings from the current season's shoots during late summer. Place in a cold frame.

↕ 3½–4 ft (1–1.2 m)   ↔ 3½–4 ft (1–1.2 m)

Salvia officinalis 'Icterina'

Slightly tender, short-lived, evergreen shrub (semi-evergreen in cold areas) with green-and-gold variegated leaves. Related forms include 'Purpurescens' (young leaves suffused purple) and 'Tricolor' (gray-green leaves splashed creamy-white).

Soil and situation: light, well-drained soil in full sun, sheltered from cold wind.

Increasing plants: take 3 in (7.5 cm) long cuttings in late summer and insert in equal parts moist peat and coarse sand. Place in a cold frame.

↕ 1½–2 ft (45–60 cm)   ↔ 15–18 in (38–45 cm)

Spiraea 'Arguta'

Bridal Wreath (UK)

Spirea (USA)
Hardy, deciduous shrub with attractive mid-green leaves and masses of pure white flowers in mid- and late spring.

Soil and situation: fertile, deep-prepared, moisture-retentive but well-drained soil in full sun.

Increasing plants: take 3–4 in (7.5–10 cm) long cuttings from the current season's shoots in mid-summer. Insert in pots of equal parts moist peat and sharp sand and place in a cold frame.

⬆ 6–8 ft (1.8–2.4 m)   ↔ 5–6 ft (1.5–1.8 m)

Syringa meyeri

Hardy, deciduous, small-leaved lilac with violet-purple flowers borne in small, rounded clusters up to 4 in (10 cm) long during early summer. Occasionally, there is a further flush of flowers.

Soil and situation: fertile, deep prepared, well-drained but moisture-retentive soil in light shade or full sun.

Increasing plants: take 3 in (7.5 cm) long cuttings with heels during mid-summer and insert in pots of equal parts moist peat and coarse sand. Place in gentle warmth.

⬆ 5–6 ft (1.5–1.8 m)   ↔ 4–5 ft (1.2–1.5 m)

Weigela Hybrids

Hardy, deciduous shrubs with arching branches and masses of flowers during early summer. There are many superb varieties, including 'Abel Carrière' (bright red), 'Bristol Ruby' (ruby-red) and 'Newport Red' (bright red).

Soil and situation: fertile, deeply prepared, well-drained but moisture-retentive soil in light shade or full sun.

Increasing plants: take 10–12 in (25–30 cm) long cuttings from mature shoots of the current season's growth during autumn. Insert them about 6 in (15 cm) deep in a nursery bed.

⬆ 5–6 ft (1.5–1.8 m)   ↔ 5–8 ft (1.5–2.4 m)

OTHER SHRUBS AND TREES

- *Berberis darwinii* (**Darwin's Berberis**): hardy, evergreen shrub with deep yellow flowers in mid- and late spring. Small, prickly, holly-like leaves.
- *Buddleja davidii* (**Butterfly Bush/Orange-eye Buddleia/ Summer Lilac**): also known as *Buddleia davidii*, this hardy, deciduous shrub is well known for its long, often arching stems that bear large, plume-like heads of fragrant, lilac-purple flowers during mid- and late summer. There are many varieties, in colors including dark violet, mauve, and white.
- *Calluna vulgaris* '**Gold Haze**' (**Heather/Ling/Scotch Heather**): hardy, evergreen, low, mound-forming shrub with golden-yellow foliage; white flowers during late summer and into early autumn.
- *Cytisus* x *kewensis*: sprawling, deciduous shrub with mid-green leaves and masses of pale yellow flowers during late spring and early summer.
- *Cytisus* x *praecox* (**Warminster Broom**): hardy, deciduous shrub with creamy-white flowers during late spring and early summer.
- *Daphne mezereum* (**February Daphne/Mezereon/ Mezereum**): hardy, deciduous shrub with purple-red flowers from late winter to spring. These are borne on bare stems and followed by scarlet, poisonous berries.
- *Fuchsia magellanica* (**Hardy Fuchsia/Lady's Eardrops**): slightly tender shrub with crimson-and-purple flowers from mid-summer to autumn.
- *Hamamelis mollis* (**Chinese Witch Hazel**): hardy, deciduous shrub or small tree that produces sweetly scented, rich golden-yellow, spider-like flowers during early and mid-winter.
- *Hydrangea macrophylla* (**Common Hydrangea/French Hydrangea**): hardy, deciduous shrub; there are two forms – Hortensias with mop-like flower heads and Lacecaps which have a more lax nature.
- *Kerria japonica* '**Pleniflora**' (**Bachelor's Buttons/Japanese Rose**): hardy, deciduous shrub with long, slender stems and double, orange-yellow flowers during late spring and early summer.
- *Mahonia* x *media* '**Charity**': hardy, evergreen shrub with distinctive, leathery leaves and long spires of fragrant, deep lemon-yellow flowers from early to late winter.
- *Paeonia suffruticosa* subsp. *rockii:* also known as 'Joseph Rock' and 'Rock's Variety,' this slightly tender deciduous shrub bears white flowers, richly and prominently blotched in maroon-crimson, during early summer.
- *Philadelphus coronarius* '**Aureus**': hardy, deciduous shrub with a bushy nature and orange-blossom-scented, creamy-white flowers during early and mid-summer. However, it is best known for its beautiful golden-yellow foliage.
- *Romneya coulteri* var. *trichocalyx* (**Californian Tree Poppy/Tree Poppy**): hardy, semi-woody shrub with blue-green leaves and slightly fragrant, poppy-like, white flowers from mid- to late summer.

SMALL CONIFERS

Slow-growing and small conifers have many uses, especially in small gardens. Small and upright types, such as *Juniperus communis* 'Compressa' (see below), can be used in winter-flowering window boxes, and others in tubs and large pots (see below for suitable types). They are also ideal in rock gardens and alpine gardens, where they create height and miniature focal points among spring-flowering bulbs. They also do well in sink-garden displays.

Are they suitable for small gardens?

SLOW-GROWING CONIFERS FOR CONTAINERS

- *Chamaecyparis pisifera* **'Filifera Aurea':** evergreen conifer with a conical outline and spreading branches that are packed with thread-like, golden-yellow foliage. Eventually, it has a mop-like outline.
- *Chamaecyparis lawsoniana* **'Ellwoodii':** evergreen conifer with short, feather-like sprays of gray-green leaves that, in winter, assume shades of steel-blue.
- *Platycladus orientalis* **'Aurea Nana':** also known as *Thuja orientalis* 'Aurea Nana,' this hardy, evergreen conifer has a neat, rounded nature and light yellow-green foliage.
- *Thuja plicata* **'Stoneham Gold':** hardy, evergreen conifer with a conical outline and bright, golden foliage with coppery-bronze tips. The foliage remains attractive throughout the dull months of winter.

OTHER SLOW-GROWING AND SMALL CONIFERS

- *Abies balsamea* **'Hudsonia':** hardy, compact and very slow-growing conifer with a flattish top formed of gray leaves that turn mid-green in mid-summer.
  Height: $\frac{1}{4}$–2 ft (45–60 cm) Spread: 20–24 in (50–60 cm)
- *Chamaecyparis lawsoniana* **'Ellwood's Gold Pillar':** hardy, evergreen, spire-like, slow-growing conifer that is tightly covered with golden-yellow foliage.
  Height: $\frac{2}{4}$–3 ft (75–90 cm) Spread: 10 in (25 cm)
- *Juniperus communis* **'Compressa':** hardy, slow-growing conifer with a compact, column-like habit and green, silver-backed leaves. It is ideal for planting in a small rock garden, in a miniature garden created in a stone sink or in an alpine garden.
  Height: 1–1¼ ft (30–45 cm) Spread: 4–6 in (10–15 cm)

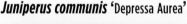

Juniperus communis 'Depressa Aurea'

Hardy, spreading, evergreen conifer with slightly feathery, bright yellow foliage in spring and summer, turning bronze by autumn. It is ideal for a large rock garden, or alongside a path where its branches cloak the edges.

Soil and situation: well-drained but moisture-retentive soil in light shade or full sun.

Pruning: no pruning is needed.

↕ 12–15 in (30–38 cm) ↔ 4–5 ft (1.2–1.5 m)

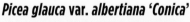

Picea glauca var. *albertiana* 'Conica'

Also known as *Picea glauca* 'Albertiana Conica,' this hardy, slow-growing conifer forms a distinctive conical outline. It is densely packed with soft, grass-green foliage and is especially attractive in spring when new growth appears.

Soil and situation: well-drained soil in full sun.

Pruning: no pruning is needed.

↕ 2½–3 ft (75–90 cm) ↔ 2½–3 ft (75–90 cm)

Taxus baccata 'Standishii'

Also known as *Taxus baccata* 'Fastigiata Standishii,' it is hardy, evergreen, slow-growing and columnar. It is tightly packed with golden-yellow leaves and is especially attractive in winter.

Soil and situation: well-drained soil in slight shade or full sun.

Pruning: no pruning is needed.

↕ 4–5 ft (1.2–1.5 m) ↔ 10–12 in (25–30 cm)

HEDGES AND WALL SHRUBS

How can these be used?

No matter the shape of your garden, you probably have a boundary onto the road, and other boundaries that separate you from your neighbors. You could have wall shrubs disguising an ugly wall, a high, dense hedge on the windward side of the garden, a wide, spiky mix of a hedge and shrubs on one neighbor's side, a stout hedge between you and the school playing fields, and so on. Hedges are good, but be aware that they need constant attention.

Architectural arch topiary

Topiary arches are winners on three counts – they are eye-catching, they can be used as a divisions or boundaries, and they are great fun to create. If you want to go one step further, you can trim "windows" on either side of the arch, have castellation, or have secondary arches or niches.

A dramatic arch created from slow-growing *Taxus baccata* (Yew)

HEDGES AND WALL SHRUBS AS BOUNDARIES AND DESIGN FEATURES

Hedges and wall shrubs make the most attractive and long-lasting boundaries. They can be expensive and time-consuming to establish, but once in place they last a lifetime. While time is a killer for walls and wooden fence panels – they crack and crumble as the years go by – hedges and wall shrubs just get stronger and altogether more attractive. Hedges and wall shrubs can be used to add form and color to the garden. Hedges can be trimmed into just about whatever shape takes your fancy. You can have geometrical forms like cubes and cones, fun forms like animals, or even folly items like arches and seat surrounds. Wall shrubs are perfect for blocking out those ugly walls and grim sheds that some of us just have to live with.

Buxus sempervirens

Common Box USA/UK
Hardy, evergreen shrub with small, dark green leaves. Slow-growing and compact.

Soil and situation: likes well-drained, fertile soil in just about any situation.

Design notes: this is a good plant for small and topiary hedges around herb gardens – just about anywhere where you want to grow a small, tight, traditional, crisp-cut hedge.

↕ 6–7 ft (1.8–2.1 m) ↔ 6–7 ft (1.8–2.1 m)

Ceanothus thyrsiflorus var. *repens*

Blue Blossom USA
Californian Lilac UK
Dense, compact, evergreen shrub with small leaves and clusters of brilliant blue flowers in late spring to mid-summer.

Soil and situation: likes well-drained, neutral to acidic soil in full sun.

Design notes: a great "statement" plant, when you really want to create a big smack of eye-catching color. The blue color is unusual and long-lasting, and looks wonderful against weathered wood and red bricks.

↕ 4–5 ft (1.2–1.5 m) ↔ 4–6 ft (1.2–1.8 m)

Cotoneaster horizontalis

Fishbone Cotoneaster USA
Rock Cotoneaster UK
Hardy, low-growing, deciduous shrub with a spreading fan of dense branches. It has small leaves, clusters of pink flowers in spring and brilliant red-orange berries in autumn to late winter.

Soil and situation: likes well-drained soil in situations that range from full sun to dappled shade.

Design notes: a good option when you want to cover a dull wall or fence with a splash of color, particularly in winter when the berries are showing.

↕ 2–3 ft (60–90 cm) ↔ 4–6 ft (1.2–1.8 m)

OTHER WALL SHRUBS AND HEDGE PLANTS

- *Abutilon megapotamicum:* semi-hardy wall shrub with a generous show of red-purple flowers from summer to autumn. A good choice when you want a long season of color. Height: 5–7 ft (1.5–2.1 m). Spread: 5–7 ft (1.5–2.1 m).
- x *Cupressocyparis leylandii* 'Robinson's Gold' (**Leyland Cypress**): a swift-growing conifer with bronze-yellow foliage. Although this plant has slightly fallen out of favor, it is still a good option for large gardens, when there is a need for a dense hedge. If you cut it back three times in the growing season you will be able, for a moment or two, to fool the eye into believing it is a yew hedge. Height: 6–15 ft (1.8–4.5 m). Spread: 3–4 ft (0.9–1.2 m).
- *Fagus sylvatica* (**Beech**): hardy, deciduous plant, with green leaves turning to russet in autumn. The russet leaves stay in place for most of the winter. A strong beech hedge is a traditional feature, good for town and country gardens alike. A 30 ft (9 m) high beech hedge can be quite an impressive sight. Height: 4–30 ft (1.2–9 m). Spread: 3–5 ft (0.9–1.5 m).
- *Ilex aquifolium* (**Holly**): hardy, evergreen plant with spiky leaves – the male form has bright red berries. This is the hedge to choose if you are trying to create an impenetrable barrier. Cats, dogs and children will stay away from the fallen leaves that gradually form an undercarpet around it. Height: 3–25 ft (0.9–7.5 m). Spread: 2–4 ft (0.6–1.2 m).
- *Piptanthus nepalensis* (**Evergreen Laburnum**): nearly an evergreen, it produces large, bright yellow flowers. It needs the protection of a warm, wind-sheltered wall. Height: 3–5 ft (0.9–1.5 m). Spread: 3–8 ft (0.9–2.4 m).
- *Prunus spinosa* (**Blackthorn**): hardy, deciduous plant with white flowers and purple blackthorn berries that makes an impenetrable hedge. This is a good option for a country garden that backs onto a field with sheep or cattle. Height: 3–5 ft (0.9–1.5 m). Spread: 3–8 ft (0.9–2.4 m).

Euonymus radicans

'Silver Queen'

Common Radicans UK

Japonica USA
Dense, low-growing, evergreen shrub with small, variegated leaves. The flowers appear in late spring to mid-summer.

Soil and situation: likes well-drained, neutral to acidic soil in full sun.

Design notes: good as a wall shrub or low hedge, and much favored in coastal areas. Looks good growing against white-plastered block walls.

↕ 2–3 ft (60–90 cm) ↔ 2–3 ft (60–90 cm)

Fuchsia magellanica 'Riccartonii'

Fuchsia USA/UK
Dense, compact, deciduous shrub with dark green leaves, red stems, and clusters of brilliant crimson and purple, bell-like flowers from mid-summer to autumn.

Soil and situation: likes well-drained soil in full sun to dappled shade – does best in a frost-free area.

Design notes: an easy-care, good-value shrub with beautiful flowers and just as beautiful red stems. You can have it as a wall shrub, or trimmed to make a hedge.

↕ 4–5 ft (1.2–1.5 m) ↔ 4–6 ft (1.2–1.8 m)

Lavandula stoechas

French Lavender USA/UK

Spanish Lavender USA/UK
Tender, evergreen shrub with gray-green leaves and tufts of pink flowers.

Soil and situation: likes well-drained, fertile soil in full sun or dappled shade.

Design notes: this plant has long been used as low, aromatic hedging. Looks good as a low hedge around herb gardens, around patios – anywhere where you want to sit and enjoy the soothing aroma.

↕ 1–2 ft (30–60 cm) ↔ 1–2 ft (30–60 cm)

Santolina chamaecyparissus

Cotton Lavender USA/UK

Lavender Cotton USA/UK
Hardy, bushy, dense, dome-like, evergreen shrub with silver leaves and bright yellow flowers in mid- to late summer.

Soil and situation: likes well-drained, neutral soil in full sun.

Design notes: a plant traditionally used to create decorative, low, aromatic hedges. Would be good around a sitting area such as an arbor or patio.

↕ 2–3 ft (60–90 cm) ↔ 1–2 ft (30–60 cm)

CLIMBING PLANTS

How can I best use climbers?

Climbing plants have evolved in such a way that they are able to climb up or around a vertical or horizontal support. Some twist and twine around wires, rods and host plants, some send out aerial roots so that they can climb up brick and stonework, some have tendrils for clinging onto trellises and host plants, and some have a vigorous, bunching growth that enables them to scramble up a support. If you are looking for swift, high plants, climbers are the answer.

CLIMBING PLANTS AS DESIGN FEATURES

You have covered the ground with shrubs, bushes, trees, grass and so on, and you have put hedges around the boundaries of the garden, so now what can you do? The answer is to create what has been called the "vertical" part of the garden, and there are climbing plants for just about every situation that you can imagine. You could have them climbing over ugly items that are beyond your control, such as unsightly sheds and crumbling walls, you could use them to provide shade or to create private rooms within your garden, you could drape them over structures such as pergolas and arches, you could grow them on supports in containers, you could let them scramble through and over trees – there are countless options.

Front-door flowers

What can you do about a dismal front door? The answer is to build a wooden porch, put up a trellis and have climbing plants all around. One moment you have something like the front door to "Bleak House" and the next you have a friendly and inviting grand entrance with lots of glorious form, foliage and color.

Climbers and containers make a riot of color.

Clematis 'Etoile Violette'

Deciduous climber with dark green leaves and amazing mauve flowers from late spring to mid-summer.

Soil and situation: likes well-drained soil in full sun, as long as the roots are well covered.

Design notes: a great plant to have climbing up and over a trellis or an arbor seat – a plant prized for its flowers.

⬆ 6–10 ft (1.8–3 m) ↔ 4–6 ft (1.2–1.8 m)

Clematis flammula

Fragrant Virgin's Bower UK/USA
Vigorous climber with dark green leaves, purple stems and clusters of star-like, yellow-cream flowers from mid-summer to mid-autumn.

Soil and situation: likes rich, well-drained soil in full sun.

Design notes: the perfect climber for growing over a garden shed or pergola – the scent is wonderful on a warm summer's afternoon.

⬆ 20 ft (6 m) ↔ 4–6 ft (1.2–1.8 m)

Clematis hybrids

Deciduous climbers with striking flowers. Depending upon the variety, they flower from early to late summer, with hues ranging from solid color to blooms that are variously splashed and striped with color.

Soil and situation: likes well-drained, neutral to alkaline soil in full sun, with the roots in shade.

Design notes: Clematis are the show-offs of the climbing world. If you really want to go to town with a climbing plant, then Clematis hybrids are a good option. They look good climbing over fences and trellises.

⬆ 4–15 ft (1.2–4.5 m) ↔ 4–10 ft (1.2–3 m)

Fallopia baldschuanica syn. *Polygonum baldschuanicum*

Mile-a-minute Vine UK/USA

Russian Vine UK/USA
Rampant climber with pale green leaves and fluffy, creamy pink flowers from mid-summer to mid-autumn.

Soil and situation: likes well-drained soil in situations ranging from full sun to dappled shade.

Design notes: if you want to cover an unsightly building or boundary quickly, this is the ultimate answer.

↕ 40 ft (12 m) ↔ 40–60 ft (12–18 m)

Ipomoea tricolor

Morning Glory UK/USA
Semi-hardy annual with a light leaf cover, and blue, red or mauve, bell-shaped flowers from late summer to early autumn. At a quick glance, it looks a bit like a runner-bean plant.

Soil and situation: likes most soils in full sun.

Design notes: a good old-time favorite for traditional cottage gardens. Looks best draped over sheds and other structures.

↕ 8–10 ft (2.4–3 m) ↔ 8–10 ft (2.4–3 m)

Lathyrus odoratus

Sweet Pea UK/USA
Delicate climbing plant (there are lots of varieties) with beautiful, often fragrant, butterfly-like flowers from mid-summer to mid-spring.

Soil and situation: likes well-drained soil in full sun.

Design notes: Sweet Peas look so delicate and yet are hardy – the perfect answer for beginners to gardening. If you are planning a cottage garden, or looking to embellish a wall in a town garden, Sweet Peas are an attractive option.

↕ 6–8 ft (1.8–2.4 m) ↔ 6–8 ft (1.8–2.4 m)

Passiflora caerulea

Blue Passionflower UK/USA
Deciduous climber with stunningly beautiful flowers from summer to autumn, followed by bright orange, egg-sized fruits.

Soil and situation: likes well-drained soil in full sun.

Design notes: a fascinating plant – the fruits are just like big orange eggs. The flowers only open on sunny days when they are looking towards the sun.

↕ 10–30 ft (3–9 m) ↔ 5–30 ft (1.5–9 m)

Trachelospermum jasminoides

Star Jasmine UK/USA
Vigorous, hardy climber with dark green leaves and delicate, white, star-shaped flowers from mid- to late summer.

Soil and situation: likes well-drained soil in full sun but it can tolerate dappled sunlight.

Design notes: with the flowers being modest but fragrant, this climber is grown more for its foliage. Good plant for an arbor or pergola.

↕ 4–5 ft (1.2–1.5 m) ↔ 4–6 ft (1.2–1.8 m)

OTHER CLIMBING PLANTS

- *Campsis* x *tagliabuana* (**Trumpet Creeper**): vigorous climber with trumpet-shaped, orange-red flowers. Once established it flowers from summer to autumn.

- *Lonicera* (**Honeysuckle/Wild Woodbine**): climber with masses of leaves and creamy yellow flowers. Looks best when it is left alone, especially in a country garden.

- *Parthenocissus tricuspidata* '**Veitchii**' (**Boston Ivy**): densely foliaged shrub that turns dark to crimson-purple in the autumn. If you want to block out an ugly wall, this is a good option.

- *Tropaeolum majus* (**Climbing Nasturtium**): annual with green leaves and poppy-like, orange flowers, just like the ordinary Nasturtium. Ideal for quick color.

- *Wisteria sinensis* (**Chinese Wisteria**): vigorous climber with hanging bunches of brilliant blue-purple flowers. This plant does take a long time to establish, but once it has done so will last a lifetime.

HERBACEOUS PERENNIALS

What does "herbaceous" mean?

Herbaceous perennials are all the green, "non-woody" plants that just pop up year after year. They have a long-lived rootstock, and stems and leaves that die down annually. Perennials burst into fresh green growth in the spring, flower in late spring or summer, or early autumn, and generally multiply throughout the year, all before dying back in the autumn. They are almost indestructible, usually pest-free plants, and represent a good-value, relatively easy option.

Perennials on patios

Perennials can look great on patios, balconies and roof gardens. All you need to do is choose a selection of small, hardy plants, set them out in good-sized tubs – so that each tub becomes a showpiece specimen – let them all perform for 2–3 years until they are crowded out, and then lift and divide them, and start the cycle again.

A low-cost, large display option for a patio, deck or roof garden.

HERBACEOUS PERENNIALS AS DESIGN FEATURES

Traditionally, herbaceous perennials have been grown in borders with walls and fences as a backdrop – and of course they do fine in this position – but there is no reason why they should not be planted in island beds, in containers, on the fringes of wooded areas, or wherever takes your fancy. The wonderful thing is that you can let them do their thing year after year, without doing much more than cutting them back at the end of the season. After about four years, dig them up, throw away the woody center, hack the remaining ring into sections, and then plant these out and start again. From a design viewpoint, the trick is knowing about size and color. Look at display gardens so that you have some idea as to your chosen plant's potential.

Achillea 'Moonshine'

Milfoil Yarrow UK/USA
Hardy plant with fern-like leaves and large clusters of yellow, daisy-like flowers from early to late summer.

Soil and situation: does well in poor soil in full sun.

Design notes: a good choice for rock gardens and dry alpine gardens. The flowers and foliage look particularly good when the plants are mulched with something like gray-colored gravel or washed crushed shells.

↕ 1 ft (30 cm) ↔ 1 ft (30 cm)

Alstroemeria 'Golden Crest'

Peruvian Lily UK/USA
Delicate-looking, slightly tender perennial with clusters of brilliantly exotic, tiger-striped, orange, lily-like flowers in mid-summer.

Soil and situation: likes well-drained but moist soil in situations from full sun to dappled shade; avoid exposed sites.

Design notes: looks its best planted in swaths when you want to create a lush, rich effect. Would also look good as a feature in a patio garden, so that it can be viewed close up.

↕ 2–3 ft (60–90 cm) ↔ 1–2 ft (30–60 cm)

Hosta 'Wide Brim'

Funkia UK **/Plantain Lily** UK/USA **/Hosta** USA
Hardy plant from Japan with yellow-green leaves and small, white flowers; it is grown mainly for its foliage.

Soil and situation: likes well-drained, moist soil in dappled and full shade.

Design notes: looks its best in shady borders that fringe the edges of woodland, and is perfect for a Japanese garden. The disadvantage is that slugs also find it very attractive and may create holes in the leaves.

↕ 1–2 ft (30–60 cm) ↔ 2–3 ft (60–90 cm)

Iris ensata 'Yoake Mae'

Hardy, tall iris with deep, rich, mauve-purple flowers in late spring and bold, green leaves – very lush. There are many other varieties.

Soil and situation: likes well-drained, moist soil in dappled sunlight.

Design notes: irises are choice plants for damp borders and around ponds – meaning soil that is wet without being waterlogged. Some irises thrive with their roots in water, however. Although the flowers tend to be short-lived, they are spectacular.

⬆ 2–3 ft (60–90 cm) ↔ 1–2 ft (30–60 cm)

Monarda didyma 'Cambridge Scarlet'

Bee Balm UK/USA
Hardy perennial with light green leaves and spiky scarlet flowers borne in mid- to late summer.

Soil and situation: likes well-drained but moist soil in situations ranging from full sun through to dappled shade.

Design notes: a good-looking plant with leaves that are aromatic when crushed. This is a good plant for patio borders and for around seating areas. It could be included in a scented garden.

⬆ 1–2 ft (30–60 cm) ↔ 1–2 ft (30–60 cm)

Paeonia

Peony UK/USA
Hardy, leafy plants with strikingly beautiful, single and double flowers that range in color from white to salmon-pink, crimson and rose-red. Over the whole range of types, they flower from early to mid-summer.

Soil and situation: likes well-drained, moist soil in sheltered situations from full sun through to dappled shade.

Design notes: they look particularly good massed in borders; a classic option for open borders and for woodland fringes. They are much loved in Japan, so they have a place in a Japanese garden.

⬆ 1–3 ft (30–90 cm) ↔ 1–2 ft (30–60 cm)

Salvia sclarea var. turkestanica

Clary Sage UK/USA
Hardy perennial with spiky, white and purple flowers in mid-summer.

Soil and situation: likes well-drained but moist soil in situations ranging from full sun to dappled shade.

Design notes: although this plant looks good and performs well year after year, some people find the aroma less than pleasant.

⬆ 3-4 ft (0.9–1.2 m) ↔ 2–3 ft (60–90 cm)

OTHER HERBACEOUS PERENNIALS

- *Allium moly* (**Golden Garlic**): hardy plant with strap-shaped leaves and clusters of yellow, star-like flowers. Grows rapidly into solid-looking, football-sized clumps – good for new gardens.
- *Aruncus dioicus* (**Goat's Beard**): hardy plant with lax, terminal heads of creamy-white flowers produced during early summer.
- *Bergenia cordifolia* (**Elephant's Ear**): hardy plant with leathery, green leaves and drooping heads of bell-shaped, pink flowers. A good old-time favorite that grows anywhere and always looks interesting.
- *Convallaria majalis* (**Lily-of-the-valley**): hardy plant with upright, green leaves and delicate, white, bell-shaped flowers. Looks its best in borders under windows, and in swaths around trees and alongside paths. One of those plants that can stand a good amount of neglect.
- *Filipendula ulmaria* (**Meadowsweet**): very popular, hardy plant with masses of dark green leaves and fluffy, white-cream flowers that smell of almonds. A choice plant for the outer fringes of a bog garden or the edge of a woodland area.
- *Hemerocallis citrina* (**Daylily**): hardy plant with strap-like leaves and orange, star-like flowers. Another plant that you can just dig in and leave to get on with it. On a warm evening it gives off a beautiful, sweet, honeysuckle-like scent.
- *Phlox paniculata* (**Summer Phlox/Fall Phlox**): hardy plant with upright stems, green leaves and pinky purple flowers. Looks beautiful when growing in large drifts along the edges of paths, trailed alongside a wooded area, in narrow borders or around a patio.
- *Stachys byzantina* (**Lamb's Ear/Lamb's Tongue**): half-hardy plant with distinctive leaves that are covered with silvery hairs. During mid-summer it bears purple flowers.
- *Trollius* x *cultorum* (**Globe Flower**): hardy, moisture-loving plant with large, buttercup-like flowers born during late spring and early summer.

BEDDING PLANTS

What does "bedding" mean?

The "bedding method" involves autumn planting of plants that will flower in the following spring, and then in late spring removing the whole display and starting again with plants that will flower in the summer. Although bedding plants can be just about anything that fits into this scheme, they are usually broken down into two groups: spring-flowering bulbs, biennials and perennials, and summer-flowering annuals and tender perennials.

Bedding on balconies

Bedding displays can look beautiful on balconies. Just select your plants, much as you would for a small bed, and then plant them out in hanging baskets, window boxes and tubs. You could have bright red *Pelargoniums*, *Lysimachia nummularia* 'Aurea' trailing over the edge of the balcony, and so on.

A beautiful, bold balcony display can give much pleasure to passers-by.

BEDDING PLANTS AS DESIGN FEATURES

Traditionally, bedding schemes were incredibly complex, with intricately shaped borders and plants set out in all manner of patterns and colors, but there is now a move to having either very simple geometrical forms, like circles or ovals, or beds that are completely free-form in shape, with the plants being in random drifts rather than formal patterns. As for the plants, you can have bulbs, biennials, perennials, annuals or whatever you like. The trick is to choose the right plant height and spread, so that you finish up with a well-packed bed without any gaps. A good idea is to visit show gardens that specialize in informal beds, and public parks that excel in formal patterns, and to take note of what is going on in terms of color, shape and type of plant.

Alcea rosea

Hollyhock (UK/USA)
Also known as Althaea rosea, this hardy perennial is usually grown as a biennial, and occasionally as an annual. From mid- to late summer it has tall stems with flowers in colors including yellow, pink, red and white. Some have double flowers.

Soil and situation: fertile, moisture-retentive soil in a sheltered position.

Design notes: a useful plant for cloaking an ugly wall or fence panel.

↕ 5–6 ft (1.5–1.8 m) ↔ 1½–2 ft (45–60 cm)

Antirrhinum

Snapdragon UK/USA
Summer-flowering plants with trumpet- or nose-shaped flowers. Children enjoy using the flowers as finger puppets.

Soil and situation: likes well-drained, moist soil; best in a sunny but sheltered position.

Design notes: a good option in that they flower from summer right through to early autumn. There are types for every situation – miniature, intermediate and tall. Good choice for pink-red schemes.

↕ 1–3 ft (30–90 cm) ↔ 1–2 ft (30–60 cm)

Bellis perennis

Common Daisy UK/USA
Hardy biennial with white, carmine, pink or cherry-red flowers from early spring to autumn.

Soil and situation: likes well-drained, moist soil in sheltered situations that range from full sun to dappled shade.

Design notes: the shape of the Common Daisy makes it a good filler when you want a bright, punchy little flower to bridge the gaps.

↕ 2–4 in (5–10 cm) ↔ 3–4 in (7.5–10 cm)

Campanula medium

Canterbury Bell (UK/USA)
Hardy biennial with upright stems bearing white, pink, blue or violet bell-shaped flowers from late spring to mid-summer.

Soil and situation: moderately fertile, well-drained soil in full sun.

Design notes: there are lots to choose from and they are perfect for cottage gardens.

↕ 15–90 cm (38–90 cm) ↔ 9–12 in (23–30 cm)

Impatiens

Hardy or tender annual, depending on the type. The common Balsam type ranges in color from scarlet, red and salmon-pink to mauve, purple and white. The flowers appear from early to late summer.

Soil and situation: does well in poor, gritty soil in full sun.

Design notes: because the Balsam Impatiens was very popular a century or so ago, it is now commonly used to create a dreamy, old-time look, with the flowers being seen as drifts rather than patterns.

↕ 1–2 ft (30–60 cm) ↔ 1 ft (30 cm)

Petunia

Half-hardy annual with tight, trumpet-shaped flowers in a wide range of colors and sizes.

Soil and situation: likes well-drained, moist soil in a sunny, sheltered position.

Design notes: petunias are very showy flowers – perfect for summer bedding. Good choice for a traditional, cottage-type country garden.

↕ 1 ft (30 cm) ↔ 1 ft (30 cm)

Tagetes patula

French Marigold UK/USA
Half-hardy annual with striking, ruffled, ball-shaped, yellow-orange flowers from summer to autumn. There is a wide range of sizes and colors – lots of yellows and oranges.

Soil and situation: likes well-drained, moist, slightly poor soil in sunny situations.

Design notes: there are lots of varieties to choose from, making this a choice bedding plant.

↕ 8 in–3 ft (20–90 cm) ↔ 1–3 ft (30–90 cm)

OTHER BEDDING PLANTS

- *Asarina purpusii* 'Victoria Falls': half-hardy summer-bedding plant with a gushing mass of purple flowers with long trumpets. Trails to 2 ft (60 cm).
- *Begonia semperflorens* 'Stara Mixed' (**Fibrous Begonia/Waxed Begonia**): half-hardy summer-bedding plant with white, rose and scarlet flowers. Height: 1 ft (30 cm). Spread: 1 ft (30 cm).
- *Bidens ferulifolia* 'Golden Eye': half-hardy summer-bedding plant with yellow, star-like flowers and fern-like foliage. Height: to 1 ft (30 cm). Spread: tumbling.
- *Erysimum alpinum* (**Alpine Wallflower**): hardy spring-bedding plant with masses of yellow and mauve flowers. Height: to 6 in (15 cm). Spread: 6 in (15 cm).
- *Erysimum cheiri* (**Wallflower/English Wallflower**): hardy spring-bedding plant with colors including orange, red and rose pink. Height: to 1 ft (30 cm). Spread: 8 in (20 cm).
- *Lunaria annua* (**Honesty/Silver Dollar**): hardy biennial with fragrant, purple flowers from late spring to early summer, followed by attractive seedpods. Height: to 3 ft (90 cm). Spread: to 1 ft (30 cm).
- *Myosotis sylvatica* (**Forget-me-not**): hardy spring-bedding plant with characteristic, misty-blue flowers. There are lots of shades of blue. Height: to 1 ft (30 cm). Spread: 6 in (15 cm).
- *Primula x polyantha* (**Polyanthus**): hardy spring-bedding plants with flowers ranging from crimson, blue and pink to yellow, white and cream. Height and spread: variable.
- *Viola* 'Universal Citrus Mixed' (**Garden Pansy**): hardy summer-bedding plant with orange, yellow or white, pansy-like flowers. Height: to 8 in (20 cm). Spread: 10 in (25 cm).
- *Zinnia elegans* (**Youth and Old Age**): half-hardy summer-bedding plant with colors ranging from white and purple to yellow, orange, red and pink. Height: to 3 ft (90 cm). Spread: 2 ft (60 cm).

ANNUALS AND BIENNIALS

What is the difference?

Annuals are plants that go through their whole life cycle in one season, and biennials are plants that do it over a two-year period. Remember, however, that much depends on the specific plant and the climate you are growing it in. For example, a tender plant that will happily grow as a perennial in a warm region might need to be grown as an annual in a colder area. Some annuals are also successful at self-seeding, reappearing in the garden year after year.

Portable planting

If you are working in a very small space, such as a verandah, and are really unclear about terms like "hardy" and "half-hardy," then plant your annuals and biennials in portable containers – pots, baskets, tubs – and then make decisions about bringing them in and putting them out as you go along.

An eye-catching combination of color and form can be created.

ANNUALS AND BIENNIALS AS DESIGN FEATURES

The big question here for beginners to garden design, and one that pops up time after time, is – if annuals mature in one year and biennials in two, is it possible to start out with a bare-plot garden and fill it with color in the same year? The short answer is yes, and here is how to do it.

Let us say that you are starting in late summer or early autumn. You can buy in carefully selected pot-grown biennials and plant them out straight away. Then, in the following late spring or early summer, you can sow seeds of half-hardy annuals like Phlox, Asters and Marigolds. In this way, at the end of it all, by late summer – within a 12-month period – you will have had both annuals and biennials in bloom in your previously bare garden.

Anagallis monelli

Blue Pimpernel UK/USA
Half-hardy annual with tight habit, with blue flowers in summer. Sow outside in mid-spring to flower in the summer of the same year.

Soil and situation: likes well-drained, moist soil in a sunny, sheltered position.

Design notes: a beautiful feature of this plant is the fact that the flowers open and close with the sun. This being so, it is important to plant them in open, fully sunny positions.

↕ 6–10 in (15–25 cm) ↔ 6–10 in (15–25 cm)

Datura meteloides

'Evening Fragrance'

Angel's Trumpet UK/USA

Thorn Apple UK/USA
Perennial, usually treated as a half-hardy annual, with large, trumpet-shaped, white and lavender flowers. Sow under glass in spring, and plant out in early summer to flower in mid- and late summer.

Soil and situation: likes well-drained, moist, light soil in sunny situations.

Design notes: good traditional choice for borders, but also looks good as a specimen in a pot or tub. Can produce flowers up to 20 cm (8 in) long.

↕ 3–4 ft (0.9–1.2 m) ↔ 2–3 ft (60–90 cm)

Eschscholzia californica

Californian Poppy (UK/USA)
Hardy annual with blue-green leaves and masses of bright orange-yellow flowers from early to late summer. Color range now includes scarlet, crimson, rose, orange, yellow, white and red.

Soil and situation: light, poor, well-drained soil in full sun.

Design notes: these flowers are bright and tend to dominate. Ideal for informal schemes.

↕ 12–15 in (30–38 cm) ↔ 6–9 in (15–23 cm)

Myosotis sylvatica

Forget-me-not UK/USA
Hardy biennial with swaths of misty blue flowers. Sow in early spring, and plant in final positions in autumn to flower the following spring.

Soil and situation: likes well-drained, moist soil – best in a sunny but sheltered position.

Design notes: though they look good in borders, especially fringing a woodland, they also do well in rock gardens and containers.

↕ 1 ft (30 cm) ↔ 6 in (15 cm)

Nicotiana
'Avalon Lime and Purple Bicolor'

Tobacco plant UK/USA
Half-hardy annual with a compact habit and large, lime and purple, star-shaped flowers. Sow under glass in late winter to early spring, and plant out the seedlings in late spring.

Soil and situation: likes well-drained, moist soil in sunny beds.

Design notes: although this is a good option for planting in large beds and borders, it also looks good massed in a container. Suits a "tropical" garden.

↕ 8–12 in (20–30 cm) ↔ 8–12 in (20–30 cm)

Petunia 'Prism Sunshine'

Half-hardy annual with striking, bell- or trumpet-shaped, yellow-green and cream flowers. Sow under glass in late winter and plant out in early summer.

Soil and situation: likes well-drained, moist soil in sunny situations.

Design notes: there are so many varieties that you can have petunias just about everywhere – in beds and containers, in pots in the conservatory, in hanging-baskets and in window boxes. There are lots of colors and textures to choose from.

↕ 8–12 in (20–30 cm) ↔ 1–2 ft (30–60 cm)

Primula x polyantha

Primrose UK/USA
Hardy biennials with yellow, creamy white, pink or crimson flowers in spring. Sow in late spring or early summer, and plant out in late summer or early autumn to flower the following spring.

Soil and situation: likes well-drained, slightly sandy soil in situations ranging from full sun to dappled shade.

Design notes: there are primulas in just about every shape and size you can imagine. The Common Primrose and the Cowslip take a lot of beating, especially when planted on woodland banks.

↕ 6–10 in (15–25 cm) ↔ 6–10 in (15–25 cm)

OTHER ANNUALS AND BIENNIALS

- *Ageratum houstonianum* (**Floss Flower/Pussy Foot**): half-hardy annual with bluish flowers. There are many varieties in lots of colors.
- *Asarina purpusii* '**Victoria Falls**': half-hardy annual summer-bedding plant with a gushing mass of purple flowers with long trumpets; trails up to 2 ft (60 cm).
- *Chrysanthemum carinatum* (**Annual Chrysanthemum/Tricolored Chrysanthemum**): also known as **Chrysanthemum tricolor**, this hardy annual has large, daisy-like flowers with contrasting color bandings.
- *Dianthus barbatus* (**Sweet William**): hardy summer-flowering biennial with clusters of delicate, daisy-like flowers in colors that range from pink through to scarlet. Though technically a perennial, it is best treated as a biennial and raised from seed each year.
- *Digitalis* (**Foxglove**): biennial that produces delicate, rose-purple, thimble-shaped flowers. It makes a wonderful border plant and is good for shady positions and edges of woodland.
- *Echium vulgare* (**Viper's Bugloss**): fully hardy biennial with tall spikes of violet-purple flowers. This plant is a good option for a seaside garden, or for a scrubby wild corner.
- *Heliotropium arborescens* (**Cherry Pie/Heliotrope**): half-hardy perennial, invariably grown as a half-hardy annual. Fragrant, forget-me-not-like flowers, in colors ranging from dark violet, through lavender, to white.
- *Lunaria annua* (**Honesty**): hardy biennial with purplish flowers followed by silver seedpods. The dried pods make very attractive winter decorations.
- *Pelargonium Cascade Series* (**Balcon/Continental Geraniums**): half-hardy annual with trailing drifts and mounds of flowers.
- *Verbascum thapsus* (**Aaron's Rod**): fully hardy biennial with bold rosettes of silvery-white leaves topped with a spike of yellow flowers. This plant is often seen growing wild.

ROCK-GARDEN PLANTS

What are rock-garden plants?

The range of plants grown in rock gardens is exceptionally wide, from true alpines to bulbs, dwarf conifers and shrubs. Yet the majority of plants are diminutive and colorful perennials, such as *Aurinia saxatilis* (also known as *Alyssum saxatile*), *Aubretia*, *Arabis* (Rock Cress) and Saxifrages. Incidentally, true alpine plants are found on mountains, below the permanent snow line and above the tree line. In a small rock garden, miniature plants are essential.

TYPES OF PLANTS

- **Bulbs and corms:** wide range of small types – see right for a selection. They have a dainty nature and many flower during winter or in spring.
- **Rock-garden perennials:** once planted, these create magnificent displays until they become congested and need to be lifted and divided. Many die down to ground level in autumn; new shoots appear in spring.
- **Annuals:** popular, inexpensive and ideal for filling bare areas in newly constructed rock gardens. Both hardy and half-hardy types are used.
- **Dwarf shrubs and trees:** deciduous and evergreen types, some prostrate, others upright or dome-shaped.
- **Miniature conifers:** distinctive and in several shapes, including conical, flattened, and bun-shaped. If they become too large, move them into a border.

MINIATURE BULBS TO CONSIDER

- *Chionodoxa luciliae* (**Glory of the Snow**): during late winter and early spring it creates a wealth of light blue, white-centered flowers.
- *Crocus chrysanthus*: golden-yellow, globe-shaped flowers are produced during late winter and early spring. Also, there are white, blue and purple forms.
- *Eranthis hyemalis* (**Winter Aconite**): bears lemon-yellow, cup-shaped flowers backed by a light-green ruff during late winter and spring.
- *Iris danfordiae*: honey-scented, vivid lemon flowers are produced during mid- and late winter.
- *Iris reticulata*: bluish-purple flowers with orange blazes appear during late winter and early spring.
- *Narcissus bulbocodium*: bears yellow, hoop-like flowers during late winter and early spring.

Aubrieta deltoidea

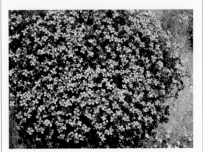

Hardy, low-growing, evergreen perennial with masses of cross-shaped flowers in shades of rose-lilac to purple from early spring to early summer.

Soil and situation: well-drained, preferably slightly chalky soil in full sun.

Increasing plants: sow seeds thinly and evenly in a seed-bed outdoors from mid-spring to early summer. Sow ¼ in (6 mm) deep in furrow 8 in (20 cm) apart. Alternatively, divide congested plants in late summer or early autumn.

↕ 3–4 in (7.5–10 cm)   ↔ ½–2 ft (45–60 cm)

Aurinia saxatilis

Gold Dust (UK)
Also known as *Alyssum saxatile*, this hardy, shrubby evergreen has gray-green leaves and masses of clustered, yellow flowers from mid-spring to early summer. Varieties include 'Citrina' (bright lemon-gold) and 'Compacta' (dwarf and golden-yellow).

Soil and situation: well-drained soil and full sun.

Increasing plants: sow seeds in pots during early spring and place in a cold frame. Alternatively, take 2 in (5 cm) long cuttings in early summer.

↕ 8–10 in (20–25 cm)   ↔ 1–1½ ft (30–45 cm)

Saxifraga cotyledon

Rosettes of dark green leaves and pure white, starry flowers borne in plume-like sprays from early to mid-summer. The form 'Southside Seedling' is ideal for planting in crevices between rocks.

Soil and situation: well-drained, gritty, slightly alkaline soil in a semi-shaded and sheltered position.

Increasing plants: detach non-flowering rosettes in early summer and insert in pots of equal parts moist peat and coarse sand. Place in a cold frame.

↕ 1–1½ ft (30–45 cm)   ↔ 12–15 in (30–38 cm)

ROCK, ALPINE AND DESERT PLANTS

Rock, alpine and desert are "shorthand" for geographical scenarios – a rocky mountainside, a gravel-covered slope, and a desert. The common factor with rock, alpine and desert plants is that they have all, to a greater or lesser degree, adapted themselves in order to thrive in harsh conditions where the soil is not much more than stone, grit and sand, and the weather is an extreme mix of very wet, very dry, very hot and very cold. This makes them useful for "difficult" spots.

What type of plants are these?

Weathered wood

If you want to go one step further and extend the dry rock theme, you could miss out on figurative sculptures and go for a completely naturalistic effect. Weathered wood looks particularly good set against a backdrop of rock, sand and gravel.

A dry garden with found sculpture.

ROCK, ALPINE AND DESERT PLANTS AS DESIGN FEATURES

Although each of these types of plant needs different soil and water conditions – swifter drainage, long periods without water and so on – they can all be grown against a backdrop of rock, sand and gravel. From a designer's viewpoint, this is exciting in that it provides a chance to get away from traditional gardens that need lots of water, rich soil, bedding plants, and so on – and allows them to try their hand at "low-maintenance dry gardening." Some designers also see rock, alpine and desert gardens as being a good way, in a world where climates are rapidly changing, to create a uniquely different type of garden. Draw inspiration from places in nature – rocky gulches, gravel pits and such like – where plants grow against all the odds.

Agave americana 'Variegatum'

Century Plant UK/USA
Distinctive succulent that produces very tall flower spikes, 15–20 ft (4.5–6 m) in height. Some types only flower in maturity and then die.

Soil and situation: likes very well-drained, poor, porous soil in a very sunny, dry position.

Design notes: this plant is grown more for its exotic "desert" looks than anything else – perfect for a dry courtyard, dry patio garden, or dry Mediterranean garden.

↕ 3–6 ft (0.9–1.8 m) ↔ 6–9 ft (1.8–2.7 m)

Artemisia armeniaca

Lad's Love UK/USA **/Southernwood** UK/USA

Wormwood UK/USA
Hardy shrub with silvery-gray leaves and small, yellow flowers.

Soil and situation: likes very well-drained soil in a sunny, dry position.

Design notes: while this plant needs more water than some of the other "dry" plants, it does look the part. A good option for a themed garden, when you want a dry, gray look with lots of sand, stone and bleached wood.

↕ 1–3 ft (30–90 cm) ↔ 1–3 ft (30–90 cm)

Aurinia saxatilis syn. *Alyssum saxatile*

Gold Dust UK/USA
Hardy, shrubby evergreen with gray-green leaves and clusters of yellow flowers produced from mid-spring to early summer.

Soil and situation: likes very well-drained soil in a sunny, dry position.

Design notes: this plant goes well with a silver-gray, dry sand or gravel theme.

↕ 8–10 in (20–25 cm) ↔ 1–2 ft (30–60 cm)

Eryngium

Sea Holly UK/USA
Hardy, bushy, thistle-like herbaceous perennials with vivid blue flowerheads, 15–20 ft (4.5–6 m) in length.

Soil and situation: likes very well-drained, poor soil in a very sunny, dry position.

Design notes: looks stunningly beautiful against dry sand or gravel. It is grown more for its color and texture than anything else, and is perfect for a dry courtyard, dry patio garden or a dry Mediterranean garden.

⬆ 3–6 ft (0.9–1.8 m) ↔ 6–9 ft (1.8–2.7 m)

Juniperus

Juniper UK/USA
Hardy, evergreen tree or shrub that is compact and slow-growing with small, spiky, scale-like leaves.

Soil and situation: likes well-drained, poor, slightly chalky soil in a sunny, dry position.

Design notes: the slow-growing characteristics of this plant makes it perfect for a dry rock, gravel or sandy garden with a desert, Mediterranean, large rock garden or high mountain theme. There are lots of varieties – some upright and others dwarf and spreading.

⬆ 3–4 ft (0.9–1.2 m) ↔ 1–3 ft (30–90 cm)

Opuntia ficus-indica

Indian Fig UK/USA

Prickly Pear UK/USA
Exotic succulent with luscious yellow, orange or red flowers on the upper part of the joints. The fruit is in the form of a pear.

Soil and situation: likes very well-drained, poor, porous soil – two parts sandy loam, one part crushed brick and one part sand – in a very sunny, dry position. Do not water until the soil becomes dry and dusty.

Design notes: just the plant for a themed Wild West garden with sand, dry sage, stone and lots of dry heat.

⬆ 3–6 ft (0.9–1.8 m) ↔ 6–9 ft (1.8–2.7 m)

OTHER ROCK, ALPINE AND DESERT PLANTS

- *Aster turbinellus:* hardy perennial with small, spiky leaves and masses of violet, daisy-like flowers. Can cope with poor, dry, well-drained soil. Grows to a height of about 3–5 ft (0.9–1.5 m).
- *Cercis siliquastrum* (**Judas Tree**): hardy plant that can be grown as a single-stemmed tree or as a scraggy shrub. Has kidney-shaped, blue-green leaves and little, pink, ball-shaped flowers. Likes a poorish soil in a dry, sunny position – good for a Mediterranean garden. Can be kept as a low shrub or allowed to grow to 25 ft (7.5 m) or more.
- *Origanum laevigatum* '**Herrenhausen**' (**Oregano**): fully hardy plant with masses of purple-pink flowers and rosettes of evergreen, aromatic leaves. Likes a sunny, dry position.
- *Salvia sclarea var. turkestanica* (**Clary Sage**): short-lived perennial or biennial with a strong, slightly rank smell. Does well in a dry, sunny spot.

Perovskia 'Blue Spire'

Azure Sage UK/USA
Hardy, deciduous, shrubby plant with dense, grayish, downy leaves and violet-blue flowers in late summer.

Soil and situation: likes very well-drained, ordinary or poor soil in a sunny, dry position.

Design notes: although it can be trimmed into shape, it looks its best when allowed to mass and go semi-wild. Good choice for the edges of a dry garden when you want to create a silver-gray backdrop.

⬆ 3–4 ft (0.9–1.2 m) ↔ 3–4 ft (0.9–1.2 m)

Yucca filamentosa

Adam's Needle UK/USA
Evergreen plant with short stems, long, strap-like leaves and small white or cream flowers on long stalks in mid- to late summer. There are many types, some subtropical and others desert.

Soil and situation: likes very well-drained, poor, porous, sandy soil in a very sunny, dry position.

Design notes: a good option for a dry garden or a Mediterranean garden.

⬆ 3-6 ft (0.9–1.8 m) ↔ 3–5 ft (0.9–1.5 m)

WATER PLANTS

There are plants for every wet and watery situation. From the outer reaches of the garden and working in towards the center of the pond, you need: waterside plants to complement and shelter the pond, bog plants for the damp ground around the water's edge, emergent or marginal plants for the shallows, floating-leaf and deep-water plants for a whole range of depths, and aquatic plants that float and/or are completely or partially submerged.

> *How do I choose water plants?*

WATER-GARDEN PLANTS AS DESIGN FEATURES

Water-garden plants are no more or less than plants that enjoy growing in, on or near water. They are a good choice if you want to have a natural wild pond, a meadow stream, a mountain brook or a Moorish pool, for example. In many ways, water plants control the pattern of planting, in as much as their needs are very specific. Although you can certainly choose what type of plants you want, you have very little choice when it comes to where they are going to fit in the watery scheme of things. Be aware that it is vital to buy plants to suit the diameter and depth of your pond. It is a good idea to start by getting one or two feature plants, and then, once they have taken hold, fill in between them with a few other, complementary, plants.

CREATING A POND

Most ponds are made from a pre-formed shell or a flexible liner. Both have merits, and their durability depends on materials and construction. Don't rush construction – ensure pre-formed shells have a firm base and are not twisted, and that sharp objects cannot puncture flexible liners. The water's surface can be at ground level, or raised to make plants and fish easier to see. There is a wide range of plants for growing in and around a pond.

TYPES OF PLANT

- **Bog-garden plants:** roots in constantly moist soil, with leaves, stems and flowers above the soil's surface. Also known as moisture-loving plants and waterside plants.
- **Deep-water aquatics:** submerged roots, with leaves and flowers on or above the water's surface.
- **Floaters:** leaves and stems float freely on the water's surface, with roots below and usually trailing.
- **Marginal plants:** roots submerged, with leaves and flowers above the water's surface. Positioned around the edge of a pond, but in the water.
- **Oxygenators:** all of the plant is submerged, with roots in a container. Also known as water weeds.
- **Waterlilies:** distinctive and popular, with roots submerged and leaves and flowers on the surface. Range of varieties and suitable for ponds of all sizes and depths.

The joy of irises

If you love water gardens, you might become one of the growing number of enthusiasts who pack their gardens with irises, since irises and water go together perfectly.

A poet once said that irises "come in three forms – beautiful, beautiful and more beautiful."

WATERLILIES FOR ALL PONDS

There are varieties for many depths of water – measured from the rim of the container to the surface.

- **Pygmy Waterlilies:** water's depth – no more than 9 in (23 cm). Spread: 1–2 ft (30–60 cm).
- **Small Waterlilies:** water's depth – 6–18 in (15–45 cm). Spread: 2–4 ft (60 cm–1.2 m).
- **Medium Waterlilies:** water's depth – 1–2 ft (30–60 cm). Spread: 4–5 ft (1.2–1.5 m).
- **Vigorous Waterlilies:** water's depth – 1½–3 ft (45–90 cm). Spread: 5–8 ft (1.5–2.4 m).

PLANTING WATERLILIES

Buy Waterlilies in late spring or early summer, just when they are starting to grow. If there is a delay in planting, remember to keep the roots moist.

Acorus calamus 'Variegatus'

Sweet Flag UK/USA
Hardy, herbaceous, aquatic plant with long, sword-like leaves and small, yellow flowers in summer.

Soil and situation: likes to have its roots in shallow water near the edge of a pool in a situation that is a mix of sun and shade.

Design notes: looks its best in a wild-type pond alongside such plants as irises, Salix (Willow) and rushes.

↕ 1–3 ft (30–90 cm) ↔ 2–3 ft (60–90 cm)

Astilbe chinensis 'Visions'

Goat's Beard UK/USA
Hardy herbaceous perennial with green leaves and masses of pink-purple flowers borne on tall, spiky stems in mid- to late summer. There are lots of other varieties to choose from in many different colors and heights.

Soil and situation: likes a deep, moist, loamy soil in a sunny or shaded position.

Design notes: a good option for a bog garden; perfect for the edge of a large natural pond running into a shady wood.

↕ 3–6 ft (0.9–1.8 m) ↔ 3–4 ft (0.9–1.2 m)

Cyperus

Umbrella Papyrus UK/USA

Umbrella Plant UK/USA
Tender perennial with long, spiky, grass-like leaves set on top of a tall stem – just like the ribs of an umbrella.

Soil and situation: likes a deep, rich, moist, loamy soil on the margins of water and a warm, sunny position.

Design notes: a good choice for growing in boggy ground alongside ponds and slow-moving streams, reminiscent of Egyptian scenes.

↕ 2–3 ft (60–90 cm) ↔ 2–3 ft (60–90 cm)

Eichhornia

Water Hyacinth UK/USA
Aquatic plant with round, glossy leaves. Can produce pale blue, hyacinth-like flowers in the right conditions.

Soil and situation: likes to be floating on the surface of the water with its
long roots anchored in the mud at the bottom of the pond. Likes warmth
and sun.

Design notes: while this is a good option for ponds, it is one of those plants that can swiftly grow out of control. That said, a carpet of Water Hyacinth floating on the warm waters of a pond looks very attractive.

↕ 6–9 in (15–23 cm) ↔ unlimited

Hosta crispula

Plantain Lily UK

Hosta USA
Hardy herbaceous perennial with variegated leaves and creamy white flowers on long stems.

Soil and situation: likes a deep, rich, moist, loamy soil in a warm, shady position.

Design notes: a good plant to have
in the areas that run down to a bog garden – moist but not wet. Looks perfect set against a backdrop of trees; also a good choice for a Japanese-style water garden.

↕ 2–3 ft (60–90 cm) ↔ 2–3 ft (60–90 cm)

Iris pseudacorus 'Variegata'

Variegated Water Flag (USA)

Variegated Yellow Flag Iris (UK)
Marginal plant, with a herbaceous nature and erect, sword-like, bluish-green leaves with yellow stripes. It bears yellow flowers during early summer.

Soil and situation: fertile soil in water 6 in (15 cm) deep and in full sun.

Increasing plants: lift and divide congested clumps immediately after the flowers fade. Alternatively, divide when plants are growing actively and positions of the rhizomatous roots can be seen.

↕ 2½–3 ft (75–90 cm) ↔ 15–18 in (38–45 cm)

Lysichiton americanus

Skunk Cabbage (USA/UK)

Western Skunk Cabbage (USA)

Yellow Skunk Cabbage (USA)
Bog-garden plant, with a hardy, herbaceous nature and oval, grass-green leaves up to 3 ft (90 cm) long. From early to late spring it produces flowers formed of deep, yellow spathes.

Soil and situation: fertile, moisture-retentive soil beside a garden pond.

Increasing plants: remove young plants from around the outside of a congested clump and plant in a pot – keep the compost moist.

⬆ 2–3 ft (60–90 cm)　↔ 2–2½ ft (60–75 cm)

Nymphaea

Waterlily UK/USA
Hardy aquatic plants with floating leaves and beautiful multi-colored flowers. There are hundreds of varieties to choose from and plants for every depth of water.

Soil and situation: likes a deep, rich, moist, loamy soil with at least 15 in (38 cm) of water above the roots, and must be in full sun. The ideal setting is a large pond at about 2 ft (60 cm) deep.

Design notes: this plant is essential for a water garden.

⬆ 10–12 in (25–30 cm)　↔ 2–3 ft (60–90 cm)

Salix 'Yelverton'

Willow UK/USA
Deciduous tree or shrub with slender, gray-green leaves and red-tinged stems. To create new plants, simply take pencil-length cuttings of ripened wood and push them into the ground.

Soil and situation: likes a moist, loamy soil next to water, in a warm, sunny position. Does not mind a flood situation, but dislikes waterlogged soil.

Design notes: if you want a natural pond, plant one or more around the fringes. This type is best cut back so that new stems grow up from the root base.

⬆ 4–5 ft (1.2–1.5 m)　↔ 4–5 ft (1.2–1.5 m)

Zantedeschia

Arum Lily UK/USA /Calla UK/USA
Dramatic, herbaceous perennial with large, arrow-shaped leaves and large, wraparound, cream-white flowers.

Soil and situation: likes a deep, rich, moist to wet, loamy soil in a warm, sunny position.

Design notes: a good option for a bog garden – say where a pond overflows into an area of bog planting. It can even be used as a marginal with its roots set in the water. A dramatic plant – perfect for an exotic, lush effect.

⬆ 2–3 ft (60–90 cm)　↔ 2–3 ft (60–90 cm)

OTHER WATER PLANTS

- *Azolla caroliniana* (**Fairy Moss**): free-floating, fast-growing perennial that has small rosettes of kidney-shaped leaves and produces small, white flowers; it will swiftly cover the surface of a pond.
- *Iris versicolor* (**Blue Flag Iris**): erect, deciduous perennial with green leaves and violet-blue flowers. Good for a boggy area.
- *Nuphar* (**Japanese Pond Lily**): beautiful perennial with floating, heart-shaped leaves and brilliant yellow flowers. Good for a deep-water pond with slow-moving water and plenty of sunshine. The leaves provide cover for fish as well as inhibiting the growth of algae by blocking out sunlight.
- *Ranunculus aquatilis* (**Water Buttercup**): pretty, delicate annual or perennial with small, green leaves and yellow-white flowers. Semi-submerged, it grows both on and under the water. A good choice for oxygenating the pond.

BAMBOOS AND GRASSES

Why should I use these plants?

Apart from the fact that bamboos and grasses belong to the same family (bamboo is a fast-growing tropical or semi-tropical grass of the genus *Bambusa*), they are also grouped because they are used more for their foliage than their flowers, and because they simply look good together. If you want to create a garden that speaks of exotic places, a Japanese garden or a green-themed garden, bamboos and grasses are ideal candidates for the job.

Grasses as design features

If you want to create a low-maintenance garden in a small space, the effect can be achieved by planting grasses in and around a terracotta pot and setting the whole against a backdrop of stones and gravel.

A beautiful arrangement of grasses and various ground-cover plants.

BAMBOOS AND GRASSES AS DESIGN FEATURES

While bamboos and grasses are good for Asian-themed gardens, they are also a great option when you want to create a cool, quiet garden that features form and texture rather than color. Bamboos and grasses invariably make good edge-of-patio plants in situations where the soil is likely to be well drained.

If you want to create a Japanese garden, or a modern "meditation" or "contemplation" garden, bamboos and grasses are the perfect plants to use. It has long been thought by Eastern artists, poets and mystics that the gentle movement and quiet rustling produced when eddies of air flow through bamboos and grasses is somehow uniquely calming and therapeutic, conducive to quiet reflection.

WHAT ARE BAMBOOS?

Bamboos belong to the grass family. They are evergreen, with stiff, hollow stems that give them support. They usually form clumps and, while some are invasive and unsuitable for small gardens, others are non-invasive or can be easily controlled (see below). Once established, bamboos need little attention, other than ensuring they are not spreading too far. Some can be grown in containers and three of them are suggested below, but there are many others.

BAMBOOS IN CONTAINERS

The range of suitable bamboos is wide, with displays in several heights. In exceptionally windy areas, choose low-growing bamboos. Alternatively, give them a sheltered position next to a wind-filtering hedge.

Low display: 3–4 ft (90 cm–1.2 m)
- *Pleioblastus viridistriatus* (**Golden-haired Bamboo**): purple-green stems and brilliant golden-yellow variegated leaves with pea-green stripes.

Medium-height display: 6–8 ft (1.8–2.4 m)
- *Fargesia murieliae* (**Umbrella Bamboo**): bright green canes that mature to dull yellow, and dark green leaves.

Tall and dominant display: 8–12 ft (2.4–3.6 m)
- *Pseudosasa japonica* (**Arrow Bamboo**): canes olive-green at first, maturing to dull matt-green. Dark, glossy-green, sharply pointed leaves.

ARE BAMBOOS TOO INVASIVE FOR A SMALL GARDEN?

Some bamboos are very invasive and in a small garden may trespass into neighboring properties. Bamboos can be classified according to their vigor.

- **Clump-forming and non-invasive:** these will not cause a problem and are ideal for small gardens. They include *Fargesia murieliae* (also known as *Arundinaria murieliae*) and *Fargesia nitida* (also known as *Arundinaria nitida*).
- **Moderately invasive but easily checked:** once established, regularly chopping back of young shoots will be necessary. Alternatively, install a proprietary metal barrier 6 in (15 cm) from the boundary and buried in a trench 20 in (50 cm) deep. Position 3 in (7.5 cm) of the barrier above the surface.
- **Invasive:** these are rampant and therefore are not at all suitable for small gardens.

WHAT ARE ORNAMENTAL GRASSES?

Unlike lawn grasses, ornamental types are ideal for planting or sowing in borders and beds in gardens. Some are annual, others herbaceous and few perennial; several uses of them are suggested below. Additionally, some grasses when dried are ideal for using in floral displays indoors. In the garden they are frequently used to introduce an artistic element, with unusual and distinctive shapes and colors that harmonize with other plants.

HOW CAN I USE ORNAMENTAL GRASSES?

These grasses can be used in many ways in gardens.

- **Annual grasses:** filling bare areas in newly planted herbaceous or mixed borders. Within a few months of being sown, they create magnificent displays.
- **Herbaceous grasses:** in beds totally devoted to them, or mixed with medleys of other plants.
- **Perennial grasses:** these include grasses such as *Cortaderia selloana* (Pampas Grass), with long, fluffy flower heads, which look good in a bed cut into a lawn.
- **Grasses in containers:** display on a patio (see right for a range of suitable plants).
- **Dominant grasses:** the majestic *Miscanthus sacchariflorus*, which grows up to 10 ft (3 m) high, can be used to create an attractive, unusual and practical screen.

GRASSES AND SEDGES IN CONTAINERS

Many grasses and sedges thrive in containers, but ensure that their roots do not become dry during summer. Sedges are especially damaged by dry soil.

- ***Acorus gramineus* 'Ogon':** initially upright, then arching, with narrow and tapering green leaves with golden variegated bands along their lengths.
- ***Carex oshimensis* 'Evergold':** arching nature, with leaves variegated green and yellow. There are several other *Carex* species that are suitable for containers.
- ***Festuca glauca:*** tufted nature, with colored leaves and including blue, blue-green and silvery-blue. Ideal for containers with ornate sides that need to be admired.
- ***Hakonechloa macra* 'Alboaurea':** cascading nature, with long, arching, narrow leaves striped gold and off-white.

Coix lacryma-jobi

Christ's Tears (UK)

Job's Tears (USA/UK)
Half-hardy annual grass with broad, lance-shaped, pale to mid-green leaves. From mid-summer to early autumn it bears gray-green, woody, edible seeds that hang in tear-like clusters.

Soil and situation: fertile, moisture-retentive but well-drained soil in full sun.

Increasing plants: during late winter and early spring sow seeds shallowly in pots in gentle warmth. Plant into a border when all risk of frost has passed.

⬆ 1½–2 ft (45–60 cm) ↔ 10–12 in (25–30 cm)

Cortaderia selloana

Pampas Grass (USA/UK)
Perennial, evergreen grass with slender leaves and tall, woody stems that bear fluffy, silvery plumes up to 18 in (45 cm) long from late summer to late winter. For a small garden, it is best to plant the form 'Pumila.'

Soil and situation: fertile, moisture-retentive soil in full sun.

Increasing plants: lift and divide large clumps in spring, replanting young parts from around the outside. However, this usually results in spoiling the mother plant's shape.

⬆ 5–8 ft (1.5–2.4 m) ↔ 5–7 ft (1.5–2.1 m)

Deschampsia cespitosa 'Goldtau'

Tufted Hair Grass UK/USA

Tussock Grass UK/USA
Hardy, ornamental grass with tall, gold-bronze flowerheads emerging from tufted green foliage.

Soil and situation: likes a slightly moist soil in a sunny or shaded position.

Design notes: this grass makes a beautiful backdrop to water, and looks good in patio planters. A good choice for a Japanese garden. A large specimen is an impressive sight.

⬆ 2–3 ft (60–90 cm) ↔ 2–3 ft (60–90 cm)

Fargesia murieliae

Umbrella Bamboo (USA/UK)
Also known as *Arundinaria murieliae*, this hardy, elegant, clump-forming and non-invasive bamboo has arching, bright green canes that mature to dull yellow. Narrow, oblong, dark green leaves.

Soil and situation: fertile, moisture-retentive but well-drained soil in light shade or full sun.

Increasing plants: lift and divide congested large clumps in spring, just as new growth is beginning.

↕ 6–8 ft (1.8–2.4 m)

Hakonechloa macra 'Alboaurea'

Hardy, cascading, perennial grass with narrow, brightly variegated leaves. It is ideal for planting at the edge of a raised bed or in a pot on a patio. There are other attractive forms, including 'Aureola' (yellow leaves striped with narrow green lines).

Soil and situation: moderately fertile, well-drained soil in full sun.

Increasing plants: lift and divide congested plants in spring.

↕ 10–12 in (25–30 cm) ↔ 2½–3 ft (75–90 cm)

Miscanthus sinensis 'Morning Light'

Zebra Grass UK/USA
Hardy, ornamental grass with narrow, green, yellow- or silver-striped leaves.

Soil and situation: likes a deep, moist, loamy soil in a sunny or shaded position.

Design notes: a good option for areas that fringe a bog garden, and perfect for a bog garden that is overhung by young trees.

↕ 3–6 ft (0.9–1.8 m) ↔ 1–3 ft (30–90 cm)

Miscanthus sinensis 'Variegatus'

Hardy, ornamental grass with narrow, green, yellow- or silver-striped leaves.

Soil and situation: likes a deep, moist, loamy soil in a sunny or shaded position.

Design notes: a good option for bordering on a bog garden, perfect against a red brick wall, and ideal for a Japanese garden.

↕ 3–6 ft (0.9–1.8 m) ↔ 1–3 ft (30–90 cm)

Pennisetum

Bristle Grass UK/USA
Half-hardy, ornamental grass with narrow, silver-gray leaves.

Soil and situation: likes a well-drained soil in a sunny position.

Design notes: a good plant for a semi-dry garden – a patio, container, or a walled, Mediterranean-type garden. There are both compact and tall-growing types.

↕ 1–10 ft (0.3–3 m) ↔ 1–2 ft (30–60 cm)

Phyllostachys aureosulcata

Bamboo with wand-like, orange-yellow branches and pale green leaves. The stems are erect and densely crowded. There are several varieties.

Soil and situation: likes a deep, moist, loamy soil in a sunny or shaded, sheltered position; needs lots of water and hates cold winds.

Design notes: a good option when you want to have a medium-sized clump of bamboo. It is much favored by designers of Japanese gardens.

↕ 10–15 ft (3–4.5 m) ↔ indefinite

Phyllostachys nigra

Black-stemmed Bamboo (USA/UK)

Black Bamboo (USA/UK)
Hardy, graceful, evergreen, clump-forming bamboo with canes first green but jet-black within 2–3 years. The leaves are dark green. It is moderately invasive but easily checked.

Soil and situation: fertile, moisture-retentive but well-drained soil in full sun. The stems achieve their best color when in dry soil.

Increasing plants: lift and divide congested large clumps in spring, just as new growth is beginning.

⬆ 8–10 ft (2.4–3 m)

Sasa veitchii

syn. *Arundinaria veitchii*

Kuma Bamboo Grass UK/USA
Hardy, low-growing bamboo with slender purple-green canes.

Soil and situation: likes a deep, moist soil in a sunny or shaded position.

Design notes: a good choice when you want a bamboo without too much height. The long leaves and the purple canes make a fine contrasting backdrop for grasses and dry-garden plants.

⬆ 3–5 ft (0.9–1.5 m) ↔ indefinite

Stipa tenuissima

Feather Grass UK/USA
Hardy, ornamental grass with narrow, green leaves and feathery flowerheads.

Soil and situation: likes a well-drained soil in a sunny or shaded position.

Design notes: a good option for wild gardens, patio gardens, containers, as a backdrop to a small pond – anywhere where you want to achieve a delicate look. It looks its best when wafting in a gentle breeze.

⬆ 2–3 ft (60–90 cm) ↔ 1–3 ft (30–90 cm)

Uncinia rubra

Red Grass UK/USA
Hardy, ornamental grass with narrow, green, red- or orange-striped leaves.

Soil and situation: likes a well-drained soil in a sunny or shaded position.

Design notes: a fine choice if you want a grass, yet at the same time you want to introduce a small amount of color to offset the yellows and greens. This grass looks its best when set against a mulch of woodchip or leaf mold.

⬆ 1–2 ft (30–60 cm) ↔ 1–2 ft (30–60 cm)

OTHER BAMBOOS AND GRASSES

- *Coix lacryma-jobi* (**Christ's Tears/Job's Tears**): half-hardy grass with spear-shaped leaves. An excellent choice for a well-drained but moist spot in full sun.
- *Cortaderia selloana* (**Pampas Grass**): perennial, evergreen grass with slender leaves and tall, woody stems that bear fluffy, plume-like flowers. This plant makes a beautiful specimen for a very large pot or tub.
- *Hakonechloa macra* '**Alboaurea**': hardy grass with a low, cascading habit, with narrow, variegated leaves. A good option for a low border around a patio, or a small detail within a Japanese garden.
- *Pleioblastus viridistriatus* (**Golden-haired Bamboo**): hardy, low-growing bamboo – a good choice for a container garden.
- *Phyllostachys nigra* (**Black-stemmed Bamboo**): hardy evergreen bamboo with green canes that turn to black within 2–3 years. Looks exotic – a good choice for a Japanese garden.

CONTAINER PLANTS

Maybe you want to enjoy gardening, but have only a balcony, a backyard, a patio, a barbecue area, a roof garden, a windowsill or a front doorstep to play with. The answer is to grow your plants in containers – these can be anything from mugs, buckets, bins and barrels to old teapots, tin baths and troughs – and put them in a place that catches the sun, at least for part of the day. Matching up the plant with the container is where the design comes in.

Portable patio planters

If you live in a rented house or apartment with a small courtyard where you want a garden and yet you want to take the plants with you when you move on, the answer is to grow everything in a range of pots and containers.

An attractive corner with most of the plants in containers, ready to go.

CONTAINER PLANTS AS DESIGN FEATURES

Just about any plant can be grown in a container – if the plant is compact enough and the container is big enough – and therefore the whole subject is as much about containers as it is about plants. From the designer's viewpoint, containers can be anything from a small vase to a stone trough. Apart from the look of the actual container – its shape, color, size and texture – using containers allows the designer to change space. One moment the garden is no more than a small courtyard garden, and the next there are containers everywhere – hanging on the walls, as window boxes, hanging from chains and ropes, fixed to poles, stacked on shelves, grouped just inside the house. Suddenly the garden is much bigger and full of interest.

Anthemis punctata subsp. *cupaniana*

Golden Marguerite (USA/UK)
Also known as *Anthemis cupaniana*, this short-lived herbaceous perennial has masses of daisy-like, white flowers with bright yellow centers from early to late summer. Finely dissected, gray leaves.

Soil and situation: light, loam-based, well-drained soil in full sun and shelter from cold wind.

Increasing plants: remove and divide congested plants in spring, replanting young pieces from around the outside.

⬆ 6–8 in (15–20 cm)　↔ 12–15 in (30–38 cm)

Armeria maritima

Sea Pink UK/USA

Thrift UK/USA
Hardy, evergreen plant of low, tufted growth, with brilliant, fluffy pink flowers.

Soil and situation: likes a light, well-drained, sandy soil in a sunny position. Does well in maritime areas.

Design notes: a good plant for seaside areas – on balconies and patios – especially in flat stone troughs and in rock-type containers. Ideal for an enclosed garden or a themed Mediterranean garden.

⬆ 1–2 ft (30–60 cm)　↔ creeping

Aucuba japonica 'Variegata'

Gold Dust Plant (USA)

Spotted laurel (UK)
Also known as *Aucuba japonica* 'Maculata,' this hardy, evergreen shrub has dark green leaves splashed in yellow. It is ideal for growing in a large tub.

Soil and situation: well-drained, moisture-retentive, soil-based compost in light shade or full sun.

Increasing plants: take 4–5 in (10–13 cm) long cuttings from the current season's growth and insert in pots of equal parts moist peat and coarse sand in late summer. Place in a cold frame.

⬆ 3½–4 ft (1–1.2 m)　↔ 3–4 ft (90 cm–1.2 m)

Chamaerops humilis

Fan Palm UK/USA
Very attractive, dwarf-growing palm with slender leaves fanning out from spiny stalks, and small, yellow flowers in early spring.

Soil and situation: likes a fibrous loam with plenty of grit. Does really well in warm, sheltered, coastal areas, but must be generously watered.

Design notes: just right for a dry-type Mediterranean garden. Looks good alongside grasses and bamboos – very exciting with a white-plastered wall as a backdrop. It needs a huge pot.

↕ 4–6 ft (1.2–1.8 m) ↔ 4–6 ft (1.2–1.8 m)

Choisya ternata 'Sundance'

Yellow-leaved Mexican Orange Blossom (USA/UK)
Slightly tender, evergreen shrub with golden-yellow leaves and faintly scented white flowers in late spring and early summer, and often intermittently throughout summer.

Soil and situation: well-drained, loam-based compost in full sun and sheltered from cold wind.

Increasing plants: take 3 in (7.5 cm) long cuttings in mid-summer and insert in pots of equal parts moist peat and coarse sand. Place in gentle warmth.

↕ 2½–3½ ft (75 cm–1 m) ↔ 2½–3 ft (75–90 cm)

Clematis macropetala

Slender-stemmed, deciduous and bushy climber with light and dark blue flowers during late spring and early summer. It is spectacular when planted in the top of a large barrel or pot and allowed to trail over the sides.

Soil and situation: fertile, neutral to slightly alkaline, soil-based compost in full sun.

Increasing plants: take 3 in (7.5 cm) long stem-cuttings in mid-summer and insert in pots of equal parts moist peat and coarse sand. Place in gentle warmth.

↔ Trails for 5–7 ft (1.5–2.1m)

Erigeron

Fleabane UK/USA

Summer Starwort UK/USA
Hardy, herbaceous perennial that produces pale purple and/or deep lavender, daisy-like flowers.

Soil and situation: likes a light, well-drained, sandy soil in a sunny position.

Design notes: a very attractive, old-fashioned plant that looks just right in a low, flat container. Good choice for a seaside garden.

↕ 1–2 ft (30–60 cm) ↔ 1–2 ft (30–60 cm)

Fatsia japonica

False Castor Oil Plant (UK)

Japanese Fatsia (USA)
Slightly tender, evergreen shrub with large, glossy, hand-like leaves. White flowers appear in autumn and often throughout winter.

Soil and situation: light, well-drained but moisture-retentive soil in a tub. Position in light shade or full sun, with shelter from cold wind.

Increasing plants: detach sucker-like shoots in spring and insert in pots of equal parts moist peat and coarse sand. Place in a cold frame.

↕ 5–7 ft (1.5–2.1 m) ↔ 5–6 ft (1.5–1.8 m)

Gazania

Treasure Flower UK/USA
Half-hardy perennial that belongs to the daisy family, with brilliant orange-yellow flowers in summer.

Soil and situation: likes well-drained soil in a sunny or shaded position.

Design notes: does well in a container, as long as it is positioned in full sun. The color is striking – good for a small Mediterranean courtyard garden.

↕ 1 ft (30 cm) ↔ 1 ft (30 cm)

WHICH CONTAINERS ARE BEST?

Where possible in a small garden, use containers such as window boxes, wall baskets and hanging baskets that leave the ground area free for other features. Such containers also make gardening possible in courtyards where the ground may be totally paved. Always ensure that these containers are positioned where they cannot drip water on plants below, dribble dirty water down a color-washed wall, or be bumped by passing heads.

OTHER CONTAINER PLANTS

- **Bulbs:** winter-, spring- and summer-flowering bulbs all do well and look great in containers.
- **Climbers:** Clematis, *Lathyrus odoratus* (Sweet Pea) and plants like *Humulus lupulus* (Hop) all also do well in containers, but need supports.
- *Cortaderia selloana* (**Pampas Grass**): perennial evergreen grass with slender leaves and tall woody stems. It needs a large pot, and is good for a large patio.
- *Phyllostachys nigra* (**Black-stemmed Bamboo**): hardy evergreen with green canes that turn to black within 2–3 years. Looks exotic.
- **Small trees:** these can do well in good-sized containers. You could either choose dwarf conifers and *Acers* (Maples), or choose full-sized trees and treat them in much the same way as bonsai by top- and root-pruning to keep them small.
- **Vegetables:** potatoes, tomatoes and salad crops are good options, just right for a small-yard kitchen garden.

Hebe x andersonii 'Variegata'

Slightly tender, evergreen shrub with cream and green variegated leaves. From mid-summer to early autumn it bears lavender-blue flowers.

Soil and situation: light, well-drained but moisture-retentive loam-based compost in full sun and shelter from cold wind.

Increasing plants: take 3 in (7.5 cm) long cuttings during mid-summer and insert in pots of equal parts moist peat and coarse sand. Place in a cold frame.

↕ 2½–3 ft (75–90 cm)　↔ 2–3 ft (60–90 cm)

Single-subject displays

These are increasingly popular and without the risk of dominant plants swamping others. Here are a few displays to consider.

- *Calceolaria integrifolia* **'Sunshine' (Slipper Flower):** half-hardy perennial, creating a "ball" of yellow.
- *Cascade Geraniums* (**Continental Geraniums**): half-hardy annuals with masses of flowers in a wide color range throughout summer.
- *Lobelia erinus* (**Edging and Trailing Lobelia**): half-hardy annual with a bushy or trailing nature, in mixed or single colors.

Osteospermum ecklonis var. *prostratum*

African Daisy (UK)
Also known as *Dimorphotheca ecklonis* 'Prostrata,' this tender perennial has white-petalled flowers with mustard-yellow centers in mid- and late summer.

Soil and situation: well-drained but moisture-retentive loam-based soil in full sun.

Increasing plants: take 2 in (5 cm) long cuttings from side shoots in mid-summer and insert in pots of equal parts moist peat and coarse sand in a cold frame.

↕ 6–9 in (15–23 cm)　↔ 12–15 in (30–38 cm)

Salvia officinalis

Sage UK/USA
Very large group of hardy plants, some of which can be used as culinary herbs, with small, green leaves and brilliant blue flowers.

Soil and situation: likes a light, well-drained soil in a sunny position.

Design notes: a great option for container planting; perfect for a small kitchen porch garden.

↕ 1–3 ft (30–90 cm)　↔ 1 ft (30 cm)

Sedum

Stonecrop UK/USA
Very large group of hardy succulents. A full, plump cushion of small, yellow flowers is produced in summer, and brilliantly colored leaves in autumn.

Soil and situation: likes a light, well-drained soil in a sunny position.

Design notes: a particularly good option for container planting, in that it fills the container to overflowing, to the extent that the plant and the container become an integrated form. Just about every part of the plant will grow where it falls — leaves, roots and seeds.

⬆ 3–18 in (7.5–45 cm) ↔ 1–3 ft (30–90 cm)

Stipa arundinacea

Feather Grass UK/USA
Hardy, ornamental grass with a beautiful gold-purple tinge to the feathery heads.

Soil and situation: likes a well-drained soil in a sunny or shaded position.

Design notes: although this particular grass is more vigorous than most, it is still a good option for a container. It looks its best alongside other grasses on a patio.

⬆ 2–3 ft (60–90 cm) ↔ 1–3 ft (30–90 cm)

SUCCESS WITH HANGING BASKETS

- Don't cram masses of plants into one basket. Once established, fewer but bigger and healthier plants look better than a crowd of space-starved plants.
- Don't use too many different types of plants. A dozen totally different plants will not look as effective as 12 plants of only four kinds.
- When planting a hanging basket, choose a medley of trailing, bushy and upright plants.
- Don't be afraid to try a single-subject basket – they look distinctive and very attractive.
- Try color variations if you want lots of variety. Mixed colors of the same species give the impression of a very colorful basket without any problem of some plants physically dominating their neighbors and consequently spoiling the entire display.

Thymus

Common Creeping Thyme UK/USA

Thyme UK/USA
Group of hardy sub-shrubs and herbaceous plants, some of which can be used as culinary herbs, with small, green leaves and brilliant blue, heather-like flowers. There are lots of types – Lemon Thyme, Orange-scented Thyme, Seed Cake Thyme and more.

Soil and situation: likes a light, well-drained soil in a sunny position.

Design notes: a good option for a container just outside the back door – perfect if you enjoy cooking.

⬆ 12–18 in (30–45 cm) ↔ creeping

PLANTS FOR HANGING BASKETS

- *Antirrhinum pendula multiflora* **'Chinese Lanterns':** half-hardy annual with a cascading habit: there are many different colors, as well as bicolors, creating a distinctive feature.
- *Calceolaria integrifolia* 'Sunshine' **(Slipper Flower):** half-hardy perennial with a trailing and cascading habit and bright yellow, pouch-like flowers.
- *Campanula isophylla* **(Italian Bellflower/Star of Bethlehem):** hardy perennial with a trailing and cascading habit; it produces masses of star-shaped, blue or white flowers.
- *Cascade Geraniums* **(Continental Geraniums):** half-hardy annuals with a cascading habit; it bears masses of flowers in shades of scarlet, salmon, pink and lilac. These plants soon saturate a container in color.
- *Helichrysum petiolare:* half-hardy perennial with long, trailing stems and attractive leaves. There are several forms, some with single-colored leaves, others variegated.
- *Fuchsia* **(Lady's Eardrops):** tender perennials, many with a cascading habit and ideal as a centerpiece in a hanging basket. They become awash with distinctive, colorful flowers.
- *Lobelia erinus* **(Edging and Trailing Lobelia):** half-hardy annual with a bushy or trailing habit; it has blue, white or red flowers.
- *Lobularia maritima pendula:* also known as *Alyssum maritimum pendula*, this half-hardy annual has a trailing habit and produces cream, purple, pink, rose and purple flowers.
- *Pelargonium peltatum* **(Trailing or Ivy-leaved Geranium):** tender perennial with a trailing and cascading habit; there are many varieties, in colors including white, pink, salmon, lilac and red.
- *Petunia milliflora* **'Fantasy':** half-hardy annual, with a compact habit and trumpet-shaped flowers in many colors.

HERBS

Which plants qualify as "herbs"?

Herbs are plants that have traditionally been grown for medicinal, cosmetic and culinary uses. This book focuses on well-known, safe-to-use culinary herbs such as Sage, Rosemary and Borage, and herbs like Lavender that smell good. Other herbs are illustrated, but only for their ornamental qualities. Be warned: if you wish to turn any plant that is unknown to you into a tea, rub, balm, poultice or anything else, you must research it thoroughly first.

Fresh herbs for the taking

Herbs in pots and containers placed close to the kitchen door are a great idea. They look good, they smell good, and they are handy when you come to do the cooking.

Fresh herbs ready for picking are hard to beat.

HERBS AS DESIGN FEATURES

If, just for a moment, we forget about the culinary aspect of herbs and simply focus on what they look and smell like, then you can see that there are a lot of design options. You could grow them in containers so that they are close to hand, in a traditional knot-type garden with various colors and forms making patterns, in a small confined space so that you can enjoy their aromatic qualities, in groups – all thymes, all mints, or whatever you like – and so on. There are lots of options. All that said, however, the traditional approach of growing herbs in a small, dedicated area – so you can pop out from the kitchen and pick fresh herbs for the cooking pot – is hard to beat. There are lots of suppliers who specialize in herbs, selling both plants and related items, so check for those in your local area.

Borago officinalis

Borage UK/USA
Hardy, fragrant annual with green-gray leaves and bright blue flowers, grown both for its leaves and its looks.

Soil and situation: likes well-drained soil in a sunny, sheltered position.

Design notes: while Borage looks fine set alongside other herbs like Lavender and Rosemary, it looks particularly good when it is planted in a wild garden and allowed to do its own thing.

↕ 1–2 ft (30–60 cm) ↔ 1–2 ft (30–60 cm)

Carlina acaulis

Carlina Thistle UK/USA
Hardy plant with a thistle-like appearance and a large, spiky, ball-shaped, purple flowerhead. It was an important herb in the past, but is no longer used as one.

Soil and situation: likes a light, well-drained soil in a sunny position.

Design notes: an excellent option for a walled garden. The height of the plant and the dramatic appearance of the flowerheads makes it a good backdrop plant. It would look fine in a color-themed bed.

↕ 1–2 ft (30–60 cm) ↔ 1 ft (30 cm)

Foeniculum vulgare

Fennel UK/USA
Hardy perennial with feathery, green leaves on long, bamboo-like stems.

Soil and situation: likes well-drained soil in a sunny, sheltered position, but seems to grow just about anywhere.

Design notes: not only is Fennel a very easy-to-grow herb, but it is a beautifully tall and exotic plant, more like a grass or bamboo than anything else. Looks good in a walled garden, as a backdrop to the herb bed. Also a good container plant.

↕ 3–6 ft (0.9–1.8 m) ↔ 2–3 ft (60–90 cm)

Lavandula 'Hidcote'

Lavender UK/USA
Hardy, evergreen shrub with small, silver-gray leaves and blue flowers in summer. The particular blue is so singular that it has come to be called "lavender blue."

Soil and situation: likes a well-drained, sandy loam-type soil in a sunny, sheltered position.

Design notes: there are many other varieties of Lavender to choose from.

⬆ 1–2 ft (30–60 cm) ↔ 1–2 ft (30–60 cm)

Myrrhis odorata

Sweet Cicely UK/USA
Hardy, fragrant perennial herb with fern-like leaves, small, white, multiple flowers, and long, dark brown fruits.

Soil and situation: likes any well-drained soil in a sunny, sheltered position.

Design notes: this plant is fragrant in all its parts. The leaves are aromatic, the fruits have a sweet smell, and the whole plant has a fragrance or odor that has been likened to that of myrrh. This is a good option for an enclosed courtyard garden or a container garden. It looks good alongside Fennel.

⬆ 3–4 ft (0.9–1.2 m) ↔ 1–2 ft (30–60 cm)

Rosmarinus officinalis

Rosemary UK/USA
Hardy, shrubby, fragrant plant, with narrow leaves – glossy green on top and greeny white on the underside – with small, blue flowers.

Soil and situation: likes a light, well-drained, sandy loam-type soil in a sunny, sheltered position. Thrives in coastal areas.

Design notes: Rosemary can be kept tight and compact or "let go" to make a scraggy shrub. It looks particularly attractive in the form of a low hedge, perhaps round the herb garden.

⬆ 2–7 ft (0.6–2.1 m) ↔ 3–4 ft (0.9–1.2 m)

Ruta graveolens

Rue UK/USA

Herb of Grace UK/USA
Shrub-like and hardy, with deeply divided, blue-green leaves, and terminal clusters of yellow flowers in summer.

Soil and situation: likes a light, well-drained soil in a sunny position.

Design notes: this plant would look good anywhere, but especially in a color-themed bed.

⬆ 1–3 ft (30–90 cm) ↔ 1 ft (30 cm)

Salvia sclarea

Clary Sage UK/USA
Hardy biennial with large, hairy leaves, and blue and white, tubular flowers borne in late summer.

Soil and situation: likes a light, well-drained soil in a sunny position.

Design notes: would look good anywhere – in a container, in a walled garden, growing wild in a meadow, let go as a scraggy shrub, or in a color-themed bed.

⬆ 1–3 ft (30–90 cm) ↔ 1 ft (30 cm)

OTHER HERBS

- *Anethum graveolens* (**Dill**): aromatic annual with hollow stems, delicate, finely divided foliage, and umbels of tiny yellow flowers in summer. Grows to a height of 2 ft (60 cm).

- *Artemisia dracunculus* (**Tarragon**): shrubby plant grown for its leaves – good in a salad or in a dressing. Has woody stems, narrow leaves and inconspicuous flowers. Grows to a height of about 3 ft (90 cm).

- *Mentha* spp. (**Mint**): small group of fragrant, hardy perennials often used in cooking. The various types, such as Common Mint, Spearmint, Apple Mint and Pineapple Mint, each give off a characteristic fragrance when the leaves are bruised. A good swift-growing option for a container garden, but can be invasive in borders unless roots are contained.

- *Satureja* (**Winter Savory**): hardy, aromatic-leaved herb with small, pale green leaves and small, lilac-colored flowers. Used to flavor soups and stews. Good for a herb garden or as a specimen plant in a container.

SMALL-GARDEN HERBS

The range of small-garden herbs is very wide, and they introduce exciting and unusual flavors to vegetables as well as fish and meat dishes; sandwiches and soups also benefit from them. Pots of young herbs are relatively inexpensive to buy and most will last for several years; even then, many can be lifted, divided and replanted. Some herbs, such as Parsley, are raised each year from seeds sown in a sheltered seed bed or a pot.

PLACES TO GROW HERBS

- **Containers:** clusters of herbs in pots are convenient for placing near a kitchen door. Additionally, pots help to restrain invasive types such as mints which, in a border, would intrude on neighboring plants.
- **Cartwheel gardens:** these are often replicated by stones for the rim and spokes, with small herbs planted between them.
- **Chessboard designs:** paving slabs laid in a chessboard (checkerboard) pattern, with clusters of herbs in the spaces. This enables herbs to be easily reached.

OTHER CULINARY HERBS FOR SMALL GARDENS

The range of culinary herbs is wide and includes:

- ***Allium schoenoprasum* (Chives):** hardy perennial with a bulbous nature and grass-like, tubular, mid-green leaves. During early and mid-summer it develops globular heads of rose-pink, starry flowers. The chopped leaves are used to give a mild onion flavor to salads, omelettes and soups.
- ***Melissa officinalis* (Balm):** hardy herbaceous perennial, grown for its lemon-scented, wrinkled-surfaced and somewhat heart-shaped green leaves. The leaves are used fresh or dried in iced drinks and fruit salads.
- ***Satureja hortensis* (Summer Savory):** hardy annual with a bushy nature and spicily flavored, dark green leaves. They are used to flavor fish, meat and soups, as well as egg and cheese dishes.
- ***Thymus vulgaris* (Thyme):** also known as Common or Garden Thyme, this hardy, low-growing, evergreen shrub has aromatic, dark green leaves. They are used fresh or dried to flavor stuffings, and in fish dishes, casseroles and soups.

Mentha spicata (Common Mint)

Also known as Spearmint, this hardy, herbaceous perennial has aromatic leaves with a distinctive spearmint flavor. They are used in mint sauce and jelly, as well as for flavoring vegetables.

Soil and situation: light, fertile, moisture-retentive but well-drained soil in slight shade and a warm position. It is best grown in containers to restrict its spread.

Increasing plants: lift and divide congested plants in spring; replant young pieces direct in their growing positions.

↥ 15–18 in (38–45 cm)　↔ Vigorous and invasive

Petroselinum crispum (Parsley)

Hardy biennial invariably grown as an annual. It has branching stems, bearing curly, moss-like, mid-green leaves. It develops greenish-yellow flowers, but these should be removed. Leaves are used to garnish fish dishes and sandwiches, and to flavor sauces.

Soil and situation: light, fertile, well-drained but moisture-retentive soil in light shade or sun.

Increasing plants: sow seeds in shallow furrows in an outdoor seed bed from early spring to mid-summer.

↥ 1–1 ½ ft (30–45 cm)　↔ 9–15 in (23–38 cm)

Salvia officinalis (Sage)

Slightly tender, evergreen shrub with gray-green, wrinkled, aromatic leaves and tubular, violet-blue flowers during early and mid-summer. The leaves are used to flavor meats and stuffings.

Soil and situation: light, fertile, well-drained but moisture-retentive soil in full sun.

Increasing plants: take 3 in (7.5 cm) long cuttings from the current season's shoots in late summer. Insert them in equal parts moist peat and sharp sand, and place in a cold frame.

↥ 1 ½–2 ft (45–60 cm)　↔ 1 ½–2 ft (45–60 cm)

FRUIT

Where possible in a small garden, grow tree fruits in borders; perhaps narrow ones alongside walls for warmth-loving types (peaches and nectarines) or in beds alongside paths which give ready access to them. Fruits grown in containers – whether apples or strawberries – need regular attention, especially to ensure that the soil does not become dry. In particular, strawberries in hanging baskets need regular watering.

> *How can I grow fruits?*

PICKING FRUIT

- **Apples and pears:** test for picking by cupping individual fruits and gently lifting and twisting. If the stalk readily parts from the branch, the fruit is ready to be picked.
- **Black currants:** fruits are ready for picking about a week after turning blue-black; those at the top of each strig (bunch) ripen first and can be picked individually.
- **Peaches and nectarines:** pick when the flesh around the stalk is soft; pick in the same way as for apples.
- **Plums:** fruits are ready for picking when they easily part from the tree – the stalk usually remains on the tree. Take care not to squeeze and bruise them.
- **Raspberries:** when fruits are fully colored but still firm, pull them off; leave the plug attached to the plant.
- **Strawberries:** pick fruits when they are colored all over. Pick when dry, with the stalk attached to the fruit.

Strawberries in containers

- **Hanging baskets:** use a seed-raised variety and buy young plants in late spring or early summer. Put three plants in a large hanging basket. Do not put baskets outside until all risk of frost has passed.
- **Strawberry planters:** these have cupped holes in their sides in which plants can be placed – as well as in the top. Ensure good drainage; roll a piece of wire-netting (slightly less than the depth of the planter) to form a tube about 3 in (7.5 cm) wide. Insert this into the planter and fill with large stones. Fill the planter with loam-based compost to level with the lowest cupped hole, and put a plant in it. Continue filling and planting; lastly, put plants in the top. Thoroughly water the compost.

Apples

In confined areas, grow apples either as espaliers or cordons against walls, or as dwarf pyramids or dwarf bushes in tubs and large pots. Dwarfing rootstocks such as M27 or M9 are essential, especially for apples in containers. To ensure pollination (and subsequent development of fruit) compatible varieties close by are essential. Where only one tree is possible, choose a "family" tree, where three or four varieties have been grafted on to it. Additionally, specifically choose varieties for their flavor.

Black currants

Easily grown bush fruits, with shoots growing directly from soil level. Fruits are borne on shoots produced during the previous year – expect a yearly yield of 10–15 lb (4.5–6.8 kg) from each bush. As soon as fruits have been picked, cut out all stems that produced fruits. This leaves young shoots (produced during that season) to bear fruits during the following year. Bushes grow about 5 ft (1.5 m) high and wide, with picking mainly during mid-summer.

Gooseberries

Usually grown as bushes, with fruits borne on a permanent framework of shoots supported by a single, leg-like stem. From a bush – 3–5 ft (90 cm–1.5 m) high – expect a yearly yield of 6–12 lb (2.70–5.44 kg) fruits. Picking time is mainly in mid-summer. Prune established bushes between early winter and early spring, cutting back by half new growth at the ends of stems. Additionally, cut back side shoots to 2 in (5 cm) long.

Peaches

Succulent fruits with somewhat rough, hairy skin. In a small garden, fan-trained trees are best, positioned against a warm, wind-sheltered wall. From an established fan-trained tree expect a yield of 20 lb (9 kg) when grown on a St Julien A rootstock; space trees 15 ft (4.5 m) apart. For a small garden use Pixy rootstock, with 8 ft (2.4 m) between trees, and expect a yearly yield of 10 lb (4.5 kg) of fruits. Fruits are picked mainly during mid-summer and the early part of late summer.

Pears

In confined areas, grow pears either as espaliers, 15 ft (4.5 m) apart, or cordons, 2½ ft (75 cm) apart. Pollination partners are essential and, in a small garden, the easiest way to overcome this problem is to plant a family tree, where several varieties have been grafted onto the same tree. Fruits are ready for picking (depending on the variety) during late summer and early or mid-autumn, and usually ready for eating some time later. Established espaliers yield 15–25 lb (6.8–11.3 kg) of fruits, while a single cordon 4–6 lb (1.8–2.72 kg).

Raspberries – summer-fruiting types

Popular cane fruits, needing a supporting framework of tiered wires, 12–15 in (30–38 cm) apart to 6 ft (1.8 m) high. These are strained between strong posts and in full sun. Avoid frost-pockets on slopes. Immediately after picking, cut out all fruited canes to ground level and tie in young canes. Fertile, moisture-retentive soil is essential to encourage the yearly production of canes that during the following year bear fruits during mid- and late summer. Expect yields of 4½lb (2 kg) for each 3 ft (90 cm) of row.

Strawberries – summer-fruiting types

Popular soft fruit for growing in beds as well as in containers. Summer-fruiting types are harvested during early and mid-summer, with plants remaining productive for 3–4 years. For a worthwhile crop, you should put at least 20 plants in a bed, and expect a yield of up to 24 oz (680 g) from each plant. Other types of these fruits include Alpine Strawberries, with a productive life of one year and cropping from mid-summer to autumn. They are best grown in a container.

OTHER FRUITS FOR SMALL GARDENS

- **Blackberries:** popular cane fruit, needing a supporting framework of tiered wires, 12 in (30 cm) apart from 3 ft (90 cm) to 7 ft (2.1 m) high. These are strained between strong posts and in full sun or light shade. Immediately after picking, cut out all fruited canes to ground level and tie in young canes. Fertile, moisture-retentive soil is essential to encourage the yearly production of canes that during the following year bear fruits mainly during late summer and early autumn. Expect yields of 10–25 lb (4.5–11.3 kg) from each plant – spaced 8–12 ft (2.4–3.6 m) apart, depending on vigor.

- **Nectarines:** smooth-skinned form of the peach. There are several varieties, but all less hardy than peaches and therefore best grown as fan-trained trees against a warm, wind-sheltered wall. Grow it on the St Julien A rootstock and expect a yield of 10 lb (4.5 kg) from each fan-trained tree.

- **Raspberries - autumn-fruiting types:** fruits are similar to those of summer-fruiting types, but produce fruits from late summer to mid-autumn. Autumn-fruiting raspberries bear fruits on the tips of shoots produced earlier during the same season and for this reason pruning is easier than for summer-fruiting types. In late winter of each year, cut all canes to ground level; in spring, fresh shoots appear and these bear fruits later in the year. Expect a yield from established plants of about 1½ lb (68 g) for each 3 ft (90 cm) of row. Plants remain productive for 7–10 years, when they start to deteriorate through virus infections.

- **Red currants:** popular fruit, usually grown as a bush and growing 5-6 ft (1.5–1.8 m) high and wide. Bushes have a permanent framework of shoots supported by a single, leg-like stem. From each bush, expect a yearly yield 10 lb (4.5 kg). Bushes remain productive for 10–15 years. Picking time is usually mid-summer, although some varieties are not ready until the early part of late summer.

- **White currants:** grown in the same way as red currants (with a similar yield), and both also can be grown as single, double or triple cordons.

VEGETABLES

Should you wish to grow vegetables, there are many different ways in which you can do it. You could have a alpinened-off area with long rows for easy access, lots of small, raised beds that you can walk around and stretch over, single plants in among the flower beds, a mixture of vegetables, herbs and salad crops grown in a pattern of small, geometrical beds, plants in containers on your patio, or a whole walled garden, to mention just a few of the possibilities.

> *How can I grow vegetables?*

VEGETABLES AS DESIGN FEATURES

Most people somehow forget that fruit and vegetables are visually exciting and attractive in much the same way as a rose. What could be more beautiful than a tomato plant loaded with fruit, or an orchard tree bowed down with Victoria plums, or a good fat squash? Of course, we know that all these items taste very good, but the trick for the garden designer is not exactly to forget about the eating bit but to focus in on the whole package – the decorative potential plus the food potential. If you look at the items on this spread – tomatoes, eggplants (aubergines), beans, lettuces, zucchini (courgettes), apples and figs – you can instantly see that they would make a wonderful contribution to any garden, a joy to the eye as well as the stomach!

Tomatoes in containers

- **Hanging baskets:** use a 18 in (45 cm) wide, wire-framed basket and line with plastic. Partly fill with equal parts soil-based and peat-based compost; when all risk of frost has passed, plant a bush-type variety such as 'Tumbler.' Use a knife to slit small holes in the plastic; then, water the compost. Plants are naturally bushy and do not need to have side shoots removed.

- **Grow bags:** plant 3–4 "cordon" types in a grow bag. Supports are essential (proprietary types are available). Regularly water and feed plants. Remove side shoots and regularly pick fruits when ripe.

- **Pots:** plant a "cordon" type in a large pot of loam-based compost. Support the plant with a cane. Remove side shoots.

Beans

Semi-hardy perennial, usually treated as an annual, with broad, green leaves, pea-like flowers, and clusters of long pods. There are lots of types to choose from – fava beans, French beans and runner beans.

Soil and situation: likes deep, rich, well-dug soil, with lots of well-rotted organic matter worked into it, in a sunny, sheltered position.

Design notes: most beans produce masses of decorative foliage, which can be useful for covering an ugly wall or structure.

Beets

Choose Globe Beetroot, which are round and quick maturing and include 'Burpee's Golden' (superb flavor, with yellow flesh) and 'Detroit' (red flesh; stores well).

Sowing: in spring, shallowly fork soil and rake to a fine tilth. Form furrows 1 in (2.5 cm) deep and 12 in (30 cm) apart. Sow in clusters of 2–3 seeds, 4–6 in (10–15 cm) apart. Thin seedlings to one at each position.

Harvesting: insert a garden fork under roots and gently lift without bruising the globes. Twist off the leaves.

Carrots

Choose Short-rooted Carrots (which are finger-like) or those that resemble small golf balls; these include 'Amsterdam Forcing' (early variety with stump-end roots) and 'Parmex' (round, and ideal for containers as well as vegetable beds).

Sowing: from mid-spring to the latter part of early summer, sow seeds in furrows ½–¾ in (12–18 mm) deep and 6 in (15 cm) apart. Sow thinly and thin seedlings to about 2½ in (6 cm) apart. Refirm soil around remaining seedlings.

Harvesting: When young carrots are large enough to be eaten, pull them up. Twist off foliage, just above the roots.

Eggplant

Tender plant with broad, green leaves and large, purple or white fruits.

Soil and situation: likes much the same conditions as the tomato – deep, rich, well-dug soil, with lots of well-rotted organic matter, in a sunny, sheltered position.

Design notes: just as with tomatoes, you can grow them as bushes, up strings or wires, in containers, or as low, dwarf bushes that bow down so that the fruit is cupped in a nest of straw. They do well against the foot of a sunny wall, or you could create a cottage kitchen-garden effect and grow them among the flower beds.

French beans

These are ideal for small gardens, as well as wind-exposed positions. Choose varieties such as 'Masterpiece' (flat pods), 'Tendergreen' (pencil podded) and 'The Prince' (flat pods).

Sowing: fertile, moisture-retentive soil is essential to ensure rapid growth. In late spring or early summer, form furrows 2 in (5 cm) deep and 18 in (45 cm) apart. Sow individual seeds 3–4 in (7.5–10 cm) apart.

Harvesting: from mid-summer onwards, pick the pods when young; they should snap when bent sideways. Regular picking encourages the development of further beans.

Lettuce

Range of semi-hardy and hardy plants eaten in salads.

Soil and situation: generally likes deep, rich, well-dug soil, with lots of well-rotted organic matter, in a sunny, sheltered position.

Design notes: apart from types like round cabbage lettuce and pointed Cos, that are just cut off and taken to the kitchen, there are many other types, such as Lamb's lettuce, American cress and rocket, that are treated as nip-and-eat plants, where leaves are taken as and when required, so there is no reason why lettuces cannot be grown among flowers. Some even make good ground cover.

VEGETABLES IN GROW BAGS

Several vegetables grow well in grow bags on a sheltered patio or balcony. Plant as soon as all risk of frost has passed.

- **Bush French beans:** plant six bushy plants. The pods are ready to be picked when they snap if bent – usually when they are around 4–6 in (10–15 cm) long.
- **Zucchinis:** use two plants. Water and feed plants regularly and harvest them while young and tender. This encourages the development of further zucchinis.
- **Lettuces:** grow eight lettuces in a bag.
- **Potatoes:** in early to mid-spring cut eight 3–4 in (7.5–10 cm) long cross-slits in the top and push a tuber of an early variety of potato into each. Cover them, water them and fold back the plastic to exclude light.

Radishes

Choose summer radishes, such as 'Cherry Belle' (globular), 'French Breakfast' (oblong), 'Juliette' (globular), 'Red Prince' (globular) and 'Scarlet Globe' (globular).

Sowing: from mid-spring to late summer sow seeds every two weeks. Form furrows ½ in (12 mm) deep and 6 in (15 cm) apart and sow thinly. When the seedlings are large enough to handle, thin them 1 in (2.5 cm) apart.

Harvesting: pull up young plants when large enough to be used in salads.

Spring onions

Also known as salad onions and bunching onions, spring onions are ideal for adding to salads. Choose varieties such as 'White Lisbon' and 'Ishikuro.'

Sowing: dig the soil in winter and in early spring fork and rake it to create a fine tilth. Every two weeks from early or mid-spring to the early part of mid-summer, sow seeds in furrows ½ in (12 mm) deep and 4–5 in (10–13 cm) apart. This produces onions from early summer to early autumn.

Harvesting: use a garden fork to loosen soil and pull up the plants.

Tomato

Tender plant with broad, green leaves and bright red fruits.

Soil and situation: likes deep, rich, well-dug soil, with lots of well-rotted organic matter worked into it, in a sunny, sheltered position.

Design notes: there are lots of tomato types to choose from and lots of ways to grow them – as bushes, up strings or wires, in containers, or as low, dwarf bushes that bow down so that the fruit is cupped in a nest of straw – a bit like strawberries. Could look really attractive as a backdrop to, say, an herb bed.

Zucchini/Courgette

Tender plant with broad, green leaves, dramatic, trumpet-shaped, yellow flowers, and squash-like fruits.

Soil and situation: likes deep, rich, well-dug soil, with lots of well-rotted organic matter, in a sunny, sheltered position. Best grown on a mound of soil.

Design notes: there are lots of squash-type vegetables to choose from. Zucchinis make very dramatic, trailing plants. If you put them in a sheltered spot, the plants will send off tumbling runners and masses of luxuriant foliage with lots of flowers and fruits. They are good near a patio, and even better within reach of a barbecue.

OTHER VEGETABLES

- **Beets:** choose Globe types, which are round and quick-maturing. During spring, form furrows 1 in (2.5 cm) deep and 12 in (30 cm) apart. Sow seeds in clusters of three, 4–6 in (10–15 cm) apart. When the seedlings have formed their first leaves (other than the original seed leaves), thin them to one seedling at each position.
- **Cucumber:** can be grown in much the same way as tomatoes – either as bushes or trained up wires. Any sheltered, sunny wall or fence will do. They have lots of attractive foliage as well as yellow flowers. Good for a children's area – the kids can pick and eat the cucumbers when they are small and tender.
- **Pea:** another good plant to have growing near the barbecue area. If you get everything right, you may end up being able to cook your meat or fish, and then serve it up with fresh peas, lettuce leaves, lightly grilled (broiled) zucchini (courgettes), and perhaps a few radishes, all right there to hand.
- **Potato:** a great plant that is relatively easy to grow, and that has lots of foliage, pretty flowers, and of course all the delicious potatoes just hiding under the ground and waiting to be harvested and eaten. Potatoes are another perfect subject for a children's garden – if you want your kids to eat these vegetables, then let them have the fun of growing a few plants themselves.
- **Radish:** radishes are another good option for a children's garden. They can be sown and harvested in three weeks – this is perfect for children who always want to see swift results.
- **Spinach Beet/Perpetual Spinach:** hardy plant with green leaves tinged with red, yellow or orange. Looks good and grows vigorously. This is ideal for a children's garden; they may not like stewed cabbage-like leaves, but they will like their very own spinach leaves, lightly steamed, dribbled with tomato sauce and served with fresh bread and butter.
- **Zucchinis:** these are frost-tender plants resembling small squash. They can be grown outdoors in fertile, moisture-retentive soil in full sun, or in grow bags, wall baskets and troughs. Plant when all risk of frost has passed and harvest when 4 in (10 cm) long.

Tips for Growing Vegetables and Fruit

LAND CRESS AND OTHER SALAD LEAVES

Land cress and other salad leaves, such as rocket, lamb's lettuce and curled cress, can be eaten as a salad, cooked like spinach, chopped to make a soup, or dribbled with olive oil and stuffed between two slices of fresh brown bread to make a giant cress-like sandwich.

				SOW			**HARVEST**																
mid winter	late winter	early spring	mid spring	late spring	early summer	mid summer	late summer	early autumn	mid autumn	late autumn	early winter	mid winter	late winter	early spring	mid spring	late spring	early summer	mid summer	late summer	early autumn	mid autumn	late autumn	early winter

ABOUT LAND CRESS AND SALAD LEAVES

- While land cress and most of the other salad leaves can be grown in less favorable, damp, part-shaded areas of the garden, they do best in a well-watered area that ranges from dappled sun through to part shade.
- Used as a cress and lettuce substitute, most salad leaves can be ready 6–8 weeks after planting.
- You can use them as a cut-and-come-again crop – the more young leaves you pick, the more young leaves you get.

GROWING MEDIUM

Select a bed in a medium shaded part of the garden (not too much shade nor too much sun), and layer up mulches of well-rotted manure, garden compost and spent mushroom compost. Aim to include at least a bucketful of well-rotted manure in a 3 ft (90 cm) square bed.

SOWING AND PLANTING

- For an autumn to spring crop, sow in mid- to late summer; for a summer crop, sow from early spring to early summer. Sow little pinches of seed ¼ in (6 mm) deep on a 6–8 in (15–20 cm) grid. Compact the bed and water with a fine spray.
- As soon as the seedlings are well established, pinch weak ones out to leave the best plant at each station.

GENERAL CARE

Stir the surface of the growing medium with a hoe to create a loose mulch, and hoe and water right through the season. If birds or insects are a nuisance, arrange a tent of fine netting over the whole bed. Remember that if the weather is hot and dry and you forget to pick or water, the plants will get ragged and maybe bolt. If some plants run to seed, the resulting seedlings can be planted on to fill gaps.

HARVESTING

You can harvest the winter crop from late autumn to early winter, and the summer crop from spring onwards – the precise time depends on your chosen varieties and growing methods. A good method is to go from plant to plant picking off the tender leaves when they are as long as your hand.

Growing medium: Fertile and moisture-retentive
Situation: Part sun to part shade
Harvest: Pick regularly when leaves are 3–4 in (7.5–10 cm) long

---

Troubleshooting

Slugs and snails: The damage generally shows as holes and cuts in leaves. Remove the pests by hand on a daily basis.

Brown-edged leaves: A sign that the plant is short of water, and/or you have neglected to pick the young tender leaves.

Flea beetle: Hundreds of little holes appear in the leaves and there is general drooping of the plant. Avoid the problem next time by growing the plants under a shelter of fine horticultural netting.

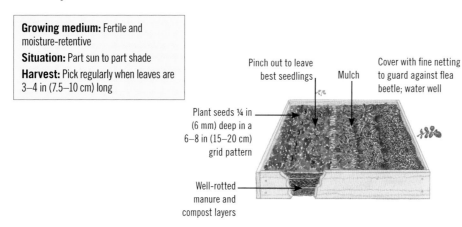

Pinch out to leave best seedlings

Mulch

Cover with fine netting to guard against flea beetle; water well

Plant seeds ¼ in (6 mm) deep in a 6–8 in (15–20 cm) grid pattern

Well-rotted manure and compost layers

LETTUCES

Not long ago, we had crunchy Romaine and soft butterhead lettuces, and that was it. Now we have leafy lettuce plants – round, soft, crisp, colored and crinkly – to suit all tastes and seasons. Try different varieties, but remember to protect the beds if the weather turns too sunny or cold.

SUMMER VARIETIES

				SOW		HARVEST																	
mid winter	late winter	early spring	mid spring	late spring	early summer	mid summer	late summer	early autumn	mid autumn	late autumn	early winter	mid winter	late winter	early spring	mid spring	late spring	early summer	mid summer	late summer	early autumn	mid autumn	late autumn	early winter

SPRING VARIETIES

					SOW										HARVEST								
mid winter	late winter	early spring	mid spring	late spring	early summer	mid summer	late summer	early autumn	mid autumn	late autumn	early winter	mid winter	late winter	early spring	mid spring	late spring	early summer	mid summer	late summer	early autumn	mid autumn	late autumn	early winter

ABOUT LETTUCES

- Lettuces do best at a temperature of about 50–60°F (10–15°C) and need shade in very hot weather.
- You can grow lettuces intercropped with radishes.
- Butterhead varieties are sown in autumn for eating in spring. Crisphead or iceberg varieties are sown in late summer for eating in late autumn. Romaine varieties are sown in autumn for eating in mid-winter through to mid-spring.

GROWING MEDIUM

Lettuces thrive on a light, friable, moisture-retentive growing medium. There must be plenty of well-rotted manure and plenty of water in summer, and the underlying ground around the bed must be well drained. Layer the bed with mulches of garden compost, old well-rotted manure and spent mushroom compost, and be prepared to add sand or other material. Allow space around the bed for a shelter.

SOWING AND PLANTING

- Sow, according to the calendar above, a pinch of seeds ½ in (12 mm) deep on a 8–10 in (20–25 cm) grid pattern. Sow thinly, compact the growing medium and use a fine spray to water. Protect with glass or plastic. Vary the spacing according to variety.
- When the seedlings are well established, thin them out to leave one good plant at each station.

> **Growing medium:** Light, fertile, moisture-retentive
> **Situation:** Light shade in hot weather
> **Harvest:** Cut when a firm heart is formed

GENERAL CARE

Stir the surface of the growing medium with a hoe to create a loose mulch. Hoe and water through the season. Spread a net over the bed to protect from birds and pests. In hot, dry weather, water at least a couple of times a day. If the weather stays hot, spread a thin mulch of spent mushroom compost over the whole bed to retain moisture.

HARVESTING

When you harvest will depend on your chosen varieties and growing methods. As a general rule, if you offer the crop full protection you will be able to maximize your yield by sowing early and harvesting both early and late. Cut lettuces close to the ground as needed. Pick cut-and-come-again leafy varieties leaf by leaf – a few leaves from one plant and a few from another – until you have enough.

Troubleshooting

Slugs and snails: Damage generally shows as holes and cuts in leaves. Remove the pests by hand on a daily basis.

Aphids: Leaves are distorted with sticky colonies of greenfly. Spray with a water to wash off the sticky mess, scrape away 1 in (2.5 cm) or so of growing medium to remove the resulting mush, and burn all the remaining debris at the end of the season.

Brown-edged leaves: These indicate that the plant is short of water. Avoid the problem by regular watering and by spreading extra mulch in long spells of hot, dry weather.

Plastic water pipe arches to support coverings against frost and excessive sun

Thin to the best seedling

Mulch

Keep well watered

Sow a pinch of seeds ½ in (12 mm) deep

Sow at 2–3-week intervals for a continuous supply

CHICORY

If you take pleasure in sharp-tasting flavors and lots of crisp and crunchy bite in your winter salad sandwiches, if you have a greenhouse or cold frame and the use of a shed, and if you do not mind waiting a good part of the year before you get a crop, chicory is a good crop to choose.

					SOW							**HARVEST**												
mid winter	late winter	early spring	mid spring	late spring	early summer	mid summer	late summer	early autumn	mid autumn	late autumn	early winter	mid winter	late winter	early spring	mid spring	late spring	early summer	mid summer	late summer	early autumn	mid autumn	late autumn	early winter

ABOUT CHICORY

- A challenging but fun aspect of growing chicory is the way in which you can take the stored roots three or four at a time, from late autumn to early spring, and grow them up as fat buds or chicons.
- The self-blanching, lettuce-like chicory varieties are often easier to grow, but are somewhat lacking in taste and bite.
- The tangy, smoky, burnt taste of chicory nicely offsets sweeter foods such as bread, butter, beets and fish. Chicory is perfect in a fat brown-bread sandwich.

GROWING MEDIUM

The growing medium needs to be soft in texture, rich in well-rotted compost, fertile and moist. Be aware that a freshly manured bed will cause the roots of the growing chicory to divide. A good option is to spread plenty of manure for one crop and then follow on with the chicory. A handful of the growing medium should feel crumbly yet moist, but not so moist that there are sticky lumps. Choose a sunny corner, well away from drafts.

SOWING AND PLANTING

- **Late spring to mid-summer** Sow a pinch of seeds ½ in (12 mm) deep about 8 in (20 cm) apart, compact the growing medium, and water with a fine sprinkler.
- Thin the seedlings to the best plants.

GENERAL CARE

Water on a daily basis. Stir the surface of the growing medium with a hoe to create a loose mulch. Nurture the plants through their growing cycle. At the end of the growing season, lift and trim off the leaves to about 1 in (2.5 cm) of the parsnip-like roots, and bed them, head to tail, flat in a box of dry sand.

HARVESTING

You can harvest and eat self-blanching varieties from mid-autumn to mid-winter. Blanch traditional types from mid- to late autumn through to mid-spring. To do this, take four roots at a time (ones that you stored in mid- to late autumn), plant them in a large pot in moist potting compost, cover the pot with black plastic sheet and put them in a medium-warm shed. They will be ready for eating in around 3–4 weeks.

Troubleshooting

Leaf and stem damage: Probably caused by a mix of slugs and cutworms. Hoe the ground around the plants, search out the pests and remove them.

Slugs: Use slug barriers or traps and/or remove the slugs by hand.

Heart rot: This shows as yellowy-brown damage to the leaves, and can be caused by frost damage or a virus. Avoid the problem next time by using frost- and virus-resistant varieties.

Growing medium: Well-rotted compost, moist
Situation (not the chicons): Sheltered and sunny
Harvest: Cut with a sharp knife at the base

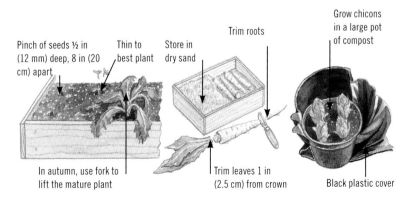

Pinch of seeds ½ in (12 mm) deep, 8 in (20 cm) apart

Thin to best plant

Store in dry sand

Trim roots

Grow chicons in a large pot of compost

In autumn, use fork to lift the mature plant

Trim leaves 1 in (2.5 cm) from crown

Black plastic cover

BEET GREENS

All the difficulties of getting a continuous supply of spinach can easily be solved by growing beet greens, also known as spinach beet, perpetual spinach and chard. It has a much stronger flavor than spinach, and the texture has a little more bite, but it is generally easier to grow.

SOW (mid spring) **HARVEST** (early autumn)

mid winter | late winter | early spring | mid spring | late spring | early summer | mid summer | late summer | early autumn | mid autumn | late autumn | early winter | mid winter | late winter | early spring | mid spring | late spring | early summer | mid summer | late summer | early autumn | mid autumn | late autumn | early winter

ABOUT BEET GREENS

- Beet greens are a good option if you are having trouble growing spinach.
- If you pick when young and tender, you can eat both the leaves and the colorful stalks.
- Late-sown roots can be lifted and grown on in the hoop house for winter use.
- The colored-stemmed varieties look good in the flower borders.
- If you grow the whole range of spinach and leaf beet varieties, you can be harvesting all year round.

GROWING MEDIUM

Beet leaf does best in a well-manured bed in a sunny position, with the growing medium being moist but well drained. Although the plants are moderately hardy, to the extent that they can take a few degrees of frost, they will do really well if you lift and grow them in a hoop house, or if you protect the beds with nets or screens.

SOWING AND PLANTING

- **Mid- to late spring** Sow a pinch of 3–4 seeds about ¾ in (18 mm) deep at 9 in (23 cm) intervals across and along the bed. Compact the growing medium and water generously with a fine spray.
- When the seedlings are big enough to handle, pinch out to leave the strongest plants.

GENERAL CARE

If the weather is overly dry, and/or the plants look tired and worse for wear, firm up the growing medium around the plants and add an extra mulch of spent mushroom compost to restrict weed growth and hold in the moisture. Water generously in dry spells. Keep the plants in good order by removing flowers and old and yellow leaves.

HARVESTING

You can harvest from mid-summer round to the following summer – the time depends on the variety, where you live and how much protection you give the plants. Pick little and often to ensure a steady supply of young and tender leaves.

Troubleshooting

Bolting: This is caused by lack of water. You can solve the problem by frequent mulching and daily watering.

Tough leaves and stalks: Prevent these by picking the leaves as soon as they are 6–8 in (15–20 cm) high. Give unwanted produce to neighbors or to your livestock, add it to the compost heap or sell it.

Growing medium: Well-manured
Situation: Sunny
Harvest: Cut stalks at the base with a sharp knife

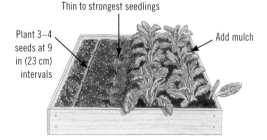

Thin to strongest seedlings

Plant 3–4 seeds at 9 in (23 cm) intervals

Add mulch

SPINACH

When it is freshly picked, swiftly steamed and carefully drained, spinach is mouthwateringly delicious. There are alternatives to spinach, however, such as perpetual spinach, Swiss chard and New Zealand spinach, that might be better suited to your area.

			SOW						**HARVEST**															
mid winter	late winter	early spring	mid spring	late spring	early summer	mid summer	late summer	early autumn	mid autumn	late autumn	early winter	mid winter	late winter	early spring	mid spring	late spring	early summer	mid summer	late summer	early autumn	mid autumn	late autumn	early winter

ABOUT SPINACH

- As with a lot of vegetables, most people only get to eat the tired and much-travelled shop-bought variety and do not know about the succulent taste of fresh, home-grown spinach.
- Popeye the cartoon character loved spinach – it made him instantly strong and bursting with iron-fuelled energy.

GROWING MEDIUM

Spinach does well on almost any growing medium, so much so that it can be grown swiftly as a catch crop in the space between other vegetables. It does not matter too much if after a few pickings it bolts, because it can be swiftly resown at intervals through to late spring. While spinach will grow just about anywhere, it does best in a moisture-retentive bed that has been well manured for a previous crop.

SOWING AND PLANTING

- **Early spring to early summer** Sow a pinch of seeds in 1 in (2.5 cm) deep dibbed holes, about 3 in (7.5 cm) apart across the bed. Compact the growing medium and use a fine spray to water generously.
- When the seedlings are big enough to handle, first pinch out to leave the strongest plants 3 in (7.5 cm) apart, and later remove every other plant to leave plants about 6 in (15 cm) apart. Water before and after thinning, and eat the thinnings.

GENERAL CARE

Stir the surface of the growing medium with a hoe to create a loose, moisture-retentive mulch. Water liberally. If the weather becomes dry, spread a generous layer of spent manure mulch between the plants, and keep watering. A shortage of water will bring about premature bolting.

HARVESTING

You can harvest for most of the year, depending on variety and growing methods. Pick the leaves by hand, breaking off old and tired leaves and removing debris as you do so.

Troubleshooting

Distorted leaves: Probably caused by spinach blight, a disease spread by aphids. Wash the aphids off with a liquid soap and water solution, pull up and burn badly affected plants, and avoid the problem next time by planting resistant varieties on a fresh bed.

Moldy leaves: These are likely to be the result of some sort of mildew. Avoid the problem by generous spacing, so that there is plenty of airflow between the plants.

Leave best seedlings 3 in (7.5 cm) apart

As leaves touch, thin to 6 in (15 cm) apart

Dibble 1 in (2.5 cm) holes to plant a pinch of seeds

Mulch in hot weather and keep well watered

As plants grow, remove and eat every other row

Growing medium: Rich, moist and fertile
Situation: Sunny
Harvest: Use scissors to cut individual leaves

BROCCOLI

Sprouting broccoli, both white and purple, is great when picked young. If you are really keen, are prepared to sow successive varieties and take care at every stage, you can, with a break in early summer, be eating broccoli – spears and flowers – from summer through to mid-autumn.

SOW **PLANT** **HARVEST** DEPENDS ON VARIETY **HARVEST**

| mid winter | late winter | early spring | mid spring | late spring | early summer | mid summer | late summer | early autumn | mid autumn | late autumn | early winter | mid winter | late winter | early spring | mid spring | late spring | early summer | mid summer | late summer | early autumn | mid autumn | late autumn | early winter |

ABOUT BROCCOLI

- If you only know about tough and stringy shop-bought broccoli (the sort that looks good to the eye but leaves a bad fibrous feel in the mouth), home-grown broccoli is going to be a tasty, sweet and tender treat.
- Once the spears show, you can lengthen the harvesting time by picking early at the shooting stage and picking late when the little flowers appear.
- The late flowers can be eaten in their own right and are very tasty.

GROWING MEDIUM

Broccoli does best on a heavy to fertile medium that is well manured and compact. A well-manured, moist but well-drained compact medium usually produces tight, compact flower heads, while a loose, over-rich medium gives loose, open heads. Ideally, the bed needs to be sited in a spot that is open and sunny, yet not windy.

SOWING AND PLANTING

- **Mid- to late spring** Sow seeds about ¼ in (6 mm) deep in prepared seed beds or in deep seed-trays.
- **Early to mid-summer** Plant out on a dull and rainy day, so that you do not have to water, and so that the tender seedlings are not baked by the hot sun. Dibble a grid of holes 12–18 in (30–45 cm) apart, and use lots of water to water the seedlings into place – the spacing depends on variety. Use your fingers to compact the growing medium around the plants.
- You can also sow seeds in early summer for eating in late autumn.

GENERAL CARE

Water the seedlings before and after planting, and then daily. Stir the surface growing medium with a hoe to create a loose mulch and to keep it clean; add an extra mulch if the weather turns dry. Add another thin mulch of well-rotted compost when the plants are well established.

HARVESTING

You can harvest from mid-winter to late spring, and mid-summer to late autumn, depending on the variety and how much protection you give the plants (whether you grow in a hoop house or cover with nets and garden fabric). Start by picking the central spear or head, and follow by picking the little side shoots. Pick every few days to encourage new growth.

Troubleshooting

Caterpillars, butterflies and pigeons: Cover the bed with netting to keep off most of the white butterflies and the pigeons, and remove caterpillars by hand. Inspect the plants daily.

Distorted leaves: These can be caused by aphids and whitefly. Spray the plants with a solution of water and liquid soap. Remove damaged leaves.

Netting protection: Make sure that you wash the netting at the start of the season, so that you remove potentially harmful insects and molds.

Sow seeds thinly in rows ¼ in (6 mm) deep, 6 in (15 cm) apart; keep well watered and thin to 2 in (5 cm) apart

Plant out firmly when 5 in (13 cm) high, water well and protect from insect attack with garden fabric

Harvest: In the following spring, cut center heads first, then every few days cut side shoots

Remove dying leaves

Growing medium: Heavy and fertile
Situation: Open and sunny

CABBAGES

Cabbages are one of the most important vegetables because they provide a year-round supply of green food. They are easy to grow and come in all manner of exciting sizes, shapes, colors and textures — big as a football, pointed, crinkly, smooth, red, white and pink.

SPRING CABBAGE

SOW | PLANT | HARVEST

mid winter	late winter	early spring	mid spring	late spring	early summer	mid summer	late summer	early autumn	mid autumn	late autumn	early winter	mid winter	late winter	early spring	mid spring	late spring	early summer	mid summer	late summer	early autumn	mid autumn	late autumn	early winter

SUMMER CABBAGE

SOW | PLANT | HARVEST

mid winter	late winter	early spring	mid spring	late spring	early summer	mid summer	late summer	early autumn	mid autumn	late autumn	early winter	mid winter	late winter	early spring	mid spring	late spring	early summer	mid summer	late summer	early autumn	mid autumn	late autumn	early winter

WINTER CABBAGE

SOW | PLANT | HARVEST

mid winter	late winter	early spring	mid spring	late spring	early summer	mid summer	late summer	early autumn	mid autumn	late autumn	early winter	mid winter	late winter	early spring	mid spring	late spring	early summer	mid summer	late summer	early autumn	mid autumn	late autumn	early winter

ABOUT CABBAGES

- With planning, you can be eating cabbages all year round.
- Cabbages easily fall victim to too much rain, too much sun, stiff frost, gusty winds, egg-laying butterflies, caterpillars, pigeons and slugs, so you will need to protect the plants.

GROWING MEDIUM

Cabbages thrive on a rich, firm, well-manured, well-drained, moist bed on a sheltered, wind-free site. Varieties like red cabbage require similar conditions, the only difference being that the growing medium needs to be richer.

SOWING AND PLANTING

- Sow seeds, according to the calendar above, ¼ in (6 mm) deep in prepared seed beds or deep seed-trays.
- Plant out according to the calendar above. Dibble holes about 1 ft (30 cm) apart, to make a grid, and water the seedlings in. Firm the growing medium up around the plants.

GENERAL CARE

Water the young plants daily. Use the hoe to pull the growing medium up around the plants to give protection against frost and wind. Once a week, in dry weather, stir the surface of the ground with a hoe to create a loose, water-holding mulch and to keep it free from weeds. Protect against pests by covering the plants with fabric, nets, or clear plastic screens.

HARVESTING

Harvest according to the calendar above. If you cut the cabbage off close to ground level and slash a deep "X" on the end of the stump, four secondary mini-cabbages will sprout up.

Growing medium: Manured, well-drained and firm
Situation: Open and sunny
Harvest: Cut stalk at the base with a sharp knife

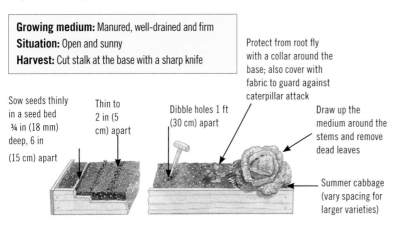

Sow seeds thinly in a seed bed ¾ in (18 mm) deep, 6 in (15 cm) apart

Thin to 2 in (5 cm) apart

Dibble holes 1 ft (30 cm) apart

Protect from root fly with a collar around the base; also cover with fabric to guard against caterpillar attack

Draw up the medium around the stems and remove dead leaves

Summer cabbage (vary spacing for larger varieties)

Troubleshooting

Root fly: Causes rotting stumps and blotchy foliage. Place a felt, plastic or carpet collar around the plant.

Leaf mold: This can seriously stunt the growth of the crop and future crops. Spray the spotted plants with an organic anti-mold mix.

Aphids: Spray with a water and soap solution, wash the mess off with clean water, burn the top 1 in (2.5 cm) or so of growing medium, and burn the plants at the end of the season.

Holes in leaves: Caused by caterpillars and birds. Avoid the problem by growing in a netted cage, like soft fruit.

Distorted roots and poor growth: Probably caused by clubroot. Pull up and burn the plants, and rotate crops in the following year.

Rotting leaves: A smelly, gray-brown rot caused by frost. Pull up and burn affected plants.

CAULIFLOWERS

Growing cauliflowers can be something of a challenge, but if they are well grown they are a joy. They can be used in soup and other dishes, but are superb when broken into large florets, swiftly steamed and served up with a hunk of home-made brown bread and a wedge of Stilton.

| | | | SOW | | | PLANT | | | | | | HARVEST | | | | | | | | | | | | | | |

ABOUT NINE MONTHS OF THE YEAR DEPENDING ON VARIETY

mid winter	late winter	early spring	mid spring	late spring	early summer	mid summer	late summer	early autumn	mid autumn	late autumn	early winter	mid winter	late winter	early spring	mid spring	late spring	early summer	mid summer	late summer	early autumn	mid autumn	late autumn	early winter

ABOUT CAULIFLOWERS

- Although cauliflowers are easy to grow – meaning that it is simple enough to get a cauliflower with an averagely acceptable head – it is very difficult to get a really good, large, firm-headed specimen.
- Cauliflowers are very sensitive to any sort of check – poor growing medium, too dry, too wet, too cold, for example. If they experience a bad time at any point, they will grow wan and loose-headed.

GROWING MEDIUM

Cauliflowers do best in a firm, well-manured, well-drained, moisture-retentive medium in a sunny location. The manure or organic matter should not be fresh, rank or sitting on the surface; rather it needs to be well rotted, positioned at a lower level and well topped with spent compost. A good method is to manure the bed for some other crop, and then to follow on with cauliflowers. If the growing medium is really poor and/or dry, it is best to give up the idea of cauliflowers and grow another crop, because while the plants will most definitely grow in poor conditions, in the sense that they will show plenty of green leaves, the heads will most likely come to nothing.

SOWING AND PLANTING

- **Early to late spring** Sow seeds about ½ in (12 mm) deep in well-prepared seed beds or seed-trays.
- **Early to mid-summer** Plant out in on a dull, rainy day, so that the young plants are not burned and dried by the hot sun. Dibble holes about 12–18 in (30–45 cm) apart, so that there are no more than four plants in a 3 ft (90 cm) square bed. Water the seedlings into the holes. Use your fingers to firm up the growing medium around the plants and water generously.
- Fit loose-fitting "collars," cut from cardboard, plastic or felt, to protect against root fly.

GENERAL CARE

Water the seedlings before and after planting. Stir the surface of the growing medium with a hoe to create a loose mulch and to keep it clean, and spread a mulch of chopped straw or torn cardboard to further hold in the moisture. Water generously. As soon as a head shows, cover by gently folding one or more leaves over to keep it clean and to stop it yellowing.

HARVESTING

If you sow early, autumn and winter varieties, you can harvest from early to mid-summer and from early autumn to the following early summer. Cut the head complete with a few inner wrap-around leaves, or lift the whole plant and store in a frost-free shed.

Troubleshooting

Leaf spot: This shows as rusty brown spots on the leaves. Do your best to get some sort of crop and then burn the rest of the plants at the end of the season, or simply cut your losses and burn the lot. Either way, use another bed next time.

Mealy aphids: A sticky blue-gray mess of aphids is seen on the undersides of the leaves. Spray with a water and liquid soap solution to wash off the aphids, scrape up and remove the top 1 in (2.5 cm) of growing medium and burn the plants at the end of the season.

Holes in leaves: Probably caused by caterpillars and/or birds. Prevent the problem by building a fine-net cage over the crop.

Growing medium: Well-rotted manure under compost
Situation: Sunny
Harvest: Use a sharp knife to cut at the base

Water 5 in (13 cm) high seedlings into planting holes and fit collars

Mulch

Sow thinly ½ in (12 mm) deep, with 8 in (20 cm) between rows

When curds form, protect by snapping two large leaves as a cover

KALE

Kale, also known also as borecole and curly kale, is a somewhat forgotten vegetable. It is hardy, it can be harvested from late autumn to mid-spring, and the young leaves and shoots are so tender and tangy that they will set your taste buds tingling.

				SOW		PLANT								HARVEST													
mid winter	late winter	early spring	mid spring	late spring	early summer	mid summer	late summer	early autumn	mid autumn	late autumn	early winter	mid winter	late winter	early spring	mid spring	late spring	early summer	mid summer	late summer	early autumn	mid autumn	late autumn	early winter

ABOUT KALE

- Although kale is a good, dependable option in its own right, it is also a good choice when you are having problems with growing other greens – for example, if you have trouble with clubroot, heavy frosts or a poor growing medium.
- Kale can be harvested from mid-autumn right through winter to early spring.
- If your plot is very windy, which is not good for Brussels sprouts or large-headed cabbages, hardy low-growing varieties of kale are a good substitute.

GROWING MEDIUM

Kale does best on a strong, deeply worked, well-compacted fertile, growing medium in a sunny corner. It needs plenty of manure, but this must not be so rich and fresh that the plants roar away and become soft – all height and no breadth. A good method is to spread the manure for one crop and then follow on with the kale. In this way, the plants will start off slowly and become hardy. Although kale will put up with just about anything, it does not like loose ground, standing water, or standing water plus a long, hard, bitter frost.

SOWING AND PLANTING

- **Mid- to late spring** Sow seeds, about ½ in (12 mm) deep, directly in the prepared raised bed or in a seed-tray.
- **Early to late summer** Plant out, preferably on a dull, rainy day so that you do not have to follow on with the watering can. Lift the seedlings, dibble holes 15–18 in (38–45 cm) apart in a grid across the bed, water the seedlings into the holes and use your fingers to compact the growing medium around the plants. Water frequently over the next few days.

GENERAL CARE

Water daily. Stir the surface of the growing medium with a hoe to create a loose mulch, and draw the earth up around to give support and to protect from wind and frost. While kale will do OK on an exposed plot, if it is extra gusty you will need to build some sort of protective screen to the windward side – use close-mesh netting or perhaps a screen made from woven wood, not a plastic sheeting screen that will get blown away.

HARVESTING

You can harvest from late autumn to late spring. Use a knife to nip out the crown, and work down the plant picking off the side shoots. Throw away all the old and yellow leaves and generally keep the surface of the bed free from any debris that might give shelter to slugs and other pests.

Troubleshooting

Mealy aphid: This shows as lumpy-looking, blue-gray colonies of sticky aphids on the undersides of the leaves. Spray them off with a water and liquid soap solution, wash with clean water, scrap the top 1 in (2.5 cm) of the bed (to remove the mess of soap and insects), and follow through by burning the plants and all debris at the end of the season.

Poor growth, yellow leaves: Probably caused by wind rock. Avoid the problem next time by supporting the plants with sticks, growing dwarf varieties, or choosing a bed that is well protected on the windward side.

Growing medium: Deeply worked, compact and fertile
Situation: Sunny
Harvest: Removing young leaves with a sharp knife

When young, earth up to the base leaves

Remove dying leaves

Sow a pinch of seeds ½ in (12 mm) deep; thin to the best seedling

Woven wood screen for exposed situations

Protect with fabric from caterpillar attack

5 plants to 3 ft (90 cm) square bed

BRUSSELS SPROUTS

Sprouts are wonderful when lightly steamed and served up firm and tight with a dab of butter or a dash of olive oil, and disgusting when they are overcooked and presented as a soft, seaweedy sludge. If you and your family do not like sprouts, maybe you just need to modify your cooking method!

		SOW			**PLANT**							**HARVEST**															
mid winter	late winter	early spring	mid spring	late spring	early summer	mid summer	late summer	early autumn	mid autumn	late autumn	early winter	mid winter	late winter	early spring	mid spring	late spring	early summer	mid summer	late summer	early autumn	mid autumn	late autumn	early winter

ABOUT BRUSSELS SPROUTS

- Brussels like to be grown in a firm medium, with no rocking in the wind or shallow roots rattling about. They will grow in a loose, rich medium, and such plants will show huge amounts of foliage, but the actual sprouts on your plate will be loose, overblown and light in weight.

GROWING MEDIUM

Brussels sprouts do best in a firm, rich and fertile medium in a good-sized bed that allows for a long season of growth. They do not like to be packed into a small space, nor an overly windy site. A good option is to plant the sprouts in a bed that has been heavily manured for a preceding crop. The ideal is to have the bed in a sunny, open location that is protected from prevailing winds. If your area is windy, choose low-growing varieties and protect the plants with nets and/or woven screens.

SOWING AND PLANTING

- **Early to mid-spring** Sow seeds about ¼ in (6 mm) deep directly in a prepared seed bed or in deep seed-trays.
- **Late spring to early summer** Plant the seedlings out – this is best done on a dull rainy day, so that the plants are not baked in the hot sun. Firm the ground with your foot and dibble holes 18–36 in (45–90 cm) apart, so that you have a staggered row with at least 18 in (45 cm) between plants. Water the seedlings into the holes and use your fingers to compact the growing medium around the plants.

GENERAL CARE

Water the seedlings before and after planting, and then daily. Stir the surface of the medium with a hoe to create a loose mulch and to discourage weeds and troublesome insects. Take away the bottom leaves as they become yellow. When the plants are happily established, spread a mulch of old spent manure or straw to further hold in the moisture. Firm up the growing medium in the autumn. Use strings, screens or nets to protect the growing plants from gusty winds.

HARVESTING

You can harvest from early autumn to early spring – the precise times depends on the variety and your growing methods. Work from bottom to top up the stem, picking only the best tight sprouts. Put tired and damaged sprouts and yellow leaves on the compost heap.

> **Growing medium:** Fertile and firm
> **Situation:** Sheltered and sunny
> **Harvest:** Pick from the bottom before sprouts open

Troubleshooting

Holes in leaves: Grow the sprouts in a netted cage to protect from birds.

Sticky distorted leaves: Caused by aphids and whitefly. Remove damaged leaves, spray with a solution of water and liquid soap, and wash the plants with clean water. Scrape off the top 1 in (2.5 cm) of growing medium and put in on the bonfire.

Distorted root and poor growth: Probably caused by clubroot. Pull up and burn the plants, and plant all future brassicas at the other end of the garden.

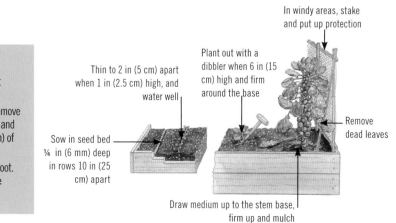

Thin to 2 in (5 cm) apart when 1 in (2.5 cm) high, and water well

Sow in seed bed ¼ in (6 mm) deep in rows 10 in (25 cm) apart

Plant out with a dibbler when 6 in (15 cm) high and firm around the base

In windy areas, stake and put up protection

Remove dead leaves

Draw medium up to the stem base, firm up and mulch

ASPARAGUS

Asparagus is now becoming a popular mainstream vegetable, although it was traditionally considered hard to grow. You might have to wait 3–4 years before you get a really good crop, but once the plants are well established you can expect them to produce for 20 years or more.

SOW | **PLANT**

| mid winter | late winter | early spring | mid spring | late spring | early summer | mid summer | late summer | early autumn | mid autumn | late autumn | early winter | mid winter | late winter | early spring | mid spring | late spring | early summer | mid summer | late summer | early autumn | mid autumn | late autumn | early winter |

YEAR 2-3 — **HARVEST**

| mid winter | late winter | early spring | mid spring | late spring | early summer | mid summer | late summer | early autumn | mid autumn | late autumn | early winter | mid winter | late winter | early spring | mid spring | late spring | early summer | mid summer | late summer | early autumn | mid autumn | late autumn | early winter |

ABOUT ASPARAGUS

- It is easier to grow from one-year-old crowns than seed.
- Some growers think that you can take a small harvest in year two; others say that you should always hold back harvesting into year three or even year four.

GROWING MEDIUM

Asparagus does best in a well-drained, deep, rich, slightly sandy medium that is layered up with a mix of well-rotted farmyard manure and spent mushroom compost. Choose a sheltered but sunny spot. Spread thin mulches of spent mushroom compost to keep down the weeds. You should have no more than one plant on a 3 ft (90 cm) square bed.

SOWING AND PLANTING

- **First year** Open up a trench about 10 in (25 cm) deep and 15 in (38 cm) wide. Cover the base with 3 in (7.5 cm) of gently mounded compost or well-rotted manure.
- **Early to mid-spring** Set the one-year-old crowns 18 in (45 cm) apart, with their roots spread over the mound, and cover with 2–3 in (5–7.5 cm) of well-rotted spent compost. Water generously.

GENERAL CARE

In the first year, let the plants grow until autumn. Just before the berries develop, cut away the foliage, clear away debris and mulch with well-rotted manure topped with spent compost. Repeat in the second year. In the third year, in early spring draw the growing medium over the plants, in mid- to late spring cut selected spears, in summer leave the spears to grow and fall, and in late autumn clear debris and remulch.

HARVESTING

In the third season, from mid-spring to early summer, when good strong spears have pushed 3–4 in (7.5–10 cm) above ground, use your fingers to gently reveal the plant, and then, one spear at a time, take a long-bladed knife and slide the blade at a flat angle into the growing medium to cut the spear at a point 3–4 in (7.5–10 cm) below the ground.

> **Growing medium:** Well-drained and fertile
> **Situation:** Open and sunny
> **Harvest:** 3rd year, sparingly; 4th year onwards, from late spring to early summer

Troubleshooting

Slugs: Use slug barriers or traps and/or remove the slugs by hand.

Roots dying: Burn all the affected plants, and restart on a fresh bed.

Frost damage: Cut away blackened shoots and protect from frost.

Poor harvest: This is probably caused by cutting too much too early.

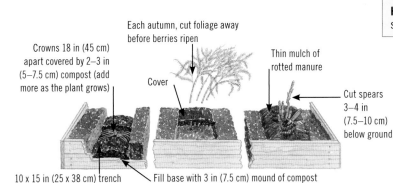

Each autumn, cut foliage away before berries ripen

Crowns 18 in (45 cm) apart covered by 2–3 in (5–7.5 cm) compost (add more as the plant grows)

Cover

Thin mulch of rotted manure

Cut spears 3–4 in (7.5–10 cm) below ground

10 x 15 in (25 x 38 cm) trench

Fill base with 3 in (7.5 cm) mound of compost

CELERY

Growing celery is something of a challenge: digging trenches, binding the plants around with cardboard collars, mounding soil, watering, more mounding soil, and so on, but eating freshly picked celery through the winter months, in soups or with bread and cheese, makes it all worthwhile.

SOW **PLANT** **HARVEST**

mid winter	late winter	early spring	mid spring	late spring	early summer	mid summer	late summer	early autumn	mid autumn	late autumn	early winter	mid winter	late winter	early spring	mid spring	late spring	early summer	mid summer	late summer	early autumn	mid autumn	late autumn	early winter

ABOUT CELERY

- Growing celery involves lots of procedures and effort such as building extra frames, planting out, and stacking the frames for blanching. It is not particularly hard work, but it is time-consuming.
- Self-blanching varieties remove the need for earthing up, but many lack the taste and texture of the old forms.
- If you grow traditional and self-blanching varieties, you can be eating celery from mid-autumn to late winter.

GROWING MEDIUM

Celery does best in a deep, rich, heavy and moist but well-drained medium in an open and sunny position. The bed needs to be damp, but not so wet that water puddles on the surface – celery needs lots of water but will not do well if the bed is waterlogged or sour. Make sure that the bed is prepared well in advance with lots of well-rotted manure. The growing medium that you have drawn to the side in preparation for mounding soil must be fine and friable.

SOWING AND PLANTING

- **Early to mid-spring** Sow seeds under glass about ½ in(12 mm) deep in prepared seed-trays. As soon as the seedlings are big enough to handle, pot them into peat pots.
- **Late spring to early summer** Plant out in a bed, 9 in (23 cm) apart.

GENERAL CARE

Water the plants daily. Stir the surface of the growing medium with a hoe to create a loose mulch. Remove suckers and debris. As the plants gain in height, add additional frames to the bed and keep topping up with mulches of well-rotted manure and garden compost so that the stalks are well covered. In frosty weather, cover the beds with a mulch of chopped straw or torn cardboard, followed by a thin mulch of spent mushroom compost topped with mats of cardboard, carpet or anything that will keep out a stiff frost. Remove the mats if the weather turns wet or mild.

HARVESTING

Harvest self-blanching varieties from late summer to late autumn, and traditional varieties from late autumn to early spring. Use a fork to ease the plant from the ground. Leave remaining plants covered. At the end of the season, when the plants look finished, there is still a chance that the hearts can be saved after cutting away the squashy brown mess.

Troubleshooting

Brown spotted leaves: Probably caused by viruses and/or fungi. Save what you can, pull up and burn the plants, and use a different bed next time.

Slugs and snails: These create open wounds that can cause secondary damage. Remove them by hand on a daily basis.

Brown rot: This shows as a rotten heart at the lifting stage. Burn the plants and try again on another plot.

Growing medium: Deep, fertile and moist
Situation: Sunny
Harvest: Use a fork to lever it out

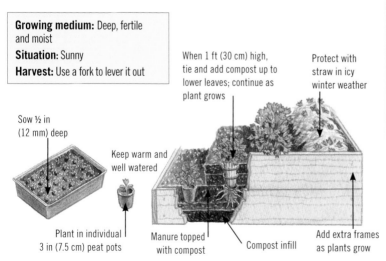

Sow ½ in (12 mm) deep

Keep warm and well watered

Plant in individual 3 in (7.5 cm) peat pots

When 1 ft (30 cm) high, tie and add compost up to lower leaves; continue as plant grows

Protect with straw in icy winter weather

Manure topped with compost

Compost infill

Add extra frames as plants grow

ARTICHOKES, GLOBE

The exotic-looking globe artichoke is grown for its flowers, which form fleshy, scale-covered heads. Although it is a perennial that can be left in place in much the same way as rhubarb, it can just as easily be grown as an annual or even as a biennial.

				SOW	PLANT			HARVEST													
mid winter	late winter	early spring	mid spring	late spring	early summer	mid summer	late summer	early autumn	mid autumn	late autumn	early winter	mid winter	late winter	early spring	mid spring	late spring	early summer	mid summer	late summer	early autumn	mid autumn	late autumn	early winter

ABOUT GLOBE ARTICHOKES

- Globe artichokes can be grown from seed, or better still from root suckers, in much the same way as rhubarb.
- A healthy plant will grow to a height of about 4 ft (1.2 m).
- Throw away the first heads in the first year, and start harvesting in earnest in the second season after planting.
- Plants reach their peak in the third or fourth year after planting.

GROWING MEDIUM

Traditionally it was grown in beds, in a deep, rich soil with full exposure to sunlight. It needs plenty of moisture throughout the summer months, and a well-drained growing medium during the winter. Prepare the bed with layers of well-rotted farmyard manure, with extra mulches of rotted manure in the spring and autumn.

SOWING AND PLANTING

- **Mid-spring** Plant the suckers singly about 4 in (10 cm) deep, say two plants to a 3 ft (90 cm) square bed.
- Tamp the plants in well, water daily and provide shade, until the plant looks to be well established.

GENERAL CARE

In the first season, water and mulch, discard the heads in the winter, cut the foliage down to the ground and cover the crowns with straw. In the second season, remove the straw, and apply a mulch of manure in the spring. Huge heads can be tough and stringy, so go for the middle size.

HARVESTING

Harvest from early summer onwards when the heads are mature but the scales still closed. Cut the crowns off with 2–3 in (5–7.5 cm) of stem and stand them in water until needed. Cut the stems down and allow the new suckers to produce a late second crop.

Troubleshooting

Slugs: Use slug barriers or traps and/or remove the slugs by hand.

Insect attack: Pinch out affected areas, spray with a solution of water and liquid soap, remove the stale top 1 in (2.5 cm) of growing medium and replace with a fresh mulch of well-rotted manure.

Rust brown heads: This is caused by fungus damage that affects the heads and flowers. Carefully cut and burn any affected plants.

Growing medium: Deep and rich
Situation: Sunny

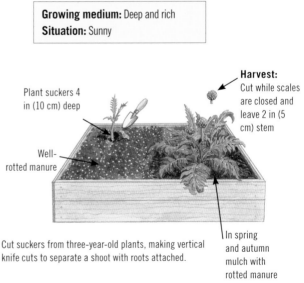

Plant suckers 4 in (10 cm) deep

Well-rotted manure

Harvest: Cut while scales are closed and leave 2 in (5 cm) stem

In spring and autumn mulch with rotted manure

Cut suckers from three-year-old plants, making vertical knife cuts to separate a shoot with roots attached.

PEAS

Although botanically the pea is defined as a fruit, most people think of it as a vegetable. The fascinating thing is that although many children will make some sort of fuss about eating most other vegetables, they tend to like the taste, texture and shape of peas.

SOW ▼   **HARVEST** ▼

| mid winter | late winter | early spring | mid spring | late spring | early summer | mid summer | late summer | early autumn | mid autumn | late autumn | early winter | mid winter | late winter | early spring | mid spring | late spring | early summer | mid summer | late summer | early autumn | mid autumn | late autumn | early winter |

ABOUT PEAS

- Peas take about 60 days to mature.
- Varieties like mangetout and sugar snap are eaten complete with their pods. Harvest when the peas just begin to show in the pods.
- Pea roots store nitrogen, so bury them at the end of the season to improve the fertility of the growing medium.

GROWING MEDIUM

Peas do well in a deep, well-drained, moist growing medium that has been well manured for a previous crop, in a warm, sheltered position. Peas need lots of moisture. If you see that the bed is dry, soak it with water and mulch the bed with well-rotted spent manure.

SOWING AND PLANTING

- **Early spring to mid-summer** Sow seeds in 1–2 in (2.5–5 cm) deep furrows in a 5–6 in (13–15 cm) grid across the bed, or under glass in lengths of 3 in (7.5 cm) wide plastic gutter; when the plants are established, slide them into place in the bed. Firm in and water generously.
- Cover the bed with wire mesh, twigs, cotton or fabric to keep the birds off.
- Watch out for pigeons, rabbits, mice and cats, which can all be a problem.

GENERAL CARE

When the plants are well established, stir the surface of the growing medium with a hoe. Repeat this at least every week, especially in dry weather. In long dry spells, drench the growing medium with water and heap a mulch of old manure over the bed. When the pods begin to fill out, cover the bed with nets and be on the lookout for mice.

HARVESTING

Harvest from early summer to mid-autumn. Peas swell rapidly, so gather them when young. Pick every 2–3 days to encourage new pods to develop.

Troubleshooting

Aphids: These show as a sticky, gray mess on the underside of the foliage. Spray the mess off with a mix of water and liquid soap, wash with clean water, then scrape the resulting soapy mess up from the bed and burn it.

Mold and mildew: This appears as yellow leaves and/or white patches, usually in dry weather. Drench with an organic spray; if this fails, save what you can of the crop, burn the plants, and choose a disease-resistant variety next time.

Mice: A terribly frustrating nuisance. The best advice is to sow in the gutters as described above, and then make a huge effort to protect the growing plants with nets, garden fabric, wire mesh and traps.

Pea moth Little maggots are found within the pod. Eat what you can, and go for a different variety and a different bed next **time.**

Growing medium: Well-drained and fertile
Situation: Sunny and sheltered
Harvest: Pick regularly before they toughen

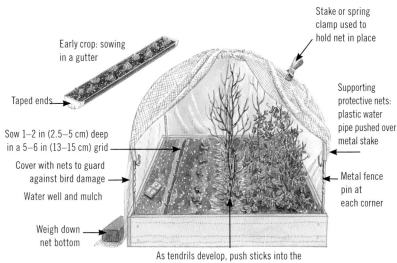

Early crop: sowing in a gutter

Taped ends

Sow 1–2 in (2.5–5 cm) deep in a 5–6 in (13–15 cm) grid

Cover with nets to guard against bird damage

Water well and mulch

Weigh down net bottom

As tendrils develop, push sticks into the soil to support the plants

Stake or spring clamp used to hold net in place

Supporting protective nets: plastic water pipe pushed over metal stake

Metal fence pin at each corner

FRENCH BEANS

The flavor of French beans may not compare with runner beans, but they are well worth planting because they can be harvested two or three weeks before runner beans. If you plant them under cover, you can enjoy your first little bean feast early in the summer.

				SOW		**HARVEST**																		
mid winter	late winter	early spring	mid spring	late spring	early summer	mid summer	late summer	early autumn	mid autumn	late autumn	early winter	mid winter	late winter	early spring	mid spring	late spring	early summer	mid summer	late summer	early autumn	mid autumn	late autumn	early winter

FRENCH BEAN FACTS

- French beans like to be in an airy situation, to the extent that some varieties will present a splotchy leaf mildew if you overdo the garden fabric protection.
- French beans are a good option if you are short of space.
- You can lengthen the total season by planting a couple of weeks early and then by protecting the young plants with garden fabric and/or plastic netting.

GROWING MEDIUM

Although just about any well-prepared soil will yield a fair crop, French beans do best in a bed that has been generously mulched with well-rotted manure in the previous season. Dust the bed with a light dressing of lime a week or two before the seeds are sown. As soon as the plants are a couple inches high, spread a mulch of old manure over the bed to hold in the moisture. Be aware, if you are planting extra early, that you must protect against gusty winds and drafts. As with runner beans, French beans must be protected against frosts and driving rain.

SOWING AND PLANTING

- **Mid- to late spring for early crop** Prepare 2 in (5 cm) deep furrows. Sow the seeds about 6 in (15 cm) apart in all directions so that you get about 20 plants in a 3 ft (90 cm) square bed. Water generously.
- **Late spring through to early summer for main crop** Sow as above.
- **Early to late summer** Sow as above.
- Early and late crops will need to be protected with cloches, nets, mini hoop houses, or anything that keeps off the wind and frost.

GENERAL CARE

When the plants are a few inches high, very carefully draw the growing medium around the stems and, if the weather looks in any way cold or gusty, ring the bed with a screen of netting. When the plants look well established, spread a mulch of old spent manure or mushroom compost to hold back the weeds and to retain moisture. Water generously at the roots – but keep the water away from the foliage. Support climbing varieties. If the weather threatens to be windy, bind the bed of beans around with soft string, so that they give each other support, and rig up a screen on the windward side

HARVESTING

You can start picking from mid-summer onwards when the pods are plump and firm. Pick with both hands, one hand supporting the stem and the other twisting off the pods.

Troubleshooting
Blackfly: Treat in the same way as broad beans.
Wilting stems: Dispose of the plants and replant new ones.
Blotchy, brown-yellow leaves: Likely to be blight. Dispose of damaged plants and avoid planting French beans on the same plot for a couple of years.

Seeds 2 in (5 cm) deep, 6 in (15 cm) apart

Pull earth up to support young plants

Old spent manure mulch

Growing medium: Medium to light
Situation: Airy
Harvest: Pick regularly before they toughen

RUNNER BEANS

The runner bean is a wonderful and popular vegetable. Building the support structures is an inventive activity, and then the mature plants are pleasing to the eye, produce well and have a long growing season. A plate of runner beans sprinkled with olive oil and cider vinegar is quite delicious!

					SOW		**HARVEST**																
mid winter	late winter	early spring	mid spring	late spring	early summer	mid summer	late summer	early autumn	mid autumn	late autumn	early winter	mid winter	late winter	early spring	mid spring	late spring	early summer	mid summer	late summer	early autumn	mid autumn	late autumn	early winter

ABOUT RUNNER BEANS

- Some growers favor sowing the seeds directly into the prepared ground between late spring and early summer. Others opt for an early start by raising seedlings under glass between mid- and late spring, and some do both.
- They can be grown as perennials if you lift and store the roots and the end of one season, and plant them afresh at the beginning of another.
- Supports – teepees, wire fences, frames and so on – must be very strong and stable.

GROWING MEDIUM

If you want a heavy crop, layer the beds up with lots of well-rotted farmyard manure, garden compost and spent mushroom compost. If your site is windy, set the seeds or plants about 8 in (20 cm) apart and build a super-strong teepee for maximum support.

SOWING AND PLANTING

- **Early in the year** Excavate the bed, fill it with rotted manure and top it off with a mulch of mushroom compost a few weeks before planting.
- **Mid-spring** Raise seedlings under glass and plant seeds about 1 in (2.5 cm) deep in compost-filled pots (then plant out in late spring to early summer); alternatively, sow seeds directly in the ground. Either way, set them about 6–8 in (15–20 cm) apart over the whole bed.

GENERAL CARE

Pull up large weeds, gently stir the growing medium with a hoe to create a loose mulch and cover with mushroom compost. In very dry weather, spread a mulch of straw or old manure over the whole bed to help hold in the moisture. Pinch out the tips when they reach the top of the frame.

HARVESTING

You can harvest from mid-summer to mid-autumn. Pick every few days rather than once a week. If you allow pods to grow to maturity, the plants will come to a halt.

Troubleshooting

Insect pests: Pinch out and remove affected areas and spray with a solution of water and liquid soap.

Blotchy leaves: Pull up and burn diseased plants, and avoid planting on the same plot for a couple of years.

Nibbles and notches: These are evidence of bean weevil. Avoid the problem by hoeing around the young plants when they are at the two- or three-leaf stage.

Mice: Damage shows as nibbles and mess. Set traps.

Withered plants: This problem can usually be prevented simply by lots of watering at the flowering stage.

Growing medium: Very rich and fertile
Situation: Open and sunny
Harvest: Pick regularly before they toughen

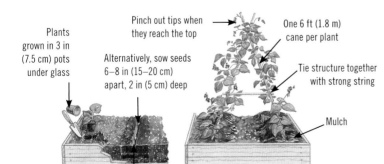

Plants grown in 3 in (7.5 cm) pots under glass

Pinch out tips when they reach the top

Alternatively, sow seeds 6–8 in (15–20 cm) apart, 2 in (5 cm) deep

One 6 ft (1.8 m) cane per plant

Tie structure together with strong string

Mulch

2 ft (60 cm) wide, 9 in (23 cm) deep trench

BROAD BEANS

Broad beans are a perfect choice for no-dig raised-bed vegetable gardening – they are hardy, they flourish in tight groups or blocks, they have a long growing season, they produce well, and, best of all, they can easily be stored by freezing or drying.

SOW · **HARVEST** · **SOW (WINTER CROP)** · **HARVEST (WINTER CROP)**

mid winter	late winter	early spring	mid spring	late spring	early summer	mid summer	late summer	early autumn	mid autumn	late autumn	early winter	mid winter	late winter	early spring	mid spring	late spring	early summer	mid summer	late summer	early autumn	mid autumn	late autumn	early winter

BROAD BEAN FACTS

- Broad beans are known variously around the world as fava beans, field beans, bell beans and tic beans.
- If you sow in mid- to late autumn in year 1, for cropping in the early summer of year 2, and also sow from late winter through to late spring in year 2, then you will be able to eat broad beans the whole summer long, and you will have a good surplus for freezing or drying.
- Overwintered plants seem to be more resistant to blackfly.

GROWING MEDIUM

Broad beans do best in a deep, rich, moisture-retentive soil that has bean enriched with well-rotted farmyard manure. A good starting point is to increase the depth of the raised bed to about 18 in (45 cm), and then increase the amount of manure for the early crop, and reduce the manure and add a bit of sand for the main crop. Generally, you should choose beds that are in a light, airy spot.

SOWING AND PLANTING

- **Late winter through to mid-spring** Sow main crop in sandy soil. Prepare 3 in (7.5 cm) deep furrows or dibbed holes and sow single seeds about 8 in (20 cm) apart in all directions. Water.
- **Winter-hardy crop through late autumn** Sow as above.
- Pick a sunny spot – and a bed which did not have beans growing in it in the previous year.

GENERAL CARE

When the plants are a few inches high, draw the soil around the stems and add a thin mulch of well-rotted manure over the whole bed. As soon as the flowers are well formed, pinch out the top shoots; this will plump up the pods and hold back the blackfly. Ring the bed with sticks and string so that the whole block of plants is well supported.

HARVESTING

Depending on the variety and the planting date, you can harvest between early summer and mid-autumn. When the beans are firm, tweak the pods from the stem. When the crop is finished, cut the plant right down to the ground to leave the roots in the soil.

Early: Rich and moisture-retentive with well-rotted manure added

Main: Less manure, add sand

Situation: Airy

Harvest: Pick when beans are formed inside pods

Troubleshooting

Wind damage: Make sure that each bed or block of plants is well supported with sticks and string, plus, if the wind is bad, ring the bed with close-mesh screen of plastic mesh or even with woven willow panels.

Blackfly: Pinch out and remove badly affected areas, and spray the plant with a solution of water and soap liquid.

Nibbles and notches: Nibbles around the leaf edges are caused by the bean weevil. Avoid the problem by spraying with an organic mix and by hoeing the area around the young plants.

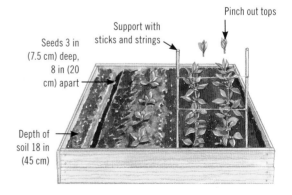

Pinch out tops

Support with sticks and strings

Seeds 3 in (7.5 cm) deep, 8 in (20 cm) apart

Depth of soil 18 in (45 cm)

SWEETCORN

Also known as Indian corn, sugar corn, pole corn, maize and many other names, sweetcorn was not so long ago thought by many British gardeners to be an outlandish item. Now it is commonplace to see fields bulging with the corn on the cob, and most keen gardeners grow it as a main crop.

| SOW | | | | | | | HARVEST | | | | | | | | | | | | | | | | | |

mid winter	late winter	early spring	mid spring	late spring	early summer	mid summer	late summer	early autumn	mid autumn	late autumn	early winter	mid winter	late winter	early spring	mid spring	late spring	early summer	mid summer	late summer	early autumn	mid autumn	late autumn	early winter

ABOUT SWEETCORN

- Sweetcorn is a good starter crop for interested children.
- Sweetcorn needs a growing season of 70–120 frost-free days after planting.
- Some varieties grow to 5–6 ft (1.5–1.8 m) in height.

GROWING MEDIUM

Sweetcorn likes a well-prepared, deeply worked, well-drained, light to sandy growing medium in a sheltered, sunny position. Dig in plenty of manure and compost in autumn, or grow it in a bed that has been well manured for a previous crop. Sweetcorn needs lots of moisture. If the medium dries out, soak it with water and cover with a mulch of well-rotted spent manure.

SOWING AND PLANTING

- **Mid-spring** Sow 1 seed 1 in (2.5 cm) deep per peat pot, put under glass or plastic and water generously. Alternatively, plant directly in the bed at a grid spacing of 1 ft (30 cm), and protect with clear plastic.
- **Late spring to early summer** Harden the plants off by standing them outside in a sheltered position in the sun for a few days, bringing them inside when the sun goes down. Dig holes 1 ft (30 cm) apart in a grid pattern, and use a fine spray to water the peat pots into place.

GENERAL CARE

Use a hoe to stir the surface of the bed to create a loose mulch, and your fingers to heap the mulch up to support the stems. Be very careful not to damage the stems when the plants are at the young and fragile stage. If the weather turns very dry, water generously and cover the ground with a thick mulch of spent mushroom compost. Protect with a net and give extra water when the cobs start to show. Support any top-heavy plants with poles.

HARVESTING

Harvest from mid-summer to mid-autumn, when the cobs show black-brown, tail-like silks. Test the grains with your nail: if they ooze a milky fluid under pressure, they are ready. Pick the cobs by hand, with a swift twist-and-down action. For maximum taste, texture and sweetness, cook and eat within 10 minutes of harvesting.

Growing medium: Fertile and well-drained
Situation: Sunny and sheltered
Harvest: When cobs have brown tails/silks

Troubleshooting

Distorted growth: Probably caused by the frit fly. You will notice distorted leaves, general weak growth and small white maggots inside the young shoots. Avoid the problem next time by growing a different variety on a different bed, and by growing under cover until the plants are beyond the five-leaf stage.

Mushroom-like growths: These growths on the cob are probably caused by smut infection. Pull up and burn at the first sign of a problem, use another bed next time, and grow a resistant variety.

Birds and mice: Protect the cobs when they begin to swell.

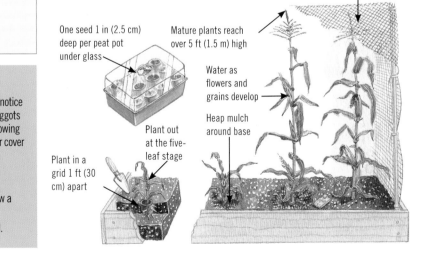

Bird damage: Net when cobs show

One seed 1 in (2.5 cm) deep per peat pot under glass

Mature plants reach over 5 ft (1.5 m) high

Water as flowers and grains develop

Heap mulch around base

Plant out at the five-leaf stage

Plant in a grid 1 ft (30 cm) apart

ONIONS AND SHALLOTS

If, like many people, you eat onions on a daily basis – in stir-fries, soups, salads, pickles, chutney, sandwiches, stews and so on – why not increase your options and potential by growing a whole range of varieties of onions and shallots? They can easily be stored for use whenever you want them.

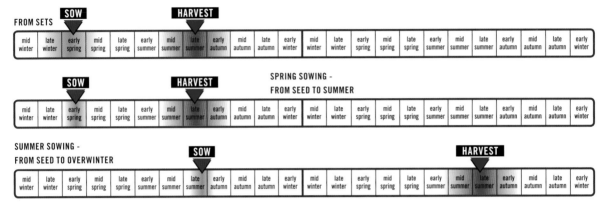

FROM SETS — SOW (early spring), HARVEST (mid/late summer)

mid winter	late winter	early spring	mid spring	late spring	early summer	mid summer	late summer	early autumn	mid autumn	late autumn	early winter	mid winter	late winter	early spring	mid spring	late spring	early summer	mid summer	late summer	early autumn	mid autumn	late autumn	early winter

SPRING SOWING – FROM SEED TO SUMMER — SOW (early spring), HARVEST (mid/late summer)

mid winter	late winter	early spring	mid spring	late spring	early summer	mid summer	late summer	early autumn	mid autumn	late autumn	early winter	mid winter	late winter	early spring	mid spring	late spring	early summer	mid summer	late summer	early autumn	mid autumn	late autumn	early winter

SUMMER SOWING – FROM SEED TO OVERWINTER — SOW (late summer), HARVEST (mid/late summer – early autumn)

mid winter	late winter	early spring	mid spring	late spring	early summer	mid summer	late summer	early autumn	mid autumn	late autumn	early winter	mid winter	late winter	early spring	mid spring	late spring	early summer	mid summer	late summer	early autumn	mid autumn	late autumn	early winter

ABOUT ONIONS AND SHALLOTS

- Onion sets are expensive, and seeds take lots of time but cost less.
- Shallots are planted singly – when they are planted in spring, they grow to produce a hand-sized cluster.

GROWING MEDIUM

Onions do best on a deeply worked, well-manured, moist, well-drained, friable, fertile, sandy growing medium in a sunny position.

SOWING AND PLANTING PROCEDURES

- Sow/plant according to the calendar.
- Sow ¼ in (6 mm) deep in boxes under cover, thin out when big enough to handle, and plant out in the beds on a 3–4 in (7.5–10 cm) grid when the plants are the size of slender pencils.
- Dig holes about 1 in (2.5 cm) deep, trim roots down to 1 in (2.5 cm), trim the leaves to remove the yellow tips, and water the onions into the holes.

GENERAL CARE

Hoe the surface to create a loose mulch. When the swelling bulb begins to show, draw the medium slightly away so the bulb sits high on the surface. Do not water, but keep hoeing the ground.

HARVESTING

Harvest from early summer to early autumn. To ripen, when the plants begin to die back bend the tops over. When they start to turn yellow, ease the onions from the ground and leave them to dry on nets or racks.

Growing medium: Light, well-drained
Situation: Sunny
Harvest: When they die back naturally

Troubleshooting

Yellow, drooping leaves: Caused by onion fly. Pull up and burn the plant if you see maggots.

Dark green, drooping leaves: Too much nitrogen in the growing medium. Avoid the problem by using well-rotted manure.

Orange-brown blotches: Caused by rust. Spray with an organic mix, or pull up and burn affected plants.

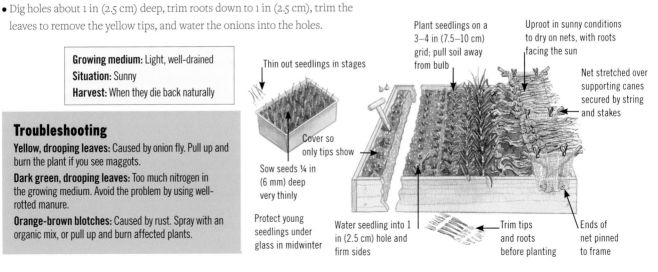

Thin out seedlings in stages

Cover so only tips show

Sow seeds ¼ in (6 mm) deep very thinly

Protect young seedlings under glass in midwinter

Plant seedlings on a 3–4 in (7.5–10 cm) grid; pull soil away from bulb

Water seedling into 1 in (2.5 cm) hole and firm sides

Trim tips and roots before planting

Uproot in sunny conditions to dry on nets, with roots facing the sun

Net stretched over supporting canes secured by string and stakes

Ends of net pinned to frame

LEEKS

If you want a really tasty item, leeks are wonderful – you can enjoy them tender and raw, cooked in soups, or chopped, steamed and served with olive oil and fresh bread, for example. The plants seem to be able to withstand any extreme of weather from wind and rain to snow and severe frosts.

		SOW				**PLANT**							**HARVEST**											
mid winter	late winter	early spring	mid spring	late spring	early summer	mid summer	late summer	early autumn	mid autumn	late autumn	early winter	mid winter	late winter	early spring	mid spring	late spring	early summer	mid summer	late summer	early autumn	mid autumn	late autumn	early winter

ABOUT LEEKS

- Leeks are grown and tended in much the same way as celery – they need a long growing season.
- Traditionally, gardeners thought that leeks improved heavy soil.
- Because they can stand frosts, leeks are a very good option for winter use, when other vegetables are scarce.
- Varieties range from small and mild to large and strong-tasting. Carefully choose a variety to suit both your tastes and your location.
- If you get it right, every plant will give you 1 lb (0.5 kg) or so of edible leek – or, put another way, it will feed two hungry adults.

GROWING MEDIUM

Leeks can be grown in an open site on just about any soil, but if you are after a really good fertile crop your growing medium needs to be of a good depth, well manured and moist (meaning that, while the growing medium within the bed feels damp to the touch, the ground around and under the bed is well drained). The drainage specifics need emphasizing, because, if you get it wrong, the hearts will rot out.

SOWING AND PLANTING

- **Mid- to late winter or early to mid-spring (depending on variety)** Sow about ¼ in (6 mm) deep in trays and keep under glass or plastic. Thin to 2 in (5 cm) apart.
- **Mid-summer** On a showery day, dibble 6 in (15 cm) deep holes at 6–8 in (15–20 cm) intervals on a grid to give you 25–30 plants to a 3 ft (90 cm) square bed. Drop one seedling into each dibbed hole and gently top up with water.

GENERAL CARE

Stir the surface of the growing medium with a hoe to create a loose mulch. Along the way the dibbled holes will gradually fill with loose medium to support and blanch the growing plants. Once the transplanted seedlings are well established, surround them with a mulch of chopped straw or old spent manure, and spend time every week with the hoe drawing the earth up. Repeat this procedure throughout the season until all but the tops of the plants are covered. Alternatievly, add extra frames on the bed and top up with mulches, so that the stems are always covered. Water frequently.

HARVESTING

You can harvest from early autumn to late spring – the precise time depends on your chosen variety and growing methods. Use a fork to help ease the roots from the ground, and lift as needed.

> **Growing medium:** Rich, moist and free-draining
> **Situation:** Open
> **Harvest when needed:** Lever with a fork to loosen soil

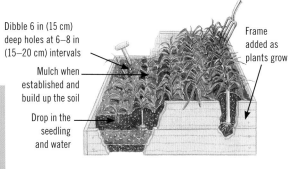

Dibble 6 in (15 cm) deep holes at 6–8 in (15–20 cm) intervals

Frame added as plants grow

Mulch when established and build up the soil

Drop in the seedling and water

Troubleshooting

Yellow drooping leaves: Most likely caused by onion fly, and shows as yellow leaves and maggots in the stem and roots. Pull up and burn badly affected plants.

Sagging stems: This suggests that the plants need additional earthing up.

Orange-brown blotches: Probably caused by rust. Pull up and burn affected plants at the first sign of a problem.

Dark green, drooping leaves: Too much nitrogen. Avoid the problem by only using well-rotted manure.

GARLIC

Many people love eating garlic in soups, stews, stir-fries, salads and numerous other dishes. One of best ways to enjoy it is to sprinkle finely chopped garlic on toast that has been drenched in high-quality olive oil. It is also very good for you – eating raw garlic is reputed to ward off colds.

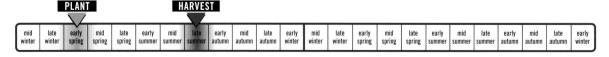

PLANT   **HARVEST**

mid winter	late winter	early spring	mid spring	late spring	early summer	mid summer	late summer	early autumn	mid autumn	late autumn	early winter	mid winter	late winter	early spring	mid spring	late spring	early summer	mid summer	late summer	early autumn	mid autumn	late autumn	early winter

ABOUT GARLIC

- Garlic is grown in much the same way as onion sets – the cloves are set just below the surface, and they like a rich, moist, well-drained growing medium in a warm, sunny position.
- Despite all the mysterious folk tales surrounding garlic, it is surprisingly simple to grow.
- Garlic is very easy to store. You just string it up, like onions, and store it in a cool, dry room or shed.
- You can plant and grow garlic cloves saved from your own crop, but cloves from shop-bought garlic do not seem to flourish.

GROWING MEDIUM

Garlic likes a light growing medium that contains plenty of well-rotted manure from a previous crop. Make sure when you are planning where to grow your garlic that you select a well-drained bed that is positioned in a warm, sunny corner – perhaps against the wall of the house or in the sunny lea of a shed.

SOWING AND PLANTING

- **Autumn or early spring** Plant single cloves 4–6 in (10–15 cm) deep, in a grid pattern that sets the mature plants about 6–8 in (15–20 cm) apart. Compact the growing medium over the clove and water generously.
- When the shoots begin to appear, use your fingertips to ease the medium gently up and around the plant to protect it.
- Water generously throughout the growing period, but never allow the plants to sit in a puddle of water.

GENERAL CARE

Every day or so, gently stir the surface of the growing medium with a hoe to create a loose mulch, maybe add a thin mulch of spent manure to keep the weeds down, and lightly water. Birds are attracted by the shoots to the extent that they will sometimes pull the little cloves out of the ground. You can prevent this by covering the bed with a net.

HARVESTING

When ready to harvest, sometime in late summer when the green foliage has fallen over and died back, use a small fork to ease the bulbs from the ground. Dry them in the sun, and string them up and store in a cool, dry place, just like onions.

Troubleshooting

Bolting: This is caused by alternating wet-drought conditions and/or too much shade. Avoid the problem next time by watering little and often, and choosing beds that are in full sun.

Birds: These can be a real nuisance when the green buds are just appearing. Avoid the problem by netting the crop until the plants are well established.

White rot: A squashy white rot appears on the bulbs. Burn the affected bulbs and plant in a fresh bed next time.

Growing medium: Rich, moist and well drained
Situation: Sunny
Harvest: When leaves turn yellow

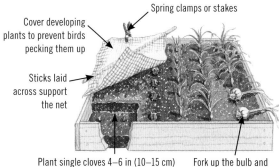

Spring clamps or stakes

Cover developing plants to prevent birds pecking them up

Sticks laid across support the net

Plant single cloves 4–6 in (10–15 cm) deep and 6–8 in (15–20 cm) apart

Fork up the bulb and leave in sun to dry

POTATOES

Most people love potatoes. It may not make economical sense to grow your own, when you can buy them cheaply from a supermarket, but when you have a plate of tasty new potatoes, freshly cooked with mint and a dab of butter or dribble of olive oil, you will be very glad that you did.

			PLANT				**HARVEST**																	
mid winter	late winter	early spring	mid spring	late spring	early summer	mid summer	late summer	early autumn	mid autumn	late autumn	early winter	mid winter	late winter	early spring	mid spring	late spring	early summer	mid summer	late summer	early autumn	mid autumn	late autumn	early winter

ABOUT POTATOES

- Potatoes are rich in vitamin C.
- The fiber content of a potato complete with skin equals that of many wholegrain cereals.

GROWING MEDIUM

Although just about any growing medium will support potatoes, the make-up of the medium in the garden contributes to the final flavor and texture of the potato on the plate. For example, a heavy, wet mix tends to result in a slick, soapy, slightly yellow potato, while potatoes grown on a dry, sandy medium are often loose and fluffy. As for the underlying soil conditions, a badly drained bed will produce good potatoes in a hot, dry year, but the potatoes will suffer if the weather becomes humid. Potatoes do best in a well-drained, clay to sandy bed, with plenty of mulches of well-rotted manure from a previous crop, in an open, sunny position.

SOWING AND PLANTING

- **Sprouting for early crop** In late winter, sit the seed potatoes, rose end up, in trays in a light, airy shed, until they produce a few 1 in (2.5 cm) shoots.
- **Sowing early** In early to mid-spring, dig 6 in (15 cm) deep holes, 12–16 in (30–40 cm) apart – say four potatoes in a 3 ft (90 cm) square bed – and set the seed potatoes in place so that the shoots are uppermost. Cover them.
- **Sowing under plastic** In early to mid-spring, set the sprouted seed potatoes on the surface of the bed 12–16 in (30–40 cm) apart as above, mulch with well-rotted garden compost and cover with black plastic sheet buried at the edges. When the shoots begin to push up against the plastic, cut slits at each planting point to allow the shoots to emerge.

GENERAL CARE

As soon as the foliage appears, mulch with well-rotted mushroom compost. Repeat this so that the foliage is always just about visible. If the weather turns frosty, cover with newspaper or garden fabric. In very hot weather, stir the surface of the bed with a hoe. Always be on the lookout for slugs. If the weather is very dry, spread a mulch of spent manure or chopped straw around the plants to hold in the residual moisture.

HARVESTING

Harvest from early summer to mid-autumn. Lift new potatoes when the flowers are fully open; otherwise wait until the tops have died down. To harvest, take a fork, push it down towards what you estimate is the outer limits of the clump, and gently undermine and lift the whole plant. Leave the potatoes on the surface until the end of the session, and then sort them into "good" and "damaged." Eat the damaged ones first. Lift new potatoes as needed. Store main crop potatoes in shallow boxes in a dry, dark, frost-free shed.

> **Growing medium:** Deep, fertile and well-drained
> **Situation:** Open and sunny
> **Harvest:** Earlies when flowers are fully open; others when tops have died down

Troubleshooting

Brown blotchy leaves: Probably caused by potato blight. Lift and burn the crop. Avoid the problem next time by using resistant seed and planting in a different bed.

Squashy potatoes: This is most likely caused by lack of water and/or repeated wet-dry-wet-dry conditions.

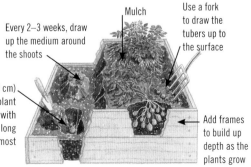

Sprouting: tubers should be rose end up

Dig 6 in (15 cm) deep holes; plant seed potatoes with 1 in (2.5 cm) long shoots uppermost

Protect from frost with garden fabric if frost is forecast

Every 2–3 weeks, draw up the medium around the shoots

Mulch

Use a fork to draw the tubers up to the surface

Add frames to build up depth as the plants grow

CARROTS

Carrots are a treat to the eye, they smell and taste good, they can be eaten cooked or raw, they are relatively easy to grow, they can be stored for long periods, they are wonderfully easy to prepare, most children like them, and they can be eaten from early summer to early winter.

			SOW			HARVEST																	
mid winter	late winter	early spring	mid spring	late spring	early summer	mid summer	late summer	early autumn	mid autumn	late autumn	early winter	mid winter	late winter	early spring	mid spring	late spring	early summer	mid summer	late summer	early autumn	mid autumn	late autumn	early winter

ABOUT CARROTS

- Small "baby" carrots are certainly juicy and succulent, but mature carrots are generally preferred when the need is for a strong taste and a good bite and texture.
- If you take care when choosing varieties, and if you are willing to protect the plants from weather extremes, you can be eating carrots for the greater part of the year.
- Deep-rooted varieties need a double-depth bed.

GROWING MEDIUM

Carrots thrive on a rich, friable, well-drained, slightly sandy medium in a sunny position. If you want to grow long-rooted types, make sure that the medium is well manured at a greater depth and the overall texture is crumbly; otherwise go for a heavy mix that has been well manured for a previous crop. If your growing medium is stony and/or stiff with fresh manure, the growing roots will divide, giving you stunted and forked carrots that are difficult to prepare.

SOWING AND PLANTING

- **Early spring to early summer (depending on variety)** Sow seeds in ¾ in (18 mm) deep furrows, 5–6 in (13–15 cm) apart across the width of the bed. Sow thinly, compact the growing medium, and water with a fine sprinkler.
- When the seedlings are big enough to handle, thin them out so they are about 2 in (5 cm) apart. Do this in the evening and remove the debris from the plot.
- Use cloches – glass, corrugated plastic or plastic hoop house – to protect the plants at both ends of the season.

GENERAL CARE

Ring the bed with a protective barrier of fine netting or clear plastic sheet. Hoe every day or so to get rid of the weeds and to loosen up the surface of the bed. The resulting loose mulch helps to hold in the moisture, which in turn prevents the roots from splitting. In extra-dry weather, increase the watering and spread an additional mulch of spent mushroom compost or garden compost over the whole bed.

HARVESTING

If you make successive sowings of a range of varieties, and protect them with a mulch of chopped straw or spent mushroom compost, you can harvest from late spring to early winter. Pull the carrots up by hand. Pack main crop carrots in boxes of sand, and store them in a frost-free shed.

Troubleshooting

Soggy holes: Probably caused by carrot fly. Limit the problem by growing onions alongside the carrots and by using a 3 ft (90 cm) high barrier of netting or plastic.

Splitting: Generally caused by alternating wet-dry-wet conditions. Avoid the problem by spreading a mulch of spent manure to retain residual moisture.

Green top: Usually caused by the top or "shoulders" of the carrot standing proud of the growing medium. Prevent it by hoeing the medium high up around the growing carrots.

Growing medium:
Well-drained, friable and slightly sandy
Situation: Sunny
Harvest: Pull by hand while easing with a fork

Plant seeds very thinly ¾ in (18 mm) deep, with 5–6 in (13–15 cm) between the rows

Thin to 2 in (5 cm) apart in the evening

Well manured for a previous crop

Protect the growing carrots from carrot fly with a 3 ft (90 cm) net or plastic barrier all around the bed

Pull up soil around plants

PARSNIPS

In times past, the good old parsnip was served up in place of the potato. They are not as versatile, maybe, but parsnips can be grown in just about any well-prepared fertile soil, they can be left in the ground over winter, and they taste amazingly good when roasted in oil or butter.

SOW **HARVEST**

mid winter	late winter	early spring	mid spring	late spring	early summer	mid summer	late summer	early autumn	mid autumn	late autumn	early winter	mid winter	late winter	early spring	mid spring	late spring	early summer	mid summer	late summer	early autumn	mid autumn	late autumn	early winter

ABOUT PARSNIPS

- Parsnips are hardy in all but the deepest frost, and generally easy to grow.
- The seeds take quite a long time to germinate and, once through, the seedlings are minute – so be patient, and do not be hasty to replant what you might see as a dud crop.
- You could maximize your space by intercropping with a swift-growing crop such as lettuces or radishes.
- Parsnips are less prone to pests and diseases than potatoes.
- They can be left in the ground over winter and lifted and eaten from mid-autumn around to the following spring. If the weather turns extra cold, cover the bed with a thick "mattress" mulch of chopped straw.

GROWING MEDIUM

Parsnips do well on just about any well-prepared, friable, fine-textured, well-drained, fertile growing medium. Choose a deep bed so that the roots can go straight down without obstruction. You can either layer up a purpose-made bed with mulches of well-rotted horse manure, or use a bed that has been well manured for a preceding crop. Be warned, however, that if you try to grow them in fresh manure the growing roots will, just like carrots, hit fresh manure and then either fork or become cankered.

SOWING AND PLANTING

- **Late winter to mid-spring** Sow a pinch of seeds in ½ in (12 mm) deep dibbled holes on a 5–6 in (13–15 cm) grid across the bed. Compact the growing medium and water generously with a fine spray. Be careful not to over-water the area.
- When the seedlings are big enough to handle, pinch out to leave a single strong plant at each station.

GENERAL CARE

Stir the surface of the growing medium to create a loose mulch, or remove weeds by hand and cover the ground with a mulch of spent mushroom compost. Either way, you must be extra careful that you do not scrape the "shoulders" of the root, as such damage might start top-rot or canker. Water little and often (never so much that the bed puddles or leaks water). If the weather turns icy, spread a mulch of chopped straw to give some protection against frost.

HARVESTING

You can harvest from mid-autumn to early spring. In all but the coldest and wet winters, parsnips can be left in the ground until they are needed. Ease them up with a fork, being careful not to break off the long root tips.

Troubleshooting

Parsnip canker: This shows itself as a rusty brown mess around the "shoulders" and is usually caused by physical damage to the root and/or contact with fresh manure. Only use well-rotted manure, and be careful not to touch the roots with the hoe.

Fresh manure: Some suppliers do not seem to understand just what "well-rotted" means and their manure is too fresh. If in doubt, simply take delivery and stack it up for next season.

Fanging: This shows as a forked root, generally caused by the presence of fresh manure and/or lots of stones. Remove all stones and avoid using fresh manure.

Splitting: This is generally caused by irregular watering.

Growing medium: Friable, well-drained and fertile
Situation: Open and sunny
Harvest: Lever with a fork to loosen the surrounding soil

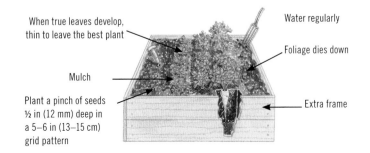

When true leaves develop, thin to leave the best plant

Water regularly

Mulch

Foliage dies down

Plant a pinch of seeds ½ in (12 mm) deep in a 5–6 in (13–15 cm) grid pattern

Extra frame

BEETS

Colorful, sweet in flavor, slightly crunchy but juicy in texture, and enjoyably easy to grow, beets are not only the perfect companion to salads but also very tasty as a hot vegetable. Beets can easily be stored by bottling it in a mixture of sugar and vinegar.

SOW   **HARVEST**

| mid winter | late winter | early spring | mid spring | late spring | early summer | mid summer | late summer | early autumn | mid autumn | late autumn | early winter | mid winter | late winter | early spring | mid spring | late spring | early summer | mid summer | late summer | early autumn | mid autumn | late autumn | early winter |

ABOUT BEETS

- Newly planted beets do not like to be disturbed or checked, so be extra careful when weeding, thinning and spreading a mulch.
- With beets, swift and young equates with texture and taste. Ideally, you need to pick the beets when they are young and tender, and cook and eat them within an hour or so of picking.
- You must carefully scrub and wash the beets prior to cooking; otherwise the food on your plate will taste dull and muddy.
- As my granny used to say, lazy bowels love beets!

GROWING MEDIUM

Beets are best grown in a light mix of well-rotted spent manure, old compost and sand. The ground needs to be well drained and well manured, but the manure must not be fresh or rank. A good method is to plant the beets on a fertile bed that has been manured for a preceding crop.

SOWING AND PLANTING

- **Early spring to early summer** Sow a pinch of 3–4 ready-soaked seeds about 1 in (2.5 cm) deep at 4–5 in (10–13 cm) intervals, so that a 3 ft (90 cm) square bed contains 36–40 plants. Compact the bed and water generously.
- When the seedlings are big enough to handle, carefully thin to leave the strongest plant.
- Firm the ground around the stems of the remaining plants, and water generously with a fine spray.

GENERAL CARE

Spread a web of black cotton threads over and around the bed, or circle it with a net, to keep off birds. Gently stir the surface of the bed with a hoe to create a loose mulch and to keep it free from weeds. If the weather is dry, spread a mulch of spent manure to further hold in the moisture, and water frequently.

HARVESTING

You can harvest from late spring through to late autumn – the time depends on the variety and growing methods. You can start harvesting by pulling every other young root, so that you can eat them small and tender in salads, and leave the rest to grow to a large size. Gently ease the roots from the ground. Twist the leaves off about 2 in (5 cm) above the crown, and eat fresh cooked, or store in boxes of sand.

Troubleshooting

Splitting roots: This is usually caused by long spells of dry weather, and the problem can be avoided by covering the ground with a deep mulch of old spent manure.

Bolting: This is usually caused by lack of water. You can avoid the difficulty by spreading a mulch of spent manure or chopped straw, and by generous watering.

Slugs: Use slug barriers or traps and/or remove the slugs by hand.

> **Growing medium:**
> **Well-drained, well-rotted manure**
> **Situation:** Open and sunny

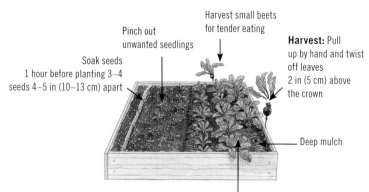

Pinch out unwanted seedlings

Harvest small beets for tender eating

Soak seeds 1 hour before planting 3–4 seeds 4–5 in (10–13 cm) apart

Harvest: Pull up by hand and twist off leaves 2 in (5 cm) above the crown

Deep mulch

Remove withered and dead leaves

RUTABAGAS

Rutabagas are easy to grow. If you have had trouble growing potatoes, and are looking to grow another primary bulk-food type of crop, they are a good option. A plate of mashed rutabagas with bread and butter on the side, topped with fried eggs, was favored by pilots in the Second World War.

				SOW								HARVEST												
mid winter	late winter	early spring	mid spring	late spring	early summer	mid summer	late summer	early autumn	mid autumn	late autumn	early winter	mid winter	late winter	early spring	mid spring	late spring	early summer	mid summer	late summer	early autumn	mid autumn	late autumn	early winter

ABOUT RUTABAGAS

- As rutabagas belong to the cabbage family, they are affected by many of the same diseases and pests.
- Do not be tempted to grow giant varieties (unless you keep goats); it is much better to choose the smaller types.
- Although rutabagas are thought to be so hardy that they can be left in the ground over winter, they do better in long periods of frost if they are protected with a thick mulch of chopped straw.
- If you are a vegetarian, try rutabagas steamed, mashed and buttered. If you eat meat, try them boiled with a ham hock.

GROWING MEDIUM

Rutabagas do best on a slightly sandy but rich growing medium, meaning a bed that is moisture-retentive and rich with mulches of well-rotted manure that have been sprinkled with sand. Above all, the bed must be moist, because if it dries the plants will swiftly bolt without swelling at the root. However, the bed must not be mushy and/or puddled with standing water. Rutabagas do best in an open, semi-shaded position with shelter to the windward side.

SOWING AND PLANTING

- **Mid-spring to early summer** Sow seeds in ½ in (12 mm) deep dibbled holes, about 9 in (23 cm) apart. Sow a pinch of seeds in each hole, cover and compact the growing medium and use a fine spray to water generously.
- When the seedlings are big enough to handle, thin to leave the strongest plant at each station.

- Water after thinning and use your fingertips to firm the growing medium up around the remaining plants.

GENERAL CARE

Stir the surface of the growing medium with a hoe to create a loose mulch. Be very careful that you do not graze the emerging root, as such damage might well result in top-rot or canker. Water little and often to avoid the flood-drought-flood conditions that cause root splitting.

HARVESTING

You can harvest from early autumn to early spring. Lift the roots as needed. In very cold weather, cover the whole bed with a mulch of chopped straw topped with a sheet of plastic – some sort of waterproof covering that you can swiftly remove to give the plants an airing.

> **Growing medium:** Light and moisture-retentive
> **Situation:** Open and semi-shaded
> **Harvest:** Pull from soil as needed

Troubleshooting

Slugs and snails: Damage shows as holes in leaves and roots. Be aware that slugs and snails can halt tender young plants. Remove the pests by hand on a daily basis.

Big foliage, little roots: This indicates that there is too much nitrogen in the growing medium. Avoid the problem by only using well-rotted manure.

Cabbage white butterflies: These insects love the leaves, so protect the crop with garden fabric (as for cabbages).

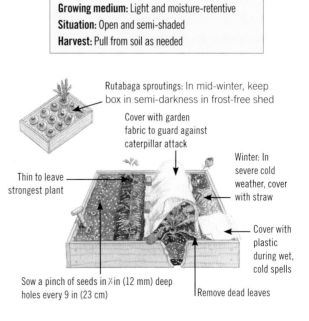

Rutabaga sproutings: In mid-winter, keep box in semi-darkness in frost-free shed

Cover with garden fabric to guard against caterpillar attack

Winter: In severe cold weather, cover with straw

Thin to leave strongest plant

Cover with plastic during wet, cold spells

Sow a pinch of seeds in ½ in (12 mm) deep holes every 9 in (23 cm)

Remove dead leaves

TURNIPS

Forget any bad memories of turnips you may have from your school-lunch days — the small, modern, tender varieties of turnip are beautiful. They are soft and white in texture and delicate in taste — wonderful in stews and curries.

| SOW DEPENDING ON VARIETY | | | | | | HARVEST | | | | | | | | | | | | | | | | | | |

| mid winter | late winter | early spring | mid spring | late spring | early summer | mid summer | late summer | early autumn | mid autumn | late autumn | early winter | mid winter | late winter | early spring | mid spring | late spring | early summer | mid summer | late summer | early autumn | mid autumn | late autumn | early winter |

ABOUT TURNIPS

- Small, fast-growing varieties can be sown as catch crops between rows of slow-growing vegetables.
- Turnips grown for their tops are sown in late summer for eating in early spring. They are very tasty!
- Turnips belong to the cabbage family, so are affected by similar pests and diseases.

GROWING MEDIUM

Turnips, just like rutabagas, do well on a rich, light, sandy, moisture-retentive growing medium that has been well manured with rotted compost. If your plot is extra dry, and/or you fail to water regularly, there is a good chance that the roots will falter and the plants bolt and come to nothing. Avoid a bed that looks to be sticky and/or puddled with standing water. Turnips do best in an open, semi-shaded bed that has plenty of shelter to the windward side.

SOWING AND PLANTING

- Sow seeds in late winter to early summer, or mid-summer to early autumn, depending on variety. Sow a pinch of seed in ½ in (12 mm) deep dibbled holes, 6–8 in (15–20 cm) apart, and cover. Firm in and water generously.
- When the seedlings are big enough to handle, thin to leave a single strong plant at each station. Water before and after thinning. Use your fingers to firm the growing medium up around the young plants.

GENERAL CARE

Stir the surface of the growing medium with your fingers to create a loose mulch. Be careful not to damage the turnips' "shoulders," as this might result in top-rot or canker. Water little and often. If it turns very dry, give the bed a good slow soaking and mulch thickly with spent mushroom compost.

HARVESTING

You can, depending on variety, harvest the roots from mid-autumn to early winter, and the tops from early to mid-spring. Lift the roots as needed. Turnips are best eaten small, young and tender.

Troubleshooting

Slugs and snails: You will find holes in the leaves and damage to the roots. Too many slugs and snails can halt the growth of the young plants. Remove the pests by hand on a daily basis.

Canker: Usually reveals itself as a rusty brown mess around the "shoulders" of the root. The problem can be caused by physical damage to the root, and/or contact with fresh manure, so only use well-rotted manure, and be careful not to scratch or graze the roots.

Clubroot: This shows as distorted roots. Pull up and burn affected plants.

Growing medium: Light and moisture-retentive
Situation: Open and semi-shaded
Harvest: Pull from soil as needed when small and tender

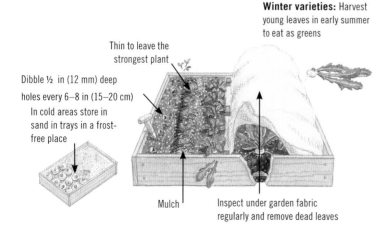

Winter varieties: Harvest young leaves in early summer to eat as greens

Thin to leave the strongest plant

Dibble ½ in (12 mm) deep holes every 6–8 in (15–20 cm)
In cold areas store in sand in trays in a frost-free place

Mulch

Inspect under garden fabric regularly and remove dead leaves

RADISHES

Radishes are extremely good as a swift fill-in or intercrop. Sprinkle the seeds around your more slow-growing crops, such as lettuces, parsnips, cabbages and cauliflowers, water daily, wait for a few weeks and you have the perfect crispy-crunchy salad bite to go with your bread and cheese.

ABOUT RADISHES

- The generic name for radishes, *Raphanus*, comes from the Greek *raphanos*, meaning "quickly appearing."
- Radishes can easily be grown all year round in temperate regions.
- The secret of growing a swift, plump crop is to choose the appropriate variety – for location and season – and sow the seeds thinly in a rich, moist growing medium.
- Never allow radishes to be short of water – they need watering a lot and often. Pick them as soon as they are ready so that they do not become old and woody.
- Children enjoy the fast results.

GROWING MEDIUM

Radishes thrive on a rich, moist, fertile growing medium in a sunny, open position. Ideally, the bed needs to be porous, easily worked and rich in old, well-rotted manure from previous crops. If the bed is overly rich in fresh manure, you will probably get fast-growing leafy plants that are small, tough and stringy at the root – they may be good on the eye but are not much fun to eat. Make sure that you compact the surface of the bed before and after sowing, so that the roots plump up.

SOWING AND PLANTING

- **Mid-winter to late summer** Sow seeds in succession every week or so in ½ in (12 mm) deep furrows, 4–6 in (10–15 cm) apart. Compact the growing medium and water generously.
- When the seedlings are big enough to handle, thin to leave the strongest plants about 1 in (2.5 cm) apart. Water generously before and after thinning.

GENERAL CARE

Stir the surface of the growing medium with a hoe at each side of the row to create a loose mulch. Water little and often to avoid the wet-drought-wet conditions that cause root splitting. If the weather turns dry, use your fingers to spread a thin mulch of spent manure around the growing plants.

HARVESTING

You can harvest from mid-spring to late winter, the precise length of time depending on variety and growing methods. Pull them up when they are small, young and tender and eat them as soon as possible after pulling.

Troubleshooting

Slugs and snails: Damage shows as slimy holes in leaves and roots. Harvest regularly and remove the pests by hand on a daily basis.

Big foliage, little roots: Probably caused by too much nitrogen in fresh manure. Avoid the problem by only using well-rotted manure.

Growing medium: Moist and fertile
Situation: Open and sunny
Harvest: By pulling them from the ground by hand

Thin to 1 in (2.5 cm) apart

Sow ½ in (12 mm) deep in rows 4–6 in (10–15 cm) apart

Sow in succession every two weeks

Mulch in dry weather

ARTICHOKES, JERUSALEM

The Jerusalem artichoke, also called sunroot and sunchoke, is very easy to grow. It produces a soaring mass of foliage, large, yellow, daisy-like flowers, and knobby, potato-like tubers. As for taste, if you think "nutty" potato with a hint of globe artichoke, you will not be far off the mark.

PLANT

HARVEST

| mid winter | late winter | early spring | mid spring | late spring | early summer | mid summer | late summer | early autumn | mid autumn | late autumn | early winter | mid winter | late winter | early spring | mid spring | late spring | early summer | mid summer | late summer | early autumn | mid autumn | late autumn | early winter |

ABOUT JERUSALEM ARTICHOKES
- They are grown just like poatoes.
- Some people find them indigestible and wind-making.
- The name Jerusalem is thought to be an American English seventeenth-century derivation of the Italian name *girasole*.
- A healthy plant will grow to a height of 10 ft (3 m) or more, so you must carefully consider where they are going to be planted. (Do you want to use them as a windbreak? Will they cast unwanted shade?)
- If all goes well, each egg-sized tuber will give you a yield of 2–3 1b (1–1.5 kg).
- If you are tempted to grow them as a permanent crop on the same bed, make sure that you lift and select the best tubers, and repeatedly mulch with well-rotted manure.

GROWING MEDIUM
Grown in beds just like potatoes, the Jerusalem artichoke does best in a dry, rich medium that has been well manured for a previous crop. Prepare the bed with layers of well-rotted farmyard manure, with extra mulches in the spring and autumn.

SOWING AND PLANTING
- **Late winter to mid-spring** Plant the tubers about 10 in (25 cm) apart at a depth of about 6 in (15 cm), say 9–11 plants to a 3 ft (90 cm) square bed.
- Tamp the plants in well, and water daily until the plant looks to be well established.

GENERAL CARE
As soon as the plants are about 1 ft (30 cm) or so high, use a hoe to earth up, and build some sort of support, using poles, a frame or a fence, up which the plants can grow. The easiest option is a pole-and-wire fence, like for runner beans or raspberries. At some point when the plants are 2–3 ft (60–90 cm) high, spread an extra mulch of spent compost and hoe it so that the tubers are topped by a ridge or mound about 6 in (15 cm) high.

HARVESTING
Harvest from mid-autumn onwards when the flowers and foliage begin to brown and die back. Cut the stems off to within 1 ft (30 cm) or so of the ground, protect with a mulch of chopped straw and lift the tubers as and when needed. Finally, remove all the tubers and keep some for planting next time.

Troubleshooting
Slugs: These can be a real tuber-eating nuisance. Use slug barriers or traps and/or remove the slugs by hand.

Troublesome tubers: When lifting, make sure that you completely remove even the smallest tubers, otherwise they will sprout and become weeds.

Growing medium: Rich, well-drained
Situation: Warm, well-drained position

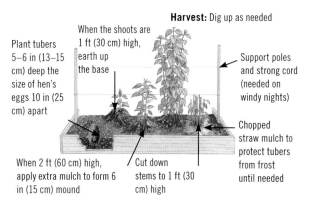

Harvest: Dig up as needed

When the shoots are 1 ft (30 cm) high, earth up the base

Plant tubers 5–6 in (13–15 cm) deep the size of hen's eggs 10 in (25 cm) apart

Support poles and strong cord (needed on windy nights)

Chopped straw mulch to protect tubers from frost until needed

When 2 ft (60 cm) high, apply extra mulch to form 6 in (15 cm) mound

Cut down stems to 1 ft (30 cm) high

CELERIAC

Although celeriac or turnip-rooted celery is related to celery, the difference is that celery is grown for its crunchy stems and for its heart, whereas celeriac is grown for its turnip-like root. Celeriac is easier to grow than celery, and is delicious in a winter soup or a winter salad.

SOW					PLANT							HARVEST													
mid winter	late winter	early spring	mid spring	late spring	early summer	mid summer	late summer	early autumn	mid autumn	late autumn	early winter	mid winter	late winter	early spring	mid spring	late spring	early summer	mid summer	late summer	early autumn	mid autumn	late autumn	early winter

ABOUT CELERIAC

- This is a relatively easy-to-grow plant, as long as it is sown under glass, carefully hardened off before planting out in the bed, and kept well watered.
- Celeriac and celery are members of the same botanical family, but they do not come from the same plant.
- Celeriac tastes good when turned into a thin, clear soup, or grated and eaten raw with a salad.

GROWING MEDIUM

Celeriac is much easier to grow than celery in that it is grown on the flat, and it does not need to have its stems covered with soil and blanched. It does best in a well-manured medium, with the manure having been put down as a thick mulch in the preceding winter, in a bed in a sunny but sheltered site where it can spend a long, uninterrupted growing season. Make sure when the root is swelling that you keep the plant well watered – give it as much water as possible in dry spells. If under-water, the swelling roots will perhaps shrink and rot, or at least stop growing.

SOWING AND PLANTING

- **Early to mid-spring** Sow seeds about ½ in (12 mm) deep under glass in prepared seed-trays (they are very slow-growing). As soon as the seedlings are big enough to handle, pot them into peat pots.
- **Late spring to early summer** Plant out 10 in (25 cm) apart, with 12–16 plants in a 3 ft (90 cm) square bed. Set the plants as "shallow" as possible so that each one is sitting in a saucer-shaped depression.
- Trim the leaves after planting.

Growing medium: Rich, well-manured and moist
Situation: Sunny and sheltered
Harvest: Pull from the ground and remove leaves

GENERAL CARE

Water the plants daily. Stir the surface of the growing medium with a hoe to create a loose mulch and to keep it clean and free from pests. Remove old leaves and any wandering shoots and roots, and generally keep the surface of the bed free from debris. You should never allow the ground to dry out.

HARVESTING

If your site is well drained, and you protect the plants with straw and garden fabric, you can leave the crop in the ground, and harvest from late autumn to early spring. If your bed is wet, lift the roots and store in a frost-free shed.

Troubleshooting

Rusty-colored tunnels: Probably caused by carrot fly. Try to avoid the problem by growing onions alongside the celeriac.

Splitting: Most likely caused by alternating wet-dry conditions. Prevent the problem by spreading a mulch of spent manure to hold in the moisture.

Slugs: Use slug barriers or traps and/or remove the slugs by hand.

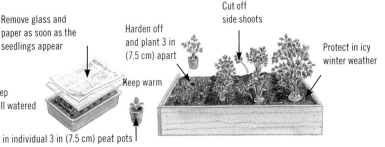

Remove glass and paper as soon as the seedlings appear

Keep well watered

Plant in individual 3 in (7.5 cm) peat pots

Keep warm

Harden off and plant 3 in (7.5 cm) apart

Cut off side shoots

Protect in icy winter weather

TOMATOES (OUTDOOR)

Some beginners to gardening think that tomatoes can only be grown in a greenhouse or hoop house, but many varieties can be grown outdoors. Tomatoes picked straight from the vine are wonderfully sweet and tasty. The unripened green ones can be used in chutneys and sauces.

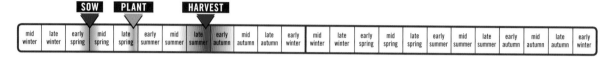

			SOW		PLANT			HARVEST																
mid winter	late winter	early spring	mid spring	late spring	early summer	mid summer	late summer	early autumn	mid autumn	late autumn	early winter	mid winter	late winter	early spring	mid spring	late spring	early summer	mid summer	late summer	early autumn	mid autumn	late autumn	early winter

ABOUT OUTDOOR TOMATOES

- Bush tomatoes are easier to grow.
- Tomatoes like dry, hot conditions with plenty of watering. The ideal is to site them in full sun, with protection on the shady sides.
- Perhaps more than anything else, tomatoes dislike drafts, uneven watering, and stagnant water.

GROWING MEDIUM

Outdoor tomatoes will do well in just about any bed, as long as the growing medium is of a good depth, richly manured, compact in texture, well drained, and in a sunny but sheltered position.

SOWING AND PLANTING

- **Early to mid-spring** Sow the seeds in a tray of moistened potting compost, and protect with a sheet of glass topped with newspaper. Keep warm.
- **Mid- to late spring** When the seedlings are large enough, plant them into 3 in (7.5 cm) peat pots. Water and keep warm.
- **Late spring to early summer (after the last frosts)** Set the peat pots 18 in (45 cm) apart in a sheltered bed, water and protect with a cloche or plastic. Plant away from potatoes.

GENERAL CARE

Support the plant with a stake and loose ties. Pinch out the side shoots. Remove the growing tip when there are 5–6 trusses. When the fruit starts to ripen, mulch with rotted manure topped with a bed of straw. Cover with the cloche and continue to water the roots.

HARVESTING

You can harvest from mid-summer to mid-autumn, the precise time depending on variety. Check that the straw is crisp and dry. Pluck the tomatoes when they are firm and nicely colored.

> **Growing medium:** Rich and well-drained
> **Situation:** Sunny and sheltered
> **Harvest:** Pick as they ripen and leave the stalk on

Troubleshooting

Discolored leaves: The cause could be lack of water, a virus or some sort of mildew. If you see that the foliage is curled and splotchy, it is likely to be mildew or a virus. Strip the damaged foliage and drench with an organic anti-mildew spray. If this has no effect, wait until the fruits ripen, and then pull up and burn the plants. Avoid the problem next time by planting virus-resistant varieties in a different position.

Blight: This shows itself as rotten fruit. Pull up and burn affected plants, and use another bed next time. Do not follow the tomatoes with potatoes.

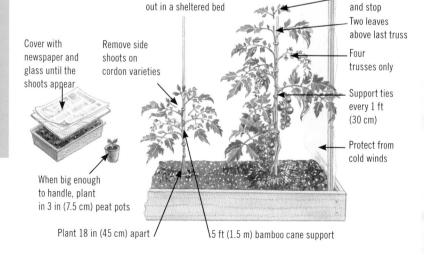

After last frosts, harden young plants before planting out in a sheltered bed

Pinch out and stop

Two leaves above last truss

Four trusses only

Support ties every 1 ft (30 cm)

Protect from cold winds

Cover with newspaper and glass until the shoots appear

Remove side shoots on cordon varieties

When big enough to handle, plant in 3 in (7.5 cm) peat pots

Plant 18 in (45 cm) apart

5 ft (1.5 m) bamboo cane support

SUMMER SQUASH AND ZUCCHINI

There are no real disadvantages to growing summer squash and zucchini. When they are grown in corners on compost and dung heaps, they make the unsightly both gorgeous and cost-effective. Their shape and speed of growth is surprising, they are incredibly tasty, and they can be frozen.

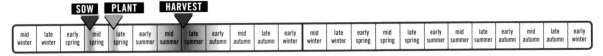

			SOW	**PLANT**		**HARVEST**																	
mid winter	late winter	early spring	mid spring	late spring	early summer	mid summer	late summer	early autumn	mid autumn	late autumn	early winter	mid winter	late winter	early spring	mid spring	late spring	early summer	mid summer	late summer	early autumn	mid autumn	late autumn	early winter

ABOUT SUMMER SQUASH AND ZUCCHINI

- Zucchinis are easier to grow.
- Summer squash can be steamed, stuffed, roasted and pickled.

GROWING MEDIUM

Summer squash and zucchini do best on a deeply worked, well-manured, moist, well-drained growing medium. Either grow them on a heap of well-rotted manure and compost or fill a bed with layered mulches of garden compost, farmyard compost and mushroom compost.

SOWING AND PLANTING

- **Mid- to late spring** Sow two seeds about ¾ in (18 mm) deep in peat pots under glass or plastic. Thin the seedlings to one good plant.
- **Late spring to early summer** When the stems are hairy, dig holes 1 ft (30 cm) deep and 1 ft (30 cm) wide, and set one plant to a 3 ft (90 cm) square bed. Fill a hole with well-rotted manure, cover it with a flat mound of manure topped with a shallow layer of soil, and put the seedling in its peat pot in place. If the growing medium spills over, you might need to add an extra frame to increase the overall depth of the bed.

GENERAL CARE

Stir the surface of the growing medium with a hoe to create a loose mulch. Once the plants are hardened off and under way, cover the mound with a mulch of spent manure to hold in the moisture. When the plants have run or grown out to cover the bed, gently pinch out the end of each leading shoot to cause them to branch. Keep watering and mulching throughout the season – mulch with grass clippings, more spent manure, or anything that will hold in the water and help plump up the crop.

HARVESTING

Harvest from mid-summer to mid-autumn. Cut zucchinis every few days. Cut summer squash as needed. At the end of the season, hang them in nets and store in a frost-free shed.

> **Growing medium:** Well-manured and free-draining
> **Situation:** Sunny and sheltered
> **Zucchinis:** Harvest with a sharp knife when about 4 in (10 cm) long
> **Summer squash:** Harvest 7–8 weeks after planting

Troubleshooting

Slugs and snails: Don't plant out the seedlings until they show two good leaves and the stems are hairy. Keep on top of the slugs by tidying up dead leaves and debris, and by removing them by hand daily.

Mottled leaves: Possible sign of mosaic virus. Spray with a soapy water mix to wash off aphids, scrape away and remove the top 1 in (2.5 cm) of growing medium, and remove and burn debris.

Sow two seeds ¾ in (18 mm) deep in peat pots; pinch out to leave the best seedling

Plant out in peat pots when stems become hairy

Fabric used at start of the season to protect against frost

Plastic water pipe arches will support a protective cover for windy areas

Mulch

Pinch out end of leader when it reaches the side

Compost

Manure

Extra frame

Rotted manure

CUCUMBERS (OUTDOOR OR RIDGE TYPE)

Growing cucumbers outdoors is surprisingly easy, especially if you protect them with some sort of screen. If you want cucumbers with a strong taste and good bite and texture, and are not worried about them being a bit short and lumpy, the outdoor or ridge types are the ones to go for.

OUTDOORS

SOW · PLANT · HARVEST

mid winter	late winter	early spring	mid spring	late spring	early summer	mid summer	late summer	early autumn	mid autumn	late autumn	early winter	mid winter	late winter	early spring	mid spring	late spring	early summer	mid summer	late summer	early autumn	mid autumn	late autumn	early winter

INDOORS

SOW · PLANT · HARVEST

mid winter	late winter	early spring	mid spring	late spring	early summer	mid summer	late summer	early autumn	mid autumn	late autumn	early winter	mid winter	late winter	early spring	mid spring	late spring	early summer	mid summer	late summer	early autumn	mid autumn	late autumn	early winter

ABOUT CUCUMBERS

- Choose a suitable outdoor variety – meaning true ridge or gherkin types.
- If you want to harvest extra early, turn one of your beds into a hotbed by adding huge amounts of fresh stable manure.

GROWING MEDIUM

The growing medium needs to be soft, of a good depth, well manured and moist. The easiest way is to build one or more extra-deep beds about 18 in (45 cm) deep and quarter-fill them with fresh stable manure topped with soil and/or well-rotted manure. Choose a sheltered spot in full sun, away from drafts, and build a plastic screen to the windward side. Mound up the growing medium.

SOWING AND PLANTING

- **Mid- to late spring** Sow seeds of outdoor varieties about ¾ in (18 mm) deep directly into 3 in (7.5 cm) peat pots and cover with glass or plastic.
- As soon as the plants have two true leaves, test the bed to make sure that it is not too hot – it needs to be about 64–86°F (18–30°C) – and set them in place, with no more than one plant in a 3 ft (90 cm) square bed.
- Cover the bed with a cloche or screen, or a build a teepee of sticks and cover it with plastic sheet or fabric.
- Water the plants daily.

GENERAL CARE

If you have made a hotbed, just prior to planting test the temperature to ensure that the bed is not too hot. Nip out the growing point after 5–6 leaves. Water every day and stop the side shoots when they reach the boundary of their allotted area. Once the small cucumbers begin to show, spread a generous mulch of well-rotted manure over the bed and continue watering copiously.

HARVESTING

Harvest outdoor varieties from early summer to early autumn, depending on variety. Support the weight of the fruit in one hand and cut off with a sharp knife in the other. Gather every other day, and remove yellow leaves, stunted fruits and general debris as you go.

> **Growing medium:** Well-manured and free-draining
> **Situation:** Full sun, sheltered
> **Harvest:** With a sharp knife

Troubleshooting

Withered fruit: Root rot or some other root problem caused by drought. Remove the damaged fruit and, if lack of water might be a problem, increase watering

Slugs and snail: Damaged trails and pits to the fruit. Remove the pests by hand daily.

Bitter fruit: From drafty, wet, cold conditions. Water twice daily and surround with a plastic or garden fabric screen.

Sow 2–3 seeds ¾ in (18 mm) deep in 3 in (7.5 cm) pots

Cover

Plant out when true leaves appear; nip out growing point after 5–6 leaves

Choose the best seedlings and discard the others

Spread out the lateral as they grow; stop them when they reach the sides

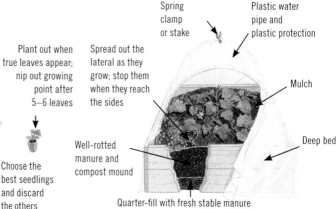

Spring clamp or stake

Plastic water pipe and plastic protection

Mulch

Deep bed

Well-rotted manure and compost mound

Quarter-fill with fresh stable manure

EGGPLANTS

If you can locate a bed in a sunny, sheltered corner, are prepared to spend time building clear plastic screens to make the most of the sun and netted screens to keep off gusty drafts, and you enjoy growing crops such as tomatoes and cucumbers, eggplants are a good choice for you.

		SOW		**PLANT**				**HARVEST**															
mid winter	late winter	early spring	mid spring	late spring	early summer	mid summer	late summer	early autumn	mid autumn	late autumn	early winter	mid winter	late winter	early spring	mid spring	late spring	early summer	mid summer	late summer	early autumn	mid autumn	late autumn	early winter

ABOUT EGGPLANTS

- Apart from the need for constant watering, eggplants are surprisingly easy to grow.
- They are grown from seed, in much the same way as tomatoes, cucumbers and sweet peppers.
- They can be grown outside in a sheltered corner of the garden as long as they are protected with screens – plastic screens to make the most of the sun, and net or woven willow ones to protect from cold winds.

GROWING MEDIUM

Eggplants like a rich, moist, well-drained growing medium in a sunny, sheltered position. A good option is to grow them in a bed that has been layered up with a mix of well-rotted farmyard compost, spent mushroom compost and lots of leaf mold. You should have no more than four plants to a 3 ft (90 cm) square bed. Build a plastic screen to the windward side.

SOWING AND PLANTING

- **Early spring** Sow the seeds about ½ in (12 mm) deep, on a bed of moistened potting compost in a seed-tray, protect with a sheet of glass topped with newspaper, and keep warm and well watered.
- **Mid- to late spring** When the seedlings are large enough to handle, prick them out into 3 in (7.5 cm) peat pots, water and keep warm.
- **Mid- to late spring** Set the peat pots in place in the bed, water generously and protect with a plastic or net screen/shelter of your choice.

GENERAL CARE

When the plant is about 1 ft (30 cm) high, remove the growing tip to encourage branching, and support with a stick. Prune to leave the best six fruits, and vigilantly remove subsequent flowers. Spray with water to discourage aphids. Apply a mulch of well-rotted manure and gradually remove older leaves.

HARVESTING

You can harvest between early summer and mid-autumn. When the fruits are 6–9 in (15–23 cm) long and nicely plump, slice them off with a sharp knife.

Troubleshooting

Insect pests: Spray the insects off with a water/liquid soap solution and then wash the leaves with plain water. Remove larger insects by hand.

Splitting fruit: Prevent the problem by surrounding the plants with a mulch of well-rotted manure, and water daily.

Growing medium: Rich moist well drained
Situation: Sheltered and sunny against a protective wall
Harvest: Cut away fruits with a sharp knife

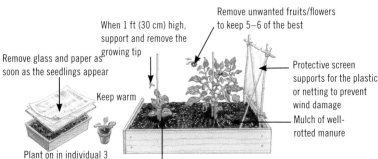

Remove glass and paper as soon as the seedlings appear

Keep warm

Plant on in individual 3 in (7.5 cm) pots

When 1 ft (30 cm) high, support and remove the growing tip

Remove unwanted fruits/flowers to keep 5–6 of the best

Protective screen supports for the plastic or netting to prevent wind damage

Mulch of well-rotted manure

In mid- to late spring, plant in the bed

SWEET PEPPERS

Sweet peppers are grown in much the same way as tomatoes and eggplants – they need relatively warm and sheltered conditions – but are usually easier to grow than tomatoes. If you like salads, stir-fries and roasts with stuffed vegetables, sweet peppers are a good choice.

ABOUT SWEET PEPPERS

- You might need to use screens and/or hoop house cloches to protect them from cold winds.
- You can sow them directly in peat pots, bring them on under glass or plastic, and then transfer them to the beds.
- If a blast of cold weather is forecast, set a teepee of bamboo canes over the plant and wrap it around with clear plastic or bubble wrap.

GROWING MEDIUM

Sweet peppers do best in a well-drained, well-manured bed in a sunny, sheltered position. A good option is an extra-high raised bed with a plastic screen windbreak all around. Failing that, you could plant them in temporary bag-beds in a hoop house or in some sort of dedicated glass or plastic shelter. If you have no choice other than to grow them in the open garden, make sure that they are in a sunny position up against a wall or fence, or perhaps against the sunny side of your shed. Load as much manure as possible on during the winter, and top it with a mulch of spent compost.

SOWING AND PLANTING

- **Late winter to early spring** Sow the seeds ¾ in (18 mm) deep in trays on a bed of moistened potting compost, and protect with a sheet of glass topped with newspaper. Keep warm.
- **Mid- to late spring** Plant the seedlings into small peat pots. Water and keep warm.
- **Around early summer** Plant outside when the plants are strong enough. Set the peat pots directly in the bed 12–18 in (30–45 cm) apart, and protect with a cloche or plastic shelter.

> **Growing medium:** Well-manured and well-drained
> **Situation:** Sheltered and warm/sunny against a protective wall
> **Harvest:** Cut the fruits off with a sharp knife

GENERAL CARE

Water the seedlings before and after planting, and then daily. Every few days or so, stir the surface of the growing medium with a hoe or trowel to create a loose mulch and to keep it free from weeds and bugs. Support the plants with a cane and ties. When the plants are happily established, spread a mulch of old spent manure or straw over the bed to further hold in the moisture.

HARVESTING

You can harvest from mid-summer to mid-autumn – the actual time depends on the variety, and whether you want to pick the peppers when they are young and green or when they are well ripened and red. Use a sharp knife to cut the fruits as needed.

Troubleshooting

Rolled leaves: Plants are too cold. Add a mulch of chopped straw or cardboard around the foot of the plants and protect the total bed with a screen or cover.

Mold: From virus diseases that take hold in wet, cold conditions. Remove affected fruit and leaves. Wash the plant with liquid soap and water, and rake up and remove the top 1 in (2.5 cm) of growing medium. If the problem persists, spray with an organic anti-mold drench.

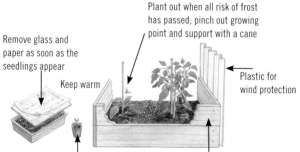

Remove glass and paper as soon as the seedlings appear

Keep warm

Plant in individual 3 in (7.5 cm) peat pots

Plant out when all risk of frost has passed; pinch out growing point and support with a cane

Plastic for wind protection

Extra frame if gales are forecast

STRAWBERRIES

With as few as 20 strawberry plants, during the fruiting season you should be able to pick plenty enough to eat every day, give some to relations and neighbors, and make jam. Colorful, juicy strawberries are an absolute joy, especially when picked and eaten fresh immediately.

| | | | | | | PLANT BARE-ROOTED | | | (PLANT CONTAINER-GROWN ANYTIME) | | | | | | | | | | | | HARVEST | | | | PRUNE | | |

| mid winter | late winter | early spring | mid spring | late spring | early summer | mid summer | late summer | early autumn | mid autumn | late autumn | early winter | mid winter | late winter | early spring | mid spring | late spring | early summer | mid summer | late summer | early autumn | mid autumn | late autumn | early winter |

ABOUT STRAWBERRIES

- Although strawberry types are described in the catalogs as "perpetual," "wild" and other names, they actually break down into early, mid-season and late varieties.
- Strawberries do best when they are grown en masse, say four to a 3 ft (90 cm) square bed.
- You can plant strawberries in late summer, mid-autumn to early winter, and spring. Only summer planting is described here, but the basics apply for all planting times.
- Strawberries can easily be propagated by layering the runners, about three from each plant, into pots or straight into the growing medium.

GROWING MEDIUM

Strawberries thrive in a well-manured bed in a sunny position with some shelter or screen to the windward side.

PLANTING (SUMMER)

- Fill the bed with plenty of well-rotted manure and/or garden compost.
- In mid-summer to early autumn, for bare-rooted plants, dig shallow holes wide enough to take the roots at full spread, say four plants in a 3 ft (90 cm) square bed.
- Carefully spread the roots out to their full extent, top the holes up with well-rotted garden compost and friable soil, ease and lift the plant slightly, and press firmly so that the crown is just above ground level. Gently water plants into place.

GENERAL CARE

When the fruits start to form, keep up the watering and spread a thick mulch of fresh straw around the plants to keep them warm and clean, and to hold back the weeds. Push in sticks or wires to make a low bowed support, and spread a net over them to keep off the birds.

HARVESTING

Pick the strawberries as they ripen, as soon as the color is uniform. The best time is early morning when the berries are dry. Pick the berries complete with the stalks and plugs. It is best if the fruit is eaten or cooked on the day of picking.

Growing medium: Fertile and well-drained
Situation: Sunny
Harvest: Stalk and plug when evenly red

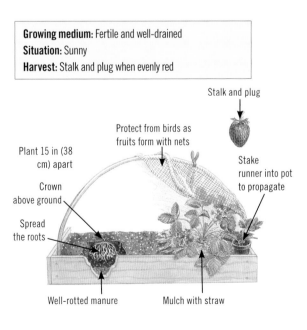

Stalk and plug

Protect from birds as fruits form with nets

Stake runner into pot to propagate

Plant 15 in (38 cm) apart

Crown above ground

Spread the roots

Well-rotted manure

Mulch with straw

Troubleshooting

Slugs and snails: Damage shows as slimy bites and holes in the fruit. Remove the pests by hand.

Mold and mildew: This shows as limp, moldy foliage and fruit drop. Clean up and remove the debris, and drench the plants with an organic mold spray. Once fruiting is over, cut off the foliage, gather all the straw mulch and debris and burn the lot. This helps to keep diseases down. Avoid the problem next time by growing a disease-resistant variety in a different bed in a well-ventilated, sunny spot.

Blackened flowers: Probably frost or wind damage. Avoid the problem by covering with a fine garden fabric if a cold spell is forecast and by watering the ground rather than the plants.

RASPBERRIES

Raspberries and their close hybrid cousins loganberries, veitchberries and lowberries are a good option for a medium-sized no-dig garden. Choose a suitable variety (summer- or autumn-fruiting, vigorous, restrained growth, heavy-fruiting, disease-resistant) to match your requirements.

(PLANT CONTAINER-GROWN ANYTIME) **PLANT BARE-ROOTED** **PRUNE** **HARVEST** **PRUNE**

mid winter	late winter	early spring	mid spring	late spring	early summer	mid summer	late summer	early autumn	mid autumn	late autumn	early winter	mid winter	late winter	early spring	mid spring	late spring	early summer	mid summer	late summer	early autumn	mid autumn	late autumn	early winter

ABOUT RASPBERRIES

- The raspberry is a hardy deciduous shrub – a member of the rose family.
- There are two kinds of raspberries – those that fruit in the summer and those that fruit in the autumn.
- The tender fruits should be eaten raw or cooked on the day of picking.

GROWING MEDIUM

Although generally summer- and autumn-fruiting raspberries have much the same needs – a well-drained bed with plenty of rotted manure in a well-sheltered, sunny position, away from drafts and deep shade – autumn-fruiting raspberries need just that bit more sun, air and shelter. A good option in an existing no-dig raised bed garden is to convert a number of side-by-side square beds into a single long, narrow bed to give you a bed about 3 ft (90 cm) wide by 6–12 ft (1.8–3.5 m) long.

PLANTING

- **Late autumn to early winter** For bare-rooted canes, dig a trench 1 ft (30 cm) deep and 18 in (45 cm) wide (length to suit you) and half-fill it with well-rotted farmyard manure. Set the bare-rooted canes in place about 15 in (38 cm) apart.
- Fill the trench with a mix of garden compost and old manure and tamp firm. Cut the canes down to about 1 ft (30 cm) from the ground.
- Along the length of the bed, build a support frame or fence that has horizontal wires at 2 ft (60 cm), 3 ft (90 cm) and 5 ft (1.5 m) from the ground.

GENERAL CARE

Summer-fruiting varieties In spring, when young canes start to grow, cut the old dead wood down to ground level. Tie the new growing canes to the support wires. After fruiting, cut all fruiting canes down to ground level, and tie up all the new canes.

Autumn-fruiting varieties After fruiting, cut all the canes down to ground level.

HARVESTING

Pick the raspberries on a dry, sunny day, as soon as they are fully colored. Snip them off complete with the stalk, or pull the fruit clear of the stalks. Remove, gather and burn the debris.

Troubleshooting

Curling leaf aphids: Damage shows as curled edges to the leaves, premature fruit fall and general weakening of the canes. Drench with an organic spray, wash with clean water and remove the mess from the surface of the bed. At the end of the season, spray the canes with winter wash and burn the debris.

Maggoty fruit: Most likely raspberry beetles, which feed on the flowers and lay eggs that eventually produce grubs that attack the berries. Avoid the problem next time by burning old canes as soon as they are cut, generally clearing up rubbish, and spraying with a winter wash at the end of the season.

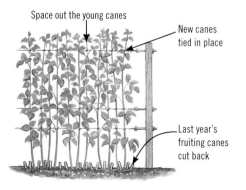

Space out the young canes

New canes tied in place

Last year's fruiting canes cut back

BLACKBERRIES

There is no doubt that blackberries are easy to grow and fruitful – an average plant will give 10–25 lb (4.5–11 kg) of fruit – but you will need lots of space. Blackberries can be eaten fresh or used in desserts, jams, juices and sauces. They also make a good cough syrup.

PLANT BARE-ROOTED (PLANT CONTAINER-GROWN ANYTIME)												**PRUNE**							**HARVEST**				
mid winter	late winter	early spring	mid spring	late spring	early summer	mid summer	late summer	early autumn	mid autumn	late autumn	early winter	mid winter	late winter	early spring	mid spring	late spring	early summer	mid summer	late summer	early autumn	mid autumn	late autumn	early winter

ABOUT BLACKBERRIES

- Most people know a blackberry when they see one. In the UK and many parts of Europe, collecting wild blackberries is a traditional activity that can evoke strong memories of childhood, rural hardship and wartime food shortages.
- There are small, thornless varieties that are good for small gardens.
- Blackberries can be grown more or less anywhere, as long as there is plenty of sun and dry air.

GROWING MEDIUM

Blackberries thrive in just about any growing medium as long as it is well manured, free from standing water and of a good depth. In a no-dig raised bed garden, they do best when planted as free-standing clumps so that they receive all-round sun.

PLANTING

- In late autumn to early winter for bare-rooted canes, and at any time for container-grown ones, dig a hole that is 9 in (23 cm) deep and 2 ft (60 cm) wide. Spread about 4 in (10 cm) of well-rotted manure in the bottom of the hole and set the bare-rooted canes or container-grown plants in place so that the roots are only just covered. Fill the hole with well-rotted manure and top with compacted mushroom compost or garden compost.
- Build a 6 ft (1.8 m) high post-and-wire support frame, with horizontal wires at 1 ft (30 cm) intervals.

GENERAL CARE

After planting, cut down the canes to about 9 in (23 cm) above the bed – each cut should be just above a strong, healthy bud. During the first summer, weave and train the young canes along all but the top wire. In the second year, train the new canes up through to the top wire. In the autumn, cut down all fruiting canes. Repeat the procedure in all following years.

HARVESTING

Pick the berries when the color has just changed from red to black, while they are still firm. As a test, take a berry and gently ease it away – if it comes cleanly away from its plug and stalk, it is ready. Blackberries need to be eaten fresh on the day of picking or swiftly canned or frozen.

Troubleshooting

Sticky curling leaves: These indicate aphids. Large colonies of aphids will result in distorted shoots and fruit drop. Minimize the problem by burning all the cuttings and debris at the end of the season. Avoid it next time by spraying with a winter oil wash to destroy the aphid eggs.

Gray mold: This shows itself as a gray-white powder on the foliage, indicating humid, stale-air, cold conditions. Avoid the problem by cutting back the lower foliage to let in the air, and by generally clearing away all the debris on the ground.

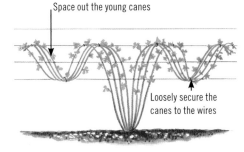

Space out the young canes

Loosely secure the canes to the wires

CURRANTS (BLACK, RED AND WHITE)

Although each of the currants needs slightly different treatment, they are grouped together here because most people think of them as being very similar. Black currants are more popular than either red or white currants.

PLANT BARE-ROOTED (PLANT CONTAINER-GROWN ANYTIME)												**PRUNE**						**HARVEST**							
mid winter	late winter	early spring	mid spring	late spring	early summer	mid summer	late summer	early autumn	mid autumn	late autumn	early winter	mid winter	late winter	early spring	mid spring	late spring	early summer	mid summer	late summer	early autumn	mid autumn	late autumn	early winter

ABOUT CURRANTS

- Black currants need to be treated differently from red and white currants, and they are easier to grow and care for.
- Black currants are usually made into jam, while red and white currants tend to be made into sauces and jellies.
- While red and white currants can be trained up wires, in a no-dig raised bed garden it is easiest to grow all three types as bush forms.

GROWING MEDIUM

Currants do best in a well-drained, deeply worked, well-manured growing medium. Select a deep bed, break up the hard subsoil and layer up with alternate mulches of farmyard manure, leaf mold and garden compost. The ideal site is moist but well-drained, sunny with a good circulation of air, and with some protection to the windward side.

PLANTING

- Plant in late autumn, or late winter to early spring, for bare-rooted bushes, and at any time for container-grown bushes.
- Dig a hole that is plenty wide and deep enough for the roots to spread out.
- Spread about 4 in (10 cm) of well-rotted manure over the bottom of the hole and set the bare-rooted or container-grown plant in place. Backfill and make adjustments so that the ground mark on the stem is level with the surface of the growing medium within the bed.
- Fill the hole up with well-rotted manure topped with well-compacted garden compost.

GENERAL CARE

After planting black currants, cut all stems down to about 1 in (2.5 cm) above soil level, and in the following season cut out all shoots that have produced fruit. With red and white currants, cut the main shoots back by half immediately after planting. In late winter, cut out shoots that cross the plant's center. When the fruit starts to form, protect the whole bush with fine netting to keep off the birds.

HARVESTING

Pick the fruit immediately after the color has turned, while the berries are still firm and shiny. Pick off the whole cluster rather than individual berries. In a good year, you might need to do this once or twice a week.

Troubleshooting

Vanishing berries: Birds will strip the bushes bare if you give them a chance. Avoid the problem by covering the beds with nets or by growing the bushes in a netted cage.

Holes in leaves and distorted shoots: Probably caused by capsid bugs. Spray with a winter wash and avoid the problem next time by growing a resistant variety.

Black currant, first season after pruning

Red or white currant, pruned as a bush

GOOSEBERRIES

In earlier times, gooseberries eaten raw straight off the bush were very bristly and sharp in taste, but once they were topped, tailed, cooked and served up as pies, crumbles and jam they were wonderful. Some modern dessert varieties are described as being good eaten raw.

PRUNE   **PLANT BARE-ROOTED**   (PLANT CONTAINER-GROWN ANYTIME)   **HARVEST**

mid winter	late winter	early spring	mid spring	late spring	early summer	mid summer	late summer	early autumn	mid autumn	late autumn	early winter	mid winter	late winter	early spring	mid spring	late spring	early summer	mid summer	late summer	early autumn	mid autumn	late autumn	early winter

ABOUT GOOSEBERRIES

- Gooseberries seem to do well against all the odds. A totally neglected bush will give a surprising amount of fruit, but picking will be difficult.
- Although the gooseberry is generally the first fruit to be ready for use, it is seldom seen in shops – all the more reason perhaps to grow your own.

GROWING MEDIUM

Gooseberries thrive in just about any deeply dug, well-manured growing medium. Although they will grow in a dank corner of the garden, they will be more susceptible to molds and blights than when they are grown in a light, sunny corner. The ideal is a bed that is moist but well-drained, with plenty of well-rotted manure to hold in the moisture, situated in a sunny, open, airy spot that is sheltered on the cold, windward sides.

PLANTING

- Plant in mid- to late autumn, or late winter to early spring, for bare-rooted bushes, and at any time for container-grown ones.
- Dig a hole that is plenty wide and deep enough for the roots to spread out.
- Spread about 4 in (10 cm) of well-rotted manure over the bottom of the hole and set the bare-rooted or container-grown plants in place. Ease container-grown plants from their pots and arrange them so that they are level with the growing medium.
- Fill the hole up with a mix of well-rotted manure topped with well-compacted garden compost.

Troubleshooting

Curling, distorted leaves: Probably caused by aphids. Spray them off with organic spray, wash the resulting mess off with water, and in winter spray with an organic wash.

Holes in leaves: These are usually the work of one of the fly pests. At the end of the season, remove all the surface of the bed to a depth of 3–4 in (7.5–10 cm) and burn it, and spray with an organic winter wash. Be careful not to burn the roots that are just under the surface of the bed.

GENERAL CARE

After planting, cut back each main branch by about half. In the following autumn, cut back by half all the shoots that have formed in the year. At the end of the following season, shorten those shoots produced during the season by half and clear out any shoots that crowd out the center. An open framework will make picking easier.

HARVESTING

Pick fruit for cooking as soon as it starts to color and while it is still hard, and fruit for eating when it feels slightly soft to the touch. In a good year, you might need to gather the fruit once or twice a week. Trim off the tough tops and tails.

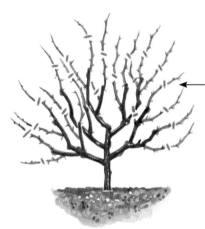

Shorten the young shoots in the first and second seasons, so that you have a well-shaped bush

RHUBARB

Fresh rhubarb stalks picked, cooked and eaten straight from the garden are tender, sweet and altogether beautiful, a real treat. The good news is that most children love garden rhubarb, especially when it is dished up with custard, yogurt or ice cream, or best of all made into a crumble.

PLANT ROOT   **HARVEST**

mid winter	late winter	early spring	mid spring	late spring	early summer	mid summer	late summer	early autumn	mid autumn	late autumn	early winter	mid winter	late winter	early spring	mid spring	late spring	early summer	mid summer	late summer	early autumn	mid autumn	late autumn	early winter

ABOUT RHUBARB

- Rhubarb is a vegetable that we treat as a fruit.
- Although rhubarb can be raised from seed, the swiftest and most common method of propagating is by root division.
- Although the plants can be grown in the same bed for 20 years or so, most keen gardeners replant every 5–10 years.
- The leaves contain high levels of toxic chemicals. Cut them off and put them on the compost heap.

GROWING MEDIUM

The ideal growing medium is a deep, rich loam that is cool, moist and well-drained. Rhubarb does not like boggy, waterlogged soil. In preparation, the beds should be generously layered up in autumn with plenty of manure. The ideal site for early varieties is warm and well drained, with protection from cold winds, with the ground sloping towards the sun. Later varieties can stand a more open position and a heavier growing medium. Although rhubarb needs plenty of moisture all through the growing season, and although a low, boggy situation is unsuitable, a very dry soil is equally bad.

PLANTING

- **Late winter to early spring** Plant divided dormant roots in ground that has been previously manured. Dig a 1 ft (30 cm) deep hole wide enough to take the spread of the roots. Set the plants 30 in (75 cm) apart, in rows 3 ft (90 cm) apart.
- Fill around the root with a mix of garden compost and old manure so that the growing tips are just showing, and firm.

GENERAL CARE

As soon as planting is complete, stir the surface of the bed to reduce compaction and cover the ground with a generous mulch of well-rotted manure. Water as often as possible. Remove flower stems as soon as they appear. Encourage an early crop by covering the plants with straw and black plastic sheet.

HARVESTING

Gather the stalks from early spring to mid-summer. Grip one stalk at a time close to the ground and give it a half-turn "yank" so that it comes away from the crown. Use a sharp knife to trim both ends of the stalk – the leaf at one end and the white piece at the other. Toss the debris on the compost heap and move on to the next stalk.

Growing medium: Deep, rich and moist
Situation: Sunny and sheltered
Harvest: Pull at base, twisting up and out by hand

Troubleshooting

Crown rot: This shows as a squashy brown area on the side of the crown, with the stalks and shoots looking generally weak and scrawny. Crown rot can devastate a bed, so burn the plants as soon as the disease shows and grow a completely different variety in a bed at the other end of the garden.

Tip rot: Avoid the problem by making sure that the tips are always visible.

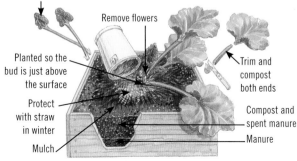

Forced rhubarb

Forcing for early crop: Use upturned bucket, box or terracotta forcer to cover the dormant buds

Remove flowers

Planted so the bud is just above the surface

Trim and compost both ends

Protect with straw in winter

Compost and spent manure

Manure

Mulch

Care and Troubleshooting

LOOKING AFTER PLANTS

Do plants need regular attention?

Plants need careful attention throughout their lives. Summer-flowering bedding plants in containers on a patio need regular watering and removal of dead flowers, while lawns require cutting and edges trimmed; also, trees must be checked to ensure stakes are not rubbing their bark. The gardening year is full of plant maintenance that turns a mediocre garden into one in which you can be especially proud. These pages show how to look after a wide range of plants.

Summer-flowering plants in hanging baskets, window boxes, troughs and tubs need watering each day, especially when the weather is hot.

DO ALL PLANTS NEED LOOKING AFTER?

Most garden plants are in an artificial environment, often radically different from their native areas. However, the majority of them are adaptive and grow surprisingly well in alien conditions – but they do benefit from extra care and attention, especially when young and becoming established.

Plants are often expected to create colorful displays year after year, while others are encouraged to put all of their endeavors into a feast of color during a few summer months.

LOW MAINTENANCE?

Trees, shrubs and conifers need less attention than summer-flowering bedding plants in borders or those planted in containers on a patio, such as hanging baskets, wall baskets and window boxes. Unless these are regularly watered, displays soon fail.

Plants in containers

- Water plants regularly throughout summer.
- Pinch off growing tips of some summer-flowering plants to encourage bushiness.
- Remove dead flowers to encourage others to develop.
- Regularly feed plants in hanging baskets, window boxes, wall baskets and tubs.
- In winter, cover soil in tubs and large pots which are homes to shrubs and trees to prevent it becoming excessively wet.

In winter, prevent soil in tubs and large pots becoming too wet by covering with plastic

In winter, cloak tender shrubs in large containers with straw

Looking after hedges

- Keep the bases of young hedges weed-free – they rob plants of moisture and food.

- Refirm soil around young hedges in spring – use the heel of your shoe.

- Water young hedges to encourage rapid establishment.

- Regularly trim formal hedges to create a neat shape.

- Brush off snow as soon as possible; use a bamboo cane or a soft brush. If left, the weight of snow deforms hedges.

- Use pruning shears – rather than hedge trimmers – to shape and remove straggly shoots from large-leaved, informal hedges. Take care not to shred leaves.

Looking after a lawn

- Regularly water lawns – especially newly established ones – throughout summer.

- Cut lawns throughout summer. During dry, hot summers leave the grass longer and cut less frequently.

- Trim lawn edges to keep the lawn neat. Pick up the cut edgings.

- Rake and scarify lawns. Additionally, in autumn rake off fallen leaves from nearby trees.

- Aerate and topdress lawns during late summer or early autumn.

Use edging shears to trim long grass along lawn edges

Repairing holes in lawns

1 Place a piece of wood, 10–12 in (25–30 cm) square and ½ in (12 mm) thick, over the hole; use an edging iron to cut around it.

2 Lift out the piece of turf and level the soil.

3 Use the same piece of wood to cut a square of turf from an out-of-the-way position.

4 Place the fresh piece of turf in the hole (above, right) and sprinkle friable soil along the joints. Firm and water the area.

Repairing lawn edges

1 Place a 8–9 in (20–23 cm) wide and 12 in (30 cm) long, ½ in (12 mm) thick piece of wood over the damaged area.

2 Use an edging knife to cut around it.

3 Lift out the tuft and turn it so that the damaged area is towards the lawn's middle.

4 Sprinkle friable soil into the damaged area, firm and dust with lawn seed; gently water.

Levelling bumps and depressions in lawns

1 Use an edging knife to cut a straight line across the bump or depression.

2 Then, use the edging knife to cut several lines, 9 in (23 cm) apart, at right angles to the first line.

3 Peel back the turf and either add or remove soil.

4 Replace the turf, firm and dribble friable soil into the cuts. Water.

Cutting off a large branch

1 Cut one-third of the way through the branch from the bottom about 2 in (5 cm) from the branch collar on the tree.

2 About 1 in (2.5 cm) further out, cut off the branch.

3 Cut the remaining stub off just outside the branch collar of the tree..

Looking after a pond

• Keep the water topped up throughout summer. Evaporation soon lowers the water's surface and may damage plants.

• If ponds need to be emptied and cleaned, choose a warm day in early summer – but first remove the fish.

• In autumn, remove leaves that have fallen into the pond. Also, pull out dead leaves from water plants.

Looking after herbaceous plants

• In late autumn or early spring, remove dead stems and supporting, twiggy sticks (if used).

• In spring, lightly fork the soil. Water the soil and add a mulch. Additionally, some plants need support.

• Throughout summer, remove dead flowers. Keep the soil moist, especially during hot weather.

Looking after annual bedding plants

• These are planted in early summer (after all risk of frost has passed); keep the soil moist, especially during hot weather.

• In mid-summer, scatter a general fertilizer around plants (but not touching) and gently water the soil.

• In autumn, pull up all plants and place on a compost heap.

Looking after biennials

• Plant them in early autumn, as soon as available. Sometimes this is combined with planting bulbs between them.

• Thoroughly water the soil to ensure that plants do not shrivel in hot autumn sunshine.

• In early spring, refirm frost-loosened soil around plants.

• Pull up and discard plants when their displays finish.

Looking after shrubs

• In spring, lightly fork soil around established shrubs. Thoroughly water and add a 3–4 in (7.5–10 cm) thick mulch.

• During hot summers, regularly and thoroughly water the soil, especially for shrubs in flower.

• Prune shrubs as required.

Shrubs such as this *Buddleja davidii* (Butterfly Bush) need yearly pruning

Cut out "reverted" shoots from variegated evergreen shrubs

Most Roses need yearly pruning to encourage theregular development of shoots and flowers

PESTS AND DISEASES

Apart from a number of very good home-made organic sprays, meaning recipes like a chopped tomato leaves soaked in water that can sprayed on aphids, and a chopped garlic and oil mix that is a great antibacterial, antifungal and insect pest spray, a very efficient way forward is to cover the crops with garden fabric, netting and such, so as to create physical barriers to keep insect and animal pests at bay.

ABOVE-GROUND PESTS AND DISEASES – SYMPTOMS AND CONTROLS

Birds

Cause damage to plants – protect with nets, or better still plant extra crops for the birds in the knowledge that some birds are beneficial in that they will eat insect pests.

Slugs and snails

Cause slimy damage to leaves and stalks – remove by hand. Some gardeners advocate ringing the beds with a copper wire stripped from an electric cable, their thinking being that something about the copper – perhaps the heat, or electric shock, or copper oxide – keeps the slimy pests away.

Cabbage caterpillars

Seen as holes, eggs and actual caterpillars – protect with fine nets to keep off the butterflies, and collect and destroy the eggs and the caterpillars.

Diamondback moths

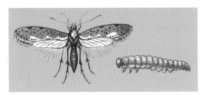

Show themselves as caterpillars feeding on the underside of leaves – protect with nets to keep of the moths and collect the caterpillars by hand.

Green capsid bugs

Makes holes in leaves and deforms growth – drench with organic spray.

Red spider mites

Causes the leafy veins of leaves to turn yellow-red-brown and results in a dusty covering – control by drenching with Neem oil (an organic pesticide), or with a homemade coriander and oil spray.

Earwigs

Show themselves as holes in leaves – can be trapped with upturned pots filled with straw and controlled with garlic and pepper spray.

Greenhouse whitefly

Shows as a sticky mess of eggs on the underside of leaves and as deformed leaves – spray with insect soap or dust with seaweed powder.

Mosaic virus

Shows as spotted green-yellow areas on the leaves and eventually results in complete plant failure – drench with a tobacco and water spray and burn badly damaged plants.

Asparagus beetles

Cause damage to leaves and stems – collect and destroy the beetles, grubs and all the debris.

Flea beetles

Cause small holes in leaves – drench with garlic and oil spray and burn debris.

Rust

Reveals itself as a brown scab-like condition on leaves – garlic and oil spray seems to work, as does a spray made from Neem oil. Limit the problem by burning all the debris at the end of the season.

Tomato leaf mold

Reveals itself as yellow-brown leaves and wilting plant. Remove damaged leaves and drench the plants with a mix of water, baking soda, veg oil and dishwashing liquid.

Aphids (greenfly)

Sticky mess indicates an infestation – drench with garlic and pepper spray and burn debris.

Smut

Shows on the leaves as a sooty looking mess that smears on contact – very difficult to control. Wash off with a thin soapy spray, and/or drench with a Neem oil spray. Burn all the debris at the end of the season and do your best to avoid the problem the next time around by planting resistant varieties on a different bed.

Mice

Cause damage to crops – especially peas – by eating seeds, munching pods and generally being a nuisance. Having tried traps, kerosene, mesh and nets, I now sow peas in the greenhouse in lengths of plastic gutter, wait until they are about 2-3 inches high, slide the young plants into place in the beds and then follow on by ringing the beds around with nets.

Black bean aphids

Show themselves as a mess of sticky black aphids on leaves and stems – drench with a mix of soft soap and white mineral oil, and do your best to encourage predatory ladybugs and other aphid-eating wildlife.

Pea and bean weevils

Cause damage as they bite and nibble around the edges of the leaves – puff organic rotenone around the leaves and burn all the ground debris.

Pea thrips

 Result in silvery brown misshaped pods – spray with insecticidal soap – avoid the problem by burning all the debris.

Pea moths

Cause maggoty peas – guard against by ringing the bed with a barrier of fine garden fabric or netting – drench with a natural soap spray.

Potato blight

Shows as black and brown spots on leaves and scabby soft potatoes – very difficult to control, the best option is to clear the beds, burn the debris, and next time around to plant resistant varieties on a new bed.

Potato leaf roll virus

Reveals itself as rolled edges to the leaves – drench with an anti-aphid mix, and use a resistant variety the next time around.

Bean halo blight

Causes squashy rusty scabs on the leaves and eventual plant failure – first try an organic spray, and if this fails pull and burn the plants, and next time around plant disease resistant varieties on new beds.

Powdery mildew

Shows as a flour-like dusting on leaves – drench with milk and water spray.

Celery heart rot

Causes a soft brown rot at the center or heart of the plant – avoid by binding the growing plant up tight with raffia and gradually mounding soil around the plant so that the stalks are hidden from view, and the center of the plant is free from standing water

Celery leaf miners

Causes brown blistering and shrivelling of the leaves – collect and kill the larvae, and drench the plants with a soft soap solution. Mound soil around the stalks to minimize the problem.

Home-made organic sprays

Be aware that in some countries it is illegal in some instances to make some home-made traditional recipes for insect and pest control.

- **Garlic and pepper** – add 3 cloves crushed garlic and 1 tablespoon vegetable oil to 3 tablespoons hot pepper sauce; let it stand overnight. Next add the mix to 1 small spoonful unscented washing-up liquid and add it all to 4 cups water. This mix can be sprayed direct as it is.

- **Garlic and oil** – add 3 cloves crushed garlic to 2 small spoonfuls mineral oil, let it sit for a day, then strain and add to 1 pint (0.5 liter) water. Shake and add 1 small spoonful washing-up liquid. When you come to spray, add 2 tablespoons of this mix to 1 pint (0.5 liter) water.

- **Tomato leaf** – soak 2 cups chopped tomato leaves in 2 cups water, leave overnight and strain. When you spray, use 1 measure of the mix to 1 of water.

- **Insecticidal soap** – 1 small spoonful pure unscented soap mixed with 2 pints (1 liter) water – dissolves insects like aphids, mites, thrips and a whole range of scale insects.

- **Neem oil** – Neem seed oil repels cabbage worm, aphids, moth larvae, and also control powdery mildew and rust. 1 oz (25 g) Neem oil and a few drops soap liquid mixed into 1 gallon (4 liters) water makes a good spray to treat all manner of mold and mites.

Slugs and snails

Signs are slimy trails and general damage to roots, fruits, shoots and indeed everything. Slugs and snails dislike barriers of wood ash, crushed eggshells, human and pet hair, oat bran and sprigs of rosemary spread around plants. Another good barrier method is to staple a continuous loop of copper wire around the top of the wooden bed. You can also try slug "traps," such as a sunken receptacle containing a little beer into which the pests fall and drown.

Warning

It is a good idea with all plant sprays – whether they be home-made, handed down, traditional or shop-bought – to have a trial run by spraying just a little on a single plant to see if it works or does damage. You must approach all sprays and cures with the assumption that they might be dangerous – meaning you must wear gloves, a mask and goggles, and you must wash your skin on contact, and safely label or dispose of all left-overs.

Woodlice

Little hard-coated lice that can often be seen crawling and rolling up into balls. They cause damage by chewing roots and seedlings. Remove and burn all the debris from around the plants, rake the ground to disturb the woodlice, and drench with a mix of mild detergent and vegetable oil – 1 part oil and a dash of liquid soap to 100 parts water.

Cabbage root fly

You will notice small white maggots in the soil and general damage to roots. The plants will wilt and die. Dust organic rotenone powder around the roots, and burn the plants at the end of the season.

Millipedes

Many-legged millipedes cause damage to roots. They can be trapped in cans filled with carrot or potato peelings, or sprayed with a garlic and pepper mix.

Crown and stem rot

You will see a soft, brown mess around the lower stem, and general wilting. Horseradish spray seems to work. Add 1 cup liquidized horseradish to 16 fl oz (475 ml) water and let it soak overnight. Strain off the liquid and mix it with 4 pints (2 liters) water. The resulting mix is a good spray for a whole range of fungal diseases.

Root rot

This is caused by various fungal diseases, shows as soggy, brown roots and general wilting. Burn damaged plants and avoid the problem next time by choosing a bed that is extra well drained and by increasing the amount of compost.

Cutworms

These are caterpillars of various moths. Symptoms show as chewed and eaten stems and roots. A sprinkling of cornmeal or bran scattered throughout the garden will kill cutworms, which munch it up and die.

Clubroot

This first shows as wart-like nodules on the roots, and the plant eventually wilts and dies. There is no cure for clubroot. Burn the diseased crops as soon as possible, and next time plant resistant varieties in different beds.

Wireworms

Green larvae of click beetles, which cause general damage to roots, stems and tubers. A garlic and oil spray works really well.

Leatherjackets

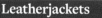

These are the fat legless grubs of craneflies, which cause general damage to roots. Spray the ground with a water and liquid soap mix. Bear in mind that, while the grubs do most certainly damage roots, this might be offset by the fact that the adult flies eat aphids, mites and leafhoppers.

Beetle grubs

You may see larvae feeding on roots and tubers, and/or damage to roots and tubers. Remove and burn all debris, and then spray with a garlic and oil mix.

Root-knot eelworms

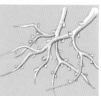

These first show themselves as galls and deforming nodules on the roots of many vegetables, and then finally as stunted growth. Remove damaged roots, leave the soil for three weeks and drench with a mix of molasses or sugar and water. Research suggests that adding a mulch of fresh chicken manure can help to reduce the problem.

YEAR-ROUND CALENDAR

The following calendar will not answer all your questions – because your growing medium and weather patterns will be specific to you and your area, and perhaps you will not want to plant all the vegetables available anyway – but it will at least give you some sort of timetable to work to.

MID-WINTER

Maintenance and preparation: Inspect your tools and sort out things like stakes, posts, string, pots, plastic sheets, netting and garden fabric. Set seed potatoes to sprout, order seeds, plan out the pattern of beds, and generally prepare.

Growing medium: Remove weeds, spread mulch, well-rotted manure or garden compost (as appropriate) and order seeds.

Sowing and planting: Plant broad beans in your chosen beds. Sow onions, leeks and radishes in a protected bed or hot bed.

Harvesting: Pick Brussels sprouts, winter cabbages, last of the carrots, celery, chicory and anything else that is ready.

LATE WINTER

Maintenance and preparation: Clean up the paths around the beds and generally make sure that all your gear is in good order. Cover beds at night with garden fabric and/or nets. Look at your master plan and see if you can get ahead with more mulching.

Growing medium: Use the hoe and rake to prepare seed beds – look for a nice warm corner and make sure that you have protective screens and garden fabric at the ready. Remove weeds; maybe add a thin mulch on selected beds, and put debris on the compost heap.

Sowing and planting: Plant artichokes and shallots. Sow early peas and maybe another row or two of broad beans. Sow carrots, lettuces and radishes under glass/plastic/mats on a hotbed. Raise seedlings of crops like leeks, cucumbers, onions and tomatoes in warm frames.

Harvesting: Pick Brussels sprouts, winter cabbages, last of the carrots, celery, chicory and anything else that is ready.

EARLY SPRING

Maintenance and preparation: Weed paths, mend frames and keep pulling up large weeds. Look at your plot and see if you want to change things around – perhaps the position of the permanent plot.

Growing medium: Keep stirring with the hoe and generally be on the lookout for weeds, especially deep-rooted perennials.

Sowing and planting: Sow hardy seeds such as lettuces and parsnips out of doors. Sow things like spinach, broccoli, leeks, onions, peas, celery, tomatoes and summer squash under glass or in a protected bed – either directly in the bed or in trays.

Harvesting: Pick sprouts, cabbages and cauliflowers.

MID-SPRING

Maintenance and preparation: Be on the lookout for slugs and snails. Watch out for problems on fruit beds. Thin seedlings as necessary. Keep pulling up large weeds and putting down mulches. Reduce the number of sprouts on seed potatoes. Cover selected beds at night.

Growing medium: Keep working the beds with the hoe and your hands, along the rows of seedlings. Draw the soil up on potatoes.

Sowing and planting: You can now sow just about everything and anything in the open. Plant main crop potatoes. Plant onions, radishes, main crop carrots, beet, salsify and scorzonera, endives, more lettuces, peas and spinach. Plant out any seedlings that you have hardened off, such as Brussels sprouts. Sow runner beans, summer squash and zucchinis under glass.

Harvesting: You can pick beet greens and broccoli.

LATE SPRING

Maintenance and preparation: Keep a watch on the weather and be ready to protect tender seedlings with glass, plastic sheeting, net screens or whatever seems to be appropriate. Be ready to deal with blackfly on beans. Set twigs among the peas. Put mulch on selected beds. Reduce the number of runners on the strawberries. Water seedlings. Keep on delicately hoeing and weeding.

Growing medium: Prepare more seed beds. Hoe and rake regularly. Heap up the growing medium to protect potatoes. Mulch between rows of more advanced vegetables.

Sowing and planting: Plant out hardy seedlings. Sow tender vegetables in vacant beds. Sow French, runner and brown beans in the open. Sow more peas, endives, radishes and summer spinach – almost anything that takes your fancy. Plant out Brussels sprouts, broccoli, cucumbers and anything else you like.

Harvesting: Pick beet leaf, broccoli, early beets, early carrots, cucumbers under cover, endives and many other vegetables.

EARLY SUMMER

Maintenance and preparation: Bring in fresh manure, well-rotted manure and spent mushroom compost. Keep everything well watered. Spread mulches around crops like turnips. Put nets over fruit. Remove weak canes from raspberries. Clean out empty beds and keep hoeing and weeding. Stake up runner beans and peas.

Growing medium: Keep hoeing. Dig up potatoes. Weed vacant seedbeds.

Sowing and planting: Plant out seedlings. Sow succession crops such as endives, lettuces and radishes.

Harvesting: Pick anything that takes your fancy.

MID-SUMMER

Maintenance and preparation: Support plants that look hot and droopy. Gather soft fruits as required. Cut mint and herbs ready for drying. Top-dress with manure mulch. Look at the tomatoes and pinch out and feed as necessary. Lift potatoes. Keep hoeing between crops. Water and weed. Make sure that any hoop houses, greenhouses and frames are open to the air.

Growing medium: Weed, hoe and mulch. Weed after lifting potatoes. Mound soil around potatoes.

Sowing and planting: Plant out the celery and crops like cabbages, sprouts and broccoli.

Harvesting: Just keep picking, eating and storing.

LATE SUMMER

Maintenance and preparation: Order seeds for autumn sowing. Keep storing vegetables for the winter by canning, drying and freezing. Bend over the necks of onions. Dry herbs. Pinch out the tops of tomatoes. Clear and mulch beds. Protect fruit crops from the birds. Plant out new strawberry beds. Keep hoeing and weeding.

Growing medium: Weed and hoe. Weed empty potato beds.

Sowing and planting: Make more sowings of endives, radishes, spinach, onions and anything else that fits the season. Sow lettuces and salad crops under cover. Sow cabbages for spring planting.

Harvesting: Just keep picking, eating and storing. Dry more herbs. Gather beans, tomatoes, and fruit as and when they are ready.

EARLY AUTUMN

Maintenance and preparation: Watch out and protect from frosts. Lift and store roots. Mound soil around celery and leeks. Watch out and destroy caterpillars. Prune raspberries. Water, weed and hoe as necessary. Blanch endives.

Growing medium: Weed, hoe and mulch the moment you have cleared the crops.

Sowing and planting: Plant out spring cabbages. Look at your seed packets and sow if possible.

Harvesting: Lift potatoes and onions. Gather runner beans. Lift and store roots. Gather and store fruit as it ripens. Keep picking and eating other crops as required.

MID-AUTUMN

Maintenance and preparation: Watch out for frost and protect as needed. Mulch vacant beds. Continue hoeing and weeding. Clear the ground and put debris on the compost heap. Clean up paths and maintain beds. Thin onions.

Growing medium: Weed, hoe and mulch beds as they become vacant.

Sowing and planting: Plant rhubarb and fruit trees. Sow peas in a protected beds. Sow salad crops under glass. Plant out seedlings. Sow early peas in warm areas.

Harvesting: Gather the remaining tomatoes. Lift and pick crops like celeriac and carrots.

LATE AUTUMN

Maintenance and preparation: Watch out for frost and protect as needed. Clean up leaves and debris, and weed and mulch vacant beds. Continue hoeing and weeding as necessary. Remove bean and pea sticks and poles.

Growing medium: Weed, hoe and mulch beds as they become vacant.

Sowing and planting: Sow broad beans in a sheltered spot.

Harvesting: Lift and store root crops. Cut, lift and eat other crops as needed.

EARLY WINTER

Maintenance and preparation: Watch out for frosts and protect as needed. Clean tools and the shed.

Growing medium: Weed hoe and mulch beds as they become vacant. Check that stored vegetables are in good order.

Sowing and planting: If the weather is very mild, you could plant broad beans. Draw growing medium up around the peas. Sow salad crops under glass and protect as needed.

Harvesting: Pick the last of the beet leaf. Pick Brussels sprouts, winter cabbages, last of the carrots, celery, chicory and anything else that is ready.

TROUBLESHOOTING

Clearing an area of the garden, building raised beds, filling the beds with various mixes of farmyard manure, garden compost and spent mushroom compost, planting up the beds, and battling with nature to achieve maximum harvests all make for an engaging experience. One year it might be all success, and the next you might have problems, but this is why growing vegetables is such a great challenge.

I have problems – can you help?

No-Dig Raised Bed Troubleshooting

QUESTION	ANSWER
The basic plot is completely overgrown with weed— an old lawn that has gone to ruin. How do I start?	Cut down and burn as many of the weeds as possible. Pull up and burn plants like nettles, thistles and docks, and then cover the whole plot with black plastic sheeting.
I have spent weeks building the beds and getting them into place, but weeds are springing up in the path areas. What can I do?	As soon as the beds are sorted and in place, cover the path areas with black plastic sheeting, old carpets, old plastic sacks, or anything that will starve the weeds of sunlight, and then spread a thick mulch of wood chips over the paths.
I am building the beds from 9 x 2 in (23 x 5 cm) rough-sawn and treated timber (as shown on page 7), but I think that some beds need to be deeper. What can I do?	The easiest option is to build more frames as already described — with the sameinternal dimensions — only this time make them from less expensive 6 x 1 in (15 x 2.5 cm) section timber. In this way you will be able to increase the depth of your beds by multiples of 6 in (15 cm).
Why do you describe the soil as "growing medium"?	The word "soil" defines the natural ground, meaning the top layer of the earth's surface that is made up of rock, mineral particles and organic matter. The content of the beds is a mix of brought-in materials, so it is not true soil. The term "growing medium" underlines the fact that it has to be created and formulated.
What do you think is a good mix for filling the beds?	Equal parts of spent mushroom compost, fresh farmyard manure, well-rotted farmyard manure, garden compost and poultry manure. Then you can use poultry manure, garden compost and the occasional load of horse manure as mulches. (Avoid the temptation to use bought-in "topsoil" in the beds, as this will contain weed seeds.)
We have a sloping site, so how can we best place the beds?	Use a spirit-level to ensure that they are true and level and you finish up with one side of the bed into the natural ground slightly, and/or prop the other side up. You can use bricks to prop up the lower side of the bed until the spirit-level shows it is level, place and screw another length of plank to the propped-up side of the bed, and remove the bricks.

No-Dig Raised Bed Troubleshooting

QUESTION	ANSWER
Can I shape the beds in height and width to suit my physical disability?	Just about everything about the beds can be modified apart from the width — the 3 ft (90 cm) width is necessary so that you can work it from both sides without actually standing on the growing medium. If you can stretch but have trouble bending, you could increase the height of the beds so that the growing surface is at a comfortable level. You could increase the width of the paths to allow for a wheelchair or walker.
How can I protect against butterflies?	The easiest option is to insert a couple of plastic water-pipe half-hoops over the bed, and then cover with very fine netting or even a found product such as net curtain, so that you finish up with a miniature hoop house-like structure. In this way you can stop the butterflies before they ever get to lay their eggs.
Could I make the sides of the beds from small bales of straw?	You can make the sides of the beds from just about any found item or material that takes your fancy — wood, brick, stone, concrete, rigid plastic sheet, galvanized sheeting, bales of straw. The only proviso is that the product or material is long-lasting and adaptable. So straw bales are fine as long as you do not mind replacing them every year or so when they rot and break down. If and when the bales break down, however, you could add them to the beds as mulch — a very nice recycling touch.
I have covered the paths with plastic sheet topped with a layer of wood chips, just as you described. What shall I do with the woodchip when it starts to rot and break down?	Woodchip is a winner on the paths on many counts: it is firm underfoot, it is not slippery, it can easily be weeded, it can be ordered in bulk, and when it rots and breaks down it can be spread on the beds as a thin mulch, andreplaced. It fits beautifully into the organic, no-dig, recycling theme.
What can I do about mice eating my peas?	Sow the seeds in the greenhouse in a length of plastic gutter (as described on page 25). When the plants are 2–3 in (5–7.5 cm) high, slide the pea plants into place in the prepared beds, and surround the bed with a fine net. You could also set two traps in each bed, and generally keep watch.
Is it true that I can keep my runner bean plants from one year to the next?	Although most people plant beans as annuals, they are in fact perennials. This being so, you can achieve early crops of runner beans by digging up the roots in autumn when the crops have been gathered in, and saving them for replanting in the following spring. Wait until the runner beans have died down, cut the old dry foliage down to about 3 in (7.5 cm) from the ground and use a fork to carefully lift out the roots. Wash the roots and bring them indoors so that they are cool and dry. Plant the roots out in spring and treat as for sown beans.
Your "distance apart" measurements seem very much closer than in traditional vegetable gardening. Why is this?	The no-dig raised bed system mimics nature in that the largely undisturbed growing medium is packed full of beneficial organisms and in near-perfect condition, and you can walk right around the bed so that there is no need to walk between lines of plants, so it is possible to set the plants closer together. The ideal is to space the plants so that the mature crop completely covers the bed and you cannot see the growing medium.